THE COMPLETE ENCYCLOPEDIA OF

CLASSIC
MOTORCYCLES

THE COMPLETE ENCYCLOPEDIA OF

CLASSIC
MOTORCYCLES

MIRCO DE CET

REBO
PUBLISHERS

© 2005 Rebo International b.v., Lisse, Netherlands

This 4th edition reprinted in 2008.

Text: Mirco De Cet
Layout: Karen Glover Graphics, East Grintead, Great Britain
General Editor: Quentin Daniel
Index: Marie Lorimer Indexing Services, Harrogate, Great Britain

The majority of pictures came from the author. Other contributors are mentioned in the acknowledgements.

Cover design: Minkowsky Graphics, Enkhuizen, Netherlands
Pre-press services: Amos Typographical Studio, Prague, Czech Republic
Proofreading: Emily Sands

ISBN 13: 978 90 366 1497 9

Contents

Forward

It is impossible to please everybody. While The Complete Encyclopedia of Classic Motorcycles *does not aspire to be the ultimate motorcycle source book, it represents my attempt to come as close as possible. For me, that meant reaching the widest possible audience, providing useful and interesting information to the knowledgeable and the curious, to the old hands and the novices, the laymen and the experts. The most famous makes can be found in these pages, along with a few lesser-known, but I have omitted some of the most obscure since I wanted the book to be as accessible as possible. For the entertainment and enlightenment of all readers, I have included some fascinating stories about the many companies and individuals who benefited from ingenuity in the workshop and courage on the racetrack, enjoyed the good times and endured the hard ones, thus furthering motorcycle design and development.*

The motorcycle has been with us for over 100 years and when you compare a modern machine to a bike from the early 1900s, you can see just how far the industry has come. Technological progress has transformed the motorcycle, increasing speed, performance, comfort and reliability, but since many of the early motorcycle companies in Europe and the United States were manufacturing bicycles or bicycle components before they started making motorcycles, the original concept of efficiently powering two wheels can still be seen. Today's machines are equipped with the latest electronic devices and the most up-to-date safety features. They are beautifully finished in bright colors or sophisticated metallic tones and are very user-friendly. The Brough Superior, often cited as the first Superbike, could reach 100 mph when most bikes of the period were struggling to do half that speed, a leap in performance so enormous that it was a positive danger in the wrong hands. It was a sign of things to come. Most of today's top sports bikes can reach speeds of over 160 mph and have phenomenal acceleration. Their power and performance capacities are even superior to certain cars.

We have become accustomed to high performance levels. However keep in mind that helmets and protective clothing, once seen as unnecessary nuisances and rarely worn, are now sleek, sharp and made from the latest hi-tech material. They remain elementary safety requirements for biking and their importance has not been diminished by even the most impressive safety features of the newer bikes.

Today, biking enthusiasts of all ages gather in large numbers, through clubs or more casually. But whether riders of veteran, vintage or modern bikes, they all share the same passion and there's much talk of side-valves, overhead cams, top speeds, oil leaks, repair remedies and, of course, spills and thrills! Curiosity and camaraderie inspire the buzz and excitement at bikers' "meets" around the world. I hope I have captured a little (at least!) of their intensity and passion in The Complete Encyclopedia of Classic Motorcycles.

Mirco De Cet

ABC All British Cycles

1913 – 1923.

The All British (Engine) Company Ltd. of London, England, was founded in 1912. The name was changed later to ABC (All British Cycles) Motors, Ltd. The company owner was Ronald Charteris and the chief engineer was Granville Bradshaw. The company made motorcycles around the turn of the century and their first machine was a 500cc twin, introduced in 1913. The engine was a flat twin and was positioned fore and aft in the frame. During the First World War, the ABC engine was used for pumping out trenches in Flanders, not for motorcycles.

The ABC Company was long associated with the Sopwith aircraft company as innovators of several designs. After the First World War, when aircraft manufacture was no longer a priority, the two worked together closely. Granville Bradshaw designed a transversely mounted, flat, twin engine five years before BMW adopted the design, also drawing up plans for a new frame. Their Sopwith 398cc 'Machine' model of 1919 was innovative enough to cause a sensation at the annual Motor Cycle Show, using front and rear leaf springs, internal front and rear expanding brakes, and featuring a cradle frame, footboards and leg shields. There was no kick-start for the early bikes - the rider had to "paddle" to get the engine running.

The ABC used a four-speed gearbox, a real innovation for the period, selected by moving the lever next to the tank.

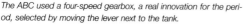

The ABC used a horizontally opposed, twin cylinder, two-valve, four-stroke, 398cc engine and could reach 60 mph.

Financial difficulties halted the introduction of an improved valve gear system.

The ABC Skootamota was designed by Granville Bradshaw and manufactured by the Campion Engineering Company.

ACE

1919 – 1929.

Ignaz Schwinn, manufacturer of bicycles, had a factory in Chicago. He also produced the Excelsior V-twin motorcycle, known in Great Britain as the American-X. Schwinn was so taken by the Henderson motorcycle design that he made a generous offer to the creators William and Tom Henderson. They accepted, and the brothers transferred from Detroit to the Excelsior concern in 1917.

By 1919, however, disagreements had arisen and the Hendersons split from Excelsior. Tom Henderson went his own way, but William started work on a new machine, eventually known as the Ace. William's new factory was located in Philadelphia and backing again came from a bicycle maker, Max Sladkin.

The change from aircraft to motorcycle production was problematic and, although the ABC name acquired respect and popularity, huge price increases did the company no favors and people looked elsewhere for cheaper machines. It is worth noting that the average motorcycle was selling for around £60, while the ABC cost nearly three times as much. Meanwhile, Bradshaw did not delay for long, coming up with a 123cc scooter, the Skootamota, which was manufactured by the Campion Engineering Company between 1919 and 1922.

Production of all ABC bikes in Britain ceased in 1923, although ABC's German factory continued to manufacture them until 1925.

The Skootamota carried its compact, single cylinder, 123cc engine at the rear, positioned above the back wheel.

After William Henderson left the Excelsior Company, he created the amazing Ace 'four,' a masive, in-line, 1229cc four cylinder motorcycle.

The new machine had a capacity of 1229cc (68.58mm bore x 82mm stroke) and was an instant success. Demand was so great that the company soon found itself in serious financial difficulties. The main problem was the need to purchase so much manufacturing material, which left the company short of cash. Fortunately, Max Sladkin, then President of Ace, managed to raise the capital needed to keep the company going. Racing and endurance events always made good publicity. In September 1922, Cannonball Baker covered the 3332 miles from Los Angeles to New York in less than seven days, taking a staggering seventeen hours off the previous trans-continental record, which incidentally went to Allan Bedell on a Henderson Four. But disaster struck in 1923 when Henderson was out testing one of the new models: he collided with a car and died upon arrival at the hospital. The Ace Company managed to tempt a young designer, Arthur Lemon, away from Excelsior. Lemon had acquired many of his skills working with Henderson and was, therefore, an ideal replacement.

For a while, Ace rode the crest of the wave. Bike sales were up and the machines were winning races in many categories, including enduro and hill climbs. By the end of 1923, however, it was clear that something had gone badly wrong and the company once again found itself struggling with financial problems. In 1924, the factory in Philadelphia closed down completely.

Because of its popularity, there were attempts to revive Ace. But even though the Michigan Motors Corporation did manufacture a number of Fours, they too had to close down.

At the Motor Cycle Show at Madison Square Gardens in 1927, there was much amazement when an Ace was exhibited on the Indian stand. It happened that the Indian Company had tied up negotiations to take over the Ace design: henceforth, the machines were to be made at the Springfield assembly plant. They came in the classic Indian red finish and bore the Indian name with a smaller Ace logo lower on the tank. The Ace, therefore, was now effectively Indian.

The in-line four firmly established the Ace tradition.

Once the big 'four' was fired up, the Ace could really motor and was used to break many speed records of the period, including the overall American coast to coast time.

Adler

1900 - 1959

A 1902 Adler with rear-wheel belt drive. Engine performance is controlled via the levers on top of the fuel tank.

Adler Fahradwerke AG was established in 1886 by Heinrich Kleyer to manufacture bicycles. After taking on typewriter production, the company changed its name to Adler Werke. Adler motorcycles were based in Frankfurt, Germany and produced motorcycles with engines of their own manufacture during the first decade of the 20th century. From 1910 until the outbreak of the Second World War, the company concentrated on the production of other items such as typewriters, bicycles and cars. During the war, they became involved

A single cylinder, 370cc, 2.5hp unit of Adler's own design. Larger capacity units were also available.

with arms production and the factory was badly bombed by the Allies.

In 1949, production of motorcycles resumed and the M100, a lightweight, 98cc, single cylinder machine, with three-speed gearbox, was introduced, followed in 1951 by three larger capacity models, the M125/150 singles and the M200 twin. In 1952, Adler produced what was probably its most popular model, the M250 two-stroke. Over the next two years, the company participated in several races, such as the Warsage 24 hour endurance and the ISDT. The machines performed extremely well and won several medals.

In 1954, Adler introduced the MB150, MB201, MB200, MB250 and the MB250S, a sports version. All had four-speed gearboxes. Adler had decided to take up road racing as well and created a race shop within the factory. Machines were ridden by Walter Vogel, Hallmeier of Nurnberg and, probably their most successful rider, Siegfried Lohmann.

The twin cylinder racing machine which took Dieter Falk to the German championship in 1955.

Sales of Adler machines started to decline in 1955, just as they did throughout the industry. An attempt was made to join the small capacity commuter market with a 98cc, two-stroke scooter, the Junior, but sales were slow. A merger with the German Triumph and Hercules companies failed. On the racing scene, Adler machines were still doing well with their 250 racer, Dieter Falk, attaining good results at the Isle of Man, Dutch TT and the Nurburgring in 1958. But in July 1958, Grundig took a stake in the company, effectively spelling the end for the motorcycle division. The company proceeded to concentrate on typewriter production.

Aermacchi

1948 – 1978

The Aermacchi Company, based in Varese, Italy, was founded in 1912 by Giulio Macchi to build aircraft. The company was moderately sucessful at first, producing both civilian and military aircraft until the end of World War II. Even today, the company is renowned for its jet trainers, which are sold around the world. Motorcycles, however, are no longer a part of its industrial make-up.

Prohibited from building aircraft after the cessation of hostilities in 1945, the company had to diversify and produced a three-wheeler truck, the MB1. The move towards actual motorcycle manufacture came with the arrival of a new designer, Lino Tonti. His first design appeared in 1950 and did not follow the traditional lines of contemporary motorcycles. An open-frame, lightweight machine with a 125cc, two-stroke engine and a single horizontal cylinder was unorthodox. A cross between a motorcycle and a scooter, the Macchi 125N was capable of 44 mph and used a three-speed transmission.

The 1954 line-up included the 125U Ghibli, a transformable scooter 125N Cigno, the lightweight 125M Monsone and the first two cylinder machine, a 250cc two-stroke.

A very good example of a 125U Ghibli. It used a two-stroke, one-cylinder engine that produced 4.5 horsepower.

The Chimera, designed by Mario Revelli de Beaumont, who also raced bikes in the 1920s. This particular machine was registered in 1965.

The original Chimera engine was a 175cc unit but graduated later to become a larger 250cc capacity machine.

Not much changed until 1955 at the Ciclo e Motociclo show in Milan. Tonti left the company and Alfredo Bianchi, who had previously worked at Parilla and Astoria, took his place. The big news at the show was the Chimera, a machine which used enclosed bodywork made from a combination of light alloy die-castings and steel pressings. The tank and seat were a single unit which could be easily removed. Bianchi was the technical director and project leader, Mario Speluzzi supervised the new engine, a 175cc, 4 stroke horizontal single. The innovative style and bodywork were designed by Mario Revelli de Beaumont. Its futuristic design was highly acclaimed and it was made until 1964, although only few examples were ever produced. Customers wanted to see the engine of the machine, the design of the Chimera was too futuristic at that time.

1956 saw Massimo Pasolini break two 75cc class world records on the highway between Varese and Milan, reaching speeds of 104 mph and 100 mph.

Two scooters were presented in 1957, both single cylinder, 150cc machines: the Zeffiro with a three-speed and Corsaro with a four-speed gearbox. Unfortunately, they never went into production.

By 1958, the Chimera had a 250cc stable mate and a whole new range of machines were presented based on the original Chimera engine. They were named the Ala Rossa, Ala d'Oro and Ala Bianca and all had a 175cc engine, whereas the Ala Azzurra had a 246cc engine.

Aermacchi has a great racing history. 1958 saw the first Aermacchi 250cc racing machines on Grand Prix circuits. Riders have been seen on winners' podiums around the world, not only for track racing, but for motorcross events as well. The machines had the Aermacchi Harley-Davidson badges on the tanks, but were basically Aermacchi road machines modified for racing. During the 1960s and 1970s, the famous Renzo Pasolini raced them successfully, sig-

nalling the beginning of the development of a more modern, two-stroke, twin cylinder, 250-350 cc machine. Sadly, both Passolini and Jarno

Two names that are inextricably linked: Renzo Pasolini (this is his helmet!) and Aermacchi race machines.

An Aermacchi Harley-Davidson Ala D'Oro of 1966 vintage with a 350cc two-stroke engine.

Shown here is an excellent example of a 1965 Aermacchi Harley-Davidson Ala D'Oro, second series racer.

The 1975 Aermacchi Harley-Davidson 125 Aletta (little wing) which used a two-stroke, 125cc horizontal engine.

A rear view of three Aermacchi Harley-Davidson racers, similar to those raced by Walter Villa in the 1970s.

Saarinen died in a first lap pile up at Monza in 1973. In 1974, Walter Villa won the first of three consecutive 250cc world titles, plus a 350 title in 1976. 1960 saw the arrival of a new machine, the Ala Verde, using the now familiar horizontal, 250cc, single engine. A scooter called 'Topper' was also shown and the Ala d'Oro was offered a 250cc engine, a machine destined to hit the racing history books. The company also produced a 500cc machine specifically for motocross racing. In Milan, Aermacchi and the American motorcycle company Harley-Davidson created a new company, called simply Aermacchi Harley-Davidson. Each company took a fifty percent share.

1961 saw the entrance of the Wisconsin, a 250cc machine aimed specifically at the North American market and little changed in 1962 and 1963, except for the introduction of the Brezza 147cc scooter and the retirement of the Zeffiro. A small two-stroke moped named the Zeffiretto was introduced in 1964. At the 1969 Milan Show, a new 125cc, two-stroke machine, the Aletta, was unveiled from which the successful racing 125 Aletta Oro was born. 1969 saw the introduction of a 350cc bike in two versions, GTS and TV, differing only in paintwork, minor details and a 5 speed gearbox for the TV. A special version was produced for the City police in Italy by Aermacchi.

By 1972, Harley-Davidson had acquired all the company's shares and took control. Aermacchi henceforth was only concerned with military aircraft production. They redesigned the range, giving two-stroke engines except the 350 four-strokes with an electric starter, dropped the name Aermacchi from the tank and replaced it with AMF Harley-Davidson. AMF put the company into receivership in May 1978 and soon after, Cagiva acquired the old Aermacchi factory and a whole new story began for a bright new company.

A 350 TV/72 model Aermacchi Harley-Davidson. It was produced only in 1972 and is therefore a rare sight.

AJS

1909 - 1932

Joseph Stevens senior was born in Wednesfield, England in 1856. He became a blacksmith whose company, J. Stevens & Co., moved in 1894 from Wednesfield to Tempest Street in Wolverhampton, where he was to have a huge influence on the manufacturing output of the town.

Joseph's son, Harry, joined the company and was taught the trade by his father. Joseph had acquired a Mitchell single cylinder, four-stroke gas engine for use in the company and Harry took a great interest in it. He realized that he too could produce a similar, but vastly improved, engine. The engine Harry produced was a great success and sold well and it soon became apparent that there was money in these engines.

In 1899, a new concern was born: the Stevens Motor Manufacturing Company. Its first machine (never commercially produced) was made in 1903. Another machine, the Motette, a powered tricycle, followed. However, this did not sell particularly well.

The company began to produce a wide range of engines and demand was so high that it had to move to larger premises in Pelham Street, Wolverhampton in 1904. The business thrived, making not just engines, but also carburettors and gearboxes. By 1907, however, a drop in demand hit the company hard and a receiver was called in. Nevertheless, they did struggle on for a few more years.

By 1908, Stevens Motors was producing frames and engines for the Wearwell Company as well as engines for Clyno. Stevens remained until 1909 when A.J. Stevens Company Limited was formed and another move was made to Retreat Street. The old works were taken over by the Clyno Company. The Stevens Company lost their main supplier,

Wearwell, but no direct impact was noticed.

Once on the new premises, Harry Stevens began on the designs for the all-new Model A and B machines, which used 2.5hp engines. Model A was the cheaper version and Model B had a lesser specification. The new machines were ready for the 1910 Cycle Show at Olympia, London, where a 3.5hp, V-twin, chain-driven machine was also displayed. These motorcycles were also very successful in endurance races, in particular at the Isle of Man TT, always a good event for advertising. Model D followed in 1912 with a 5hp V-twin engine, a two-speed gearbox, a chain-drive and a kick start.

In 1914, the AJS Company had a great triumph, which greatly enhanced its reputation. At the Isle of Man TT, the new AJS 2.75hp sports machines dominated the Junior TT by finishing 1st, 2nd, 4th, 6th and 29th. Orders poured in, not only for the machines, but also for their sidecars (another arm of the company) and they had trouble keeping up with the huge demand. It was decided that the only solution was to expand the production area, or, in other words, to find new premises. Another new company, A.J. Stevens & Co (1914) Ltd, was created to finance the project. A large plot of land was purchased

An early 1916, V-twin, 4hp model AJS.

on the corner of Graiseley Hill, off Penn road, which included Graiseley House, whose owner had emigrated. In 1915, when the new factory buildings were finished, motorcycle production was moved into the new premises. A larger complex was planned, but building work was halted due to the war. It resumed when the war ended and the office and repair departments were also moved to new buildings.

Right up to 1915, although they were heavily involved with manufacturing products for the war effort, AJS managed to keep production going. They even resorted to using gas, rather than the rationed petrol, to test their machines. By 1916, the ministry of Munitions prohibited the production of motorcycles, except for military use, and they had to stop any further production of civilian machines. They produced only military products until the relaxation of restrictions in 1919.

In 1920, AJS designed a new machine for the TT. Equipped with a 2.5hp, ohv engine and a three-speed, countershaft gearbox. Cyril Williams rode it to first place and orders flooded in. The following year was also successful in racing and trials: the Junior TT was

The 'big port' 349cc. ohv engine of the 1923 B3 model AJS. Gearchange operated through the lever on the right of the tank.

A side view of the 1923 B3 AJS. This fine machine is on exhibition at the Black Country Living Museum, Dudley, England.

dominated once again by the AJS machines, which came in 1st, 2nd, 3rd, 4th, 6th and 8th. As if this was not enough, Howard R Davies won the Senior TT on another AJS. 1920 also saw the reintroduction of the Model B with a 2.7hp, side-valve engine and many new features. About 600 people were employed in motorcycle production and the company continued to expand.

In 1922, new versions of the Model B were

introduced: the B1, a standard sports machine and the B2, a stripped sports model. At the 1922 Olympia show, a new machine, based on the TT racing machines, was presented. 'Big Port,' as it was known, used a 2.7hp engine. Other models were upgraded and tinkered-with, and the B3 and B4 models were introduced in 1924.

Throughout the early 1920s, AJS designation codes changed from B to E and then to the letter G in 1926. The GR7 and GR10 were 498cc, ohv racing machines. In 1927, there was yet another letter change to H. By 1928, there were no less than 10 production models on the books. The designation changed to K and included new ohc racing models, the K7 with a 349cc engine, and the K10 with a 498cc engine. The following year, the designation changed to M, with eleven models on show. New frames were designed to accommodate the new tank

A 1928, 799cc, K1, side-valve model V-twin. Note how high the handle bars are.

A beautifully restored AJS V-twin machine with sidecar. These combinations were a popular mode of transport.

The 1927, large capacity, 799cc, V-twin machine was more than capable of pulling a side-car and its passenger.

The 1927 'big port,' 349cc, H6 model AJS.

shape which, on some models, had flush-fitted speedometer dials. In the Junior TT, Wal Handley managed a second place on his AJS.

By now, however, the company was starting to feel the effects of the Depression.

The good news was that AJS still had a good relationship with Clyno, for whom they were manufacturing body shells. The bad news was that Clyno was soon to go out of business. Consequently, AJS decided to manufacture their own cars.

In 1930, there was another designation change, to R, although the range of models

The 349cc, single pot engine of the 1927 model H6.

The 1928 K7, single cylinder, ohc, two-valve, four-stroke model. All ohc models were stopped in 1931 when AJS became part of Matchless.

The new ohc engine was fitted to the old push-rod, 'big port', diamond frame. The 25mm Binks carburettor can be seen on the right of the cylinder.

The gears could be selected by moving this lever either up or down. The ride was quite frightening at high speeds.

was reduced. Among the models available were two 498cc machines, the ohv, two-port R8 and the side-valve R9. October 1930 also saw the production of the R7, which, at a speed of exactly 100 mph, was used by Denly and Baker to break the 350cc, three hour record at Monthlery. The Lightweight TT was won by Jimmy Guthrie on an AJS 248cc machine, though this did little to increase sales. Indeed, the company was in dire financial straits.

The 1931 line-up revealed a changed designation and five new models, all giving great value for money. Despite this, sales remained stagnant and money was borrowed to finance the commercial vehicle and car business. The company found itself at the mercy of the banks. Share prices fell on the stock market and the banks called in the loans. On 2 October 1931, shareholders were summoned to a meeting at the Victoria Hotel in Wolverhampton and the company was liquidated.

Both the AJS name and its manufacturing rights were eventually bought by Matchless motorcycles. By September 1932, all creditors had been paid. It was a sad end for a company with outlets all over the world, a company which had produced around 25,000 machines per year in its heyday. Matchless, or Associated Motor Cycles as they were now known, moved AJS to Plumstead, London where the AJS name was kept alive a little while longer, mostly by badge-engineering.

This is a 1929 model 12, which used a 248cc, single cylinder engine. The odd tank color lasted only a short period.

AJW

1928 - 1976

The AJW initials are those of the founder Arthur John Wheaton, whose family owned a printing company in Exeter, England. The first two prototypes, built in 1926, were a 500cc single and a 996cc V-twin. Both used Anzani engines. The V-twin was produced in 1928, along with the 500 model, which had a JAP rather than an Anzani engine. In 1929, the extraordinary Super Four reappeared. The Super Four made its debut at the 1928 London Motor Cycle Show, where it excited much interest. However, it was unreliable and was eventually cancelled.

Despite such setbacks, more models appeared, as did many different types of engines such as Anzani, JAP V-twins, Rudge Pithon singles and even Villiers two-strokes. The Depression affected sales, of course, and the selection of models decreased. By 1936, however, trade had improved again and models like the Silver Vixen and Silver Fox appeared.

Production halted during the Second World War, resuming only in 1948 when the firm changed hands and was now owned by Jack Ball of Bournemouth. Production of the Grey Fox began in Wimbourne in Dorset and the model was made until 1952. In 1953, the 125cc Fox Cub was introduced, but production finished when the supply of JAP engines dried up. The company made a come-back in 1958 with another Fox Cub, a 48cc which continued to sell until 1964. In 1976, the company introduced and sold a range of 50, 80 and 125cc, Italian-made, two-stroke, Wolfhound machines. In 1977, the company closed its doors and vanished.

AJW used many different makes of engine in their machines. Seen here is a Python Rudge 'twin port,' 500cc unit.

This is a 1933 AJW Flying Fox. The Rudge engine, shown above, was attached to a four-speed Rudge gearbox.

Never to see production, this is the 1952 Fox Cub prototype. It was fitted with a JAP, two-stroke, 125cc engine and a three-speed gearbox.

Aprilia

1968 to date.

aprilia

Aprilia's origins date back to immediately after the Second World War, when Cavaliere Alberto Beggio founded a bicycle production factory at Noale in the province of Venice in Italy. Alberto's son, Ivano Beggio, took over the company in 1968 and it soon became obvious that bicycles were not his main interest when, together with a dozen or so collaborators, he constructed the first Aprilia motorcycle, a gold and blue 50 cc. The first Aprilia mopeds were christened Colibrd, Daniela and Packi, but the machine most closely in line with Ivano Beggio's ideas was the Scarabeo,

This is the Daniela, one of the first machines by Aprilia. It had wheels 10 in in diameter and a Franco Morini engine.

One of the last versions of the Colibri series of machines. It used a Dellorto carburettor and had five gears.

A 1973 Scarabeo, with 125cc Franco Morini engine unit. These machines were used extensively for off-roading.

a motocross bike which came out in 1970. Produced until the end of the 1970s, the original Scarabeo was presented in various 50 and 125 cc versions, often with a truly unique and innovative look, exemplified by the 1971 metallic gold model.

In 1974, Ivano Beggio became Chairman of Aprilia and the first true motocross machine was born. It was entrusted, on an experimental basis, to Maurizio Sgarzani, a junior class rider who had made good progress in the first races. The early signs were encouraging and Aprilia technicians used the bike as the basis for the RC 125 model presented at the Milan Motor Show. A perfect combination of sport and standard production has become the trademark of the Noale Company.

In 1975, the first Aprilia Hiro racing engine was presented. The chosen rider was Ivan Alborghetti from Milan, a born champion. The results were swift. The first titles came in the Italian 125 and 250 cc championships in 1977 and the following year, Alborghetti closed the season with two third places in individual races and absolute sixth place in the World Championship, the best classification ever for an Italian rider.

The first racing successes helped raise the prestige of the new Italian make among enthusiasts. With sales of the RC and MX 125 "replicas" soaring, the newborn racing department was able to increase the budget allocated for the first season.

The Noale Company did not stop there and foreign markets soon accounted for 20 percent of production. The American market gave

Aprilia were famous for their lively graphics and color schemes. This is the replica MX125 of Alborghetti's racing machine of 1977.

Ivano Beggio's motorcycles a particularly warm welcome. The aim of the company was to become one of the sector's leading producers at an international level. The decade drew to a close with constant growth in both moped and motocross bike production.

In ten years, the company grew considerably. Between 1969 and 1979, annual production of mopeds rose from 150 to 12,000 units, while motorcycle production exceeded the 2,000 units/year mark.

The early 1980s marked a period of crisis for the motorcycle market in Europe generally and Italy in particular. Yet it was precisely during those difficult years that Ivano Beggio laid the foundations for new and prestigious achievements, fuelled by his extraordinary passion for motorcycles and his trust in the eventual rebirth of the Italian motorcycle market. No longer limited to motocross bikes and mopeds, the company's production was thus oriented along new lines, extending the range to enduro, trials and road bikes of between 50 and 600 cc. Aprilia motorcycle racing activities enhanced the company's prestige internationally and provided an opportunity to test the innovative ideas adopted by the Noale Company. So despite the crisis during the early 1980s, Aprilia became a hotbed for ideas and projects which would establish the company internationally over the coming years.

The first significant sign of this new strategy came in 1983 when the first Aprilia road bike, the ST 125, was launched. It had slender, elegant lines and behaved exceptionally well

both on the road and the track, easily winning the hearts of the specialist press. The next year saw the launch of the STX, an improved and sportier version of the ST and the company's first enduro, the ET 50, encapsulating all of Aprilia's off-road experience in one small package. In 1985, an agreement was reached between Aprilia and the Austrian company, Rotax, to supply engines and although this was the last year of the company's official participation in motocross, the ETX was launched on the market in 125 and 350cc versions.

In 1984, Aprilia announced two new machines; the MX 125 and the MX250, shown here, which by now were fitted with the Austrian Rotax engines.

In 1986, the AF1 was launched, and the ETX was joined by the Tuaregs in the enduro sector. The latter, with their maxi-tank and more precise components, drew their inspiration from the bikes used in the great African rallies so much in vogue at the time. While the ETX of the mid-1980s became the first motorcycle characterized by tone on tone coloring, the standard AF1 bikes were also highly effective between 1986 and 1991, their chromatic transformations making them look like completely different models, although all possessed the same frame.

In the 1980s, racing was successful for the Aprilia Company, which took giant steps forward. The first trials experiences began with the TL 320 in 1981, while in 1985, the first year of world championship racing, the Aprilia ridden by Philippe Berlatier reached fifth place. In 1985 as well, the extraordinary Motorcycle World Championship adventure began with the GP 250 ridden by Loris Reg-

The AF1 replica was a great machine for privateers. One of these machines took Dutchman Ven de Heijden to the European championship in 1990.

giani. Many observers felt that it was brave, to say the least, for a small, inexperienced Italian company to take on the mighty Japanese at racing. But at the end of the first season, the Aprilia GP 250 with Rotax engine came sixth in the World Championship classification. Not a bad result considering the tiny experimental racing team asssembled for the first time that year.

But the great day came two seasons later, at the San Marino Grand Prix on 30 August 1987. The Italian national anthem was played to celebrate the great win by Loris Reggiani on his AF1. It was a historic date for Ivano Beggio and his Aprilia Company. The success of the road bikes did not detract from off-road production, which remained one of the Noale Company's specialities. In 1990, they introduced the Pegaso 600, a powerful machine designed for off-road and road use.

Five years after the first victory, and following many other racing successes, Ivano Beggio's dream finally came true in 1992 when Aprilia won the World 125 Championship title with rider Alessandro Gramigni. In the same year, the World Trials Championship title was won by Tommy Ahvala on an Aprilia Climber. Since then, an incredible series of successes has made Aprilia a name to be reckoned with in the 125 and 250cc classes, with 124 Grand Prix wins, 15 World Championship titles and 16 European speed titles.

From the start, Aprilia Racing proved to be a forum for new talent and many of the top champions of recent seasons such as Biaggi, Capirossi, Gramigni, Locatelli, Sakata and, of course, Valentino Rossi, started out in the saddle of an Aprilia.

In the 1990s, Aprilia made its entry into the urban mobility vehicle sector just when the scooter market was entering a long growth period. Creativity and an unconventional approach proved to be the key to success. In 1990, Aprilia proved capable of staying one step ahead by producing Italy's first, all-plastic scooter, the Amico, while in 1992, Aprilia introduced the first scooter and first twin motorcycle with catalytic converter (the Amico LK and Pegaso 125 respectively). A year later, it developed the first, over-50cc scooter with four-stroke, four-valve engine.

Aprilia's attention to the environment was one of its primary strategic objectives. In 2000, they began production of the "cleanest" engine, the Ditech (Direct Injection Technology). Its revolutionary technology guaranteed high performance, record low consumption and very low emissions.

In 1993, an old and respected name at the Noale factory became an instant success: the Scarabeo large diameter wheel scooter. Even today, its extraordinary combination of old-fashioned and modern lines is a real benchmark for other companies. The list of successful Aprilia scooters continued with the Leonardo, the SR and the Gulliver, to name just a few better known models.

In 1995, Aprilia dazzled the motoring world

The Pegaso 600 of 1990 also used a Rotax single cylinder engine and was fitted with a 19 in rear wheel.

with the Motò, clearly a work of art on two wheels. It was created by Philippe Starck whose unique design "won" the machine a place in New York's Modern Art Museum. 1995 also saw the launch of the exceptional RS 250, possibly one of the most successful sports bikes of all time.

In 1998, Aprilia also made a successful entry into the high capacity motorcycle sector, launching the RSV 1000, followed by the Falco and the RST Futura and the ETV 1000 Caponord in 2000.

On the sports front, having extended its participation to the 500cc class of the World Motorcycle Championship in 1994, the company made its World Superbike Championship debut in 1999.

In 2000, Aprilia acquired Moto Guzzi and Laverda, part of the historic heritage of Italian and international motorcycling, thus laying the foundations for a great Italian motorcycling empire. But the story does not stop there. Over the course of 2004, new machines were presented, both in the motorcycle sector

The Scarabeo has come a long way. After the initial 50 came the 125, 150, 200 and now the 500cc version.

This is the highly innovative Ditech engine used in the SR50.

Not just a looker: high performance, ultra-low consumption and low emission make the SR50 a constant winner in the competitive scooter market.

and in the scooter range, all featuring innovative, futuristic designs. The range of machines that Aprilia have on display runs from the limited edition, awesome RSV Mille Nera to the pretty, little SR50 Ditech. Sadly, the future was changing right in front of their eyes. As of 2004, Aprilia World Service Inc., confirmed that an agreement had been finalized, finally giving the Piaggio Group a 100 percent stake in the Aprilia Group

The 2004 Pegaso ie. Through development, fuel injection is now fitted to cylinder enduro machine.

The rear suspension of the RSV 1000 Nera – a single Ohlins shock absorber with 'piggyback' cylinder.

The rear lighting of the RSV 1000 Nera is carefully designed and positioned for easy viewing.

Ready for road or track: the 2004 Aprilia RSV 1000 R Nera is a monster 1000cc machine, using all the latest technology.

The Caponord, which uses an ohc, 997cc, V-twin engine and six speed gearbox. Suitable for desert riding or even pure joy riding on normal roads. It has double front brakes discs and weighs 474 lbs empty.

Ardie

1919 -1959

In Nürnberg, Germany in 1919, Arno Dietrich created the Ardie works where he developed its first motorcycle, a 3hp, two-stroke with a 305cc engine. In 1923, a second model with a 348cc, 5hp engine was produced. Dietrich died in 1922 while test-riding one of his machines and the works were taken over by the Bendit brothers of Fürth.

By now, mainly English components were used, including engines by J.A. Prestwich (JAP), transmission from Burman and oil

Launched in 1999, the RSV Mille is still around. Its 1000cc engine and other components are upgraded on a regular basis.

The 1927 version of the TM500 was made between 1927 and 1930 and kept at the Zweirad Museum in Neckarsulm, Germany.

The semi-naked Tuono made its debut in 2002, taking many of its characteristics from the awesome RSV 1000.

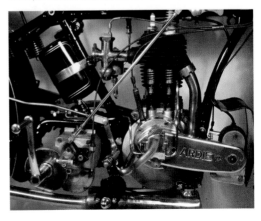

The four-stroke, single cylinder, 498cc engine could produce 9hp at 3500 rpm and had a top sped of around 56 mph.

pumps from Best&Loyd. By the mid-1920s, the TM 500 was being produced with a 490 cc, JAP engine. At the end of the decade, the 950 RM, the cheapest 500cc model in Germany, emerged. The range of engines varied from 200cc to 1000cc.

At the beginning of the 1930s, Ernst Neumann Neander came up with the idea of a pressed steel, duralumin frame, the name 'duralumin' coming from the Duerener aluminum works. These machines were equipped with JAP engines of 490cc, 345cc and 198cc, and sold under the names Silver Lightning and Silver Fox.

In 1933, however, ideas changed again and the company returned to conventional steel frames. Political circumstances forced the Bendits to leave the company. At the same time, the successful import of JAP engines had to be abandoned. A variety of engines were subsequently used, including Sachs, Bark, Kuchen and Sturmey-Archer. Although it never went to production, Kuchen also designed a transversely mounted, 348cc, V-twin machine.

After the Second World War, Ardie two-stroke engines of 124cc to 346cc were produced. The Nuremberg factory was now in the hands of the Durkopp works. It finally halted production in 1959.

This is the 305cc, single cylinder engine of the 3hp, 1923 Ardie machine. This model was made between 1919 and 1926.

The 1923 Ardie motorcycle was the first to be constructed by Arno Dietrich and could produce 3hp from its single cylinder, two-stroke engine.

Ariel

1902 – 1970

Like many motorcycle man-ufacturers, Ariel started by making bicycles and bicycle parts. The name originated with the in-vention of the tension, wire-spoke wheel patented by the Englishmen James Starley and William Hillman in 1870. They produced Britain's first, all-metal penny farthing machine and named it Ariel, Spirit of the Air, because it was lighter than most other contemporary machines. In 1896, Starley amalga-mated with the West-wood Manufacturing Company of Birming-ham to become the Starley and Westwood Company.

This company produced, among many other components, bicycle rims and tires.

The introduction to motorcycles was through a rather crude De Dion engined quadricycle, basically a bike with four wheels and a De Dion engine fitted on the rear. In 1899, they produced a tricycle – again with a De Dion engine, but mounted on the front part of the rear axle, improving weight-distribution and handling.

The first Ariel machine was not produced until 1902. Powered by a Kerry engine and pos-sessing magneto ignition and a float type car-burettor, it was chosen to participate in the 1905 International Cup Races and the 6hp machine put up the best performance at the trials with an average speed of 41 mph.

In 1905, Charles Sangster acquired the Ariel Company and designed a lightweight, two-stroke called the Areilette. It carried several advanced features such as a three-speed gear-box with clutch and kick start, but unfortunate-ly, the outbreak of the First World War put a stop to sales. After the First World War, the compa-ny introduced a 4hp, single cylinder machine

The Ariel motor tricycle has a 239cc, single cylinder, air-cooled, four-stroke engine. Although it has the Ariel casting on the side, it was in fact a de Dion-Bouton design. Top speed was about 34 mph.

with a White & Poppe engine, which served the company for many years, along with a big, V-twin machine which could use an Abingdon King Dick or Swiss-built MAG engine.

Charles Sangster took less and less interest in two wheels, concentrating on the four-wheel

This is the 1913 3.5hp model Ariel, a conventional machine. It used a 499cc, four-stroke, single cylinder engine.

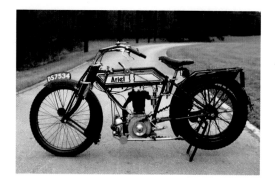

The engine used a float carburettor and a chain-driven magneto, keeping it ahead of the competition.

business. His son, Jack Gangster, now headed the Ariel works. He propositioned Valentine Page, who had designed some very sucessful engines for the JAP Company, to work for Ariel. At the 1926 Olympia show, Ariel had two new machines on their stand, a 500cc ohv and a 557cc, side-valve model. As the 1920s came to an end, the 250cc Colt was added to the line-up.

Edward Turner joined the Ariel Company as a technician, and while Val Page was busy creating his own machines, Turner was working on his pet project. Jack Sangster was one of a few to entertain Turner's idea for the Square Four and there was great excitement when production of the Four started in 1931. The machine was powered by an air-cooled, four cylinder engine, had four vertical cylinders arranged in a square configuration. The model stayed in production until 1958. Alongside "The Squariel," as it was fondly known, were the Red Hunter models, a development of Page's 500cc, ohv engine first introduced in 1932.

An early 1939 Square Four, model 4G. This was the first year suspension was used on the rear of the machine.

The Depression hit Ariel hard and the factory had to close in 1932. Jack Sangster decided to take the business into his own hands and, keeping only one part of the factory, he sold off all rest for working capital. The company became known as Ariel Motors (JS) Ltd. Val Page was one of several who left. The new company was slimmed down and the line of bikes was less ambitious. Turner tidied up some of the older designs and produced the magical Red Hunter range. The Square Four was also reworked and the buyer given a choice of two engine sizes: 600c or 1000cc.

When the Second World War broke out, the company concentrated on military production, making everything but motorcycles. They did, however, produce a few examples of the 350cc W/NG model, based on the Red Hunter. It was modified to suit the British Army, which needed higher wheel clearance and other changes.

After the Second World War, the range consisted of Red Hunter singles, ohv twins, and, of course, the Square Four. Val Page rejoined Ariel, and the 1950s saw the introduction of the twin cylinder Huntsmaster range. In 1954, the

1948 saw the launch of the KH500 Red Hunter, a parallel twin, pushrod, four-stroke machine that could reach 85 mph.

The 1956 Square Four, with its 1000cc engine, could take its rider quickly and easily to a top speed of 107 mph.

The post-war Square Four had four exhaust pipes protruding forwards. The block and cylinder head were cast alloy.

Square Four became a Mk ll 'four piper,' with two separate exhaust pipes placed on either side of the bike.

With four-strokes on their way out, much investment went into a two-stroke on which Val Page was working. This had a revolutionary frame in which the engine was suspended from the bottom of the pressed steel box member, which in turn stretched from the steering head back to the rear suspension mountings. The engine was a vertical twin two-stroke, enclosed on both sides by panels, leg shields and several other features. The

The Leader, in production between 1958 and 1965, used a parallel twin, two-stroke engine and four-speed gearbox.

The twin rear silencers of the Leader model were attached by struts to the rear mudguard. A large selection of extras were available.

machine was known as the Ariel Leader 250cc and was well-received. However, it never hit its sales target.

Ariel decided therefore to strip the panels from the machine, do away with leg shields and carry out several other alterations. The name was changed to Ariel Arrow and the factory also pro-

The engine of the Arrow, a naked version of the Leader. It too used the same two-stroke engine. A super sports version came in 1963.

duced a sports version with gold and white paintwork and whitewall tires.

Although the company did not have a racing pedigree, it did take some interest in scrambling and trials events. Among the regular riders was a young Ulsterman soon to become a biking legend: Sammy Miller.

By the early 1960s, the BSA group, of which Ariel was now part, found itself in financial difficulties. The Selly Oak factory was now a thing of the past and the Ariel

On the leader, the 6 in headlight was housed in the fairing; on the Arrow, it is attached by two extensions from the tank.

A beam frame and dummy tank can be easily spotted on the unfaired Arrow, which was introduced as a sporty alternative to the enclosed Leader.

It started as the Leader, then became the Arrow, and now, here is the sporty Golden Arrow. The engine was upgraded to 247cc.

Ascot Pullin

1928-29

The Ascot Pullin was exhibited at the 1928 Olympia show in London, England. Its beautiful blue and cream paintwork stood out from the other exhibits and created quite a stir. The machine was designed by Cyril Pullin, who had won the famous Isle of Man TT in 1914. The bike had a 500cc, flat, single, ohv engine with three-speed gearbox and featured a pressed and welded steel frame surrounding the unit. The instrumentation was more comprehensive and featured more dials than many of the cars of the period. The machine also featured hydraulic brakes, the first use of this system on a motorcycle.

works had been moved to Small Heath alongside the rest of the BSA works. One of the last bikes produced by Ariel and designed by Val Page was the 50cc Pixie, which used a pressed steel beam frame. Although there was an Ariel engine available, the Pixie was turned out with a BSA 50cc Beagle engine, a smaller version of a 75cc unit which was used for the BSA model.

Once the move to Small Heath was completed, production of the 250cc Arrow started again. It was joined by a 200cc version designed to dodge the higher rate tax, but was not a great success. The machines were disliked abroad and sales declined rapidly. By 1966, it seemed the Ariel name would come to an end. There was one last gasp: a three-wheeler developed with a Dutch-made, Anker 50cc engine. BSA named it the Ariel Three, bringing a tear to many an Ariel owner's eye. But it never really caught the public imagination and even though a contract for a military bike was on the verge of being signed, Ariel was forced to close down. Another company with a prestigious past vanished.

The Ascot Pullin was full of new features, including welded pressed steel frame and hydraulic-operated drum brakes, just to mention two.

Optional extras included adjustable windscreen with electric wiper, legshields and rearview mirror. Unfortunately, the machine suffered from handling problems and the company had difficulty meeting the orders it received. By the time the glitches were ironed out, the company had run out of money. In 1930, they filed for bankruptcy and the remaining bikes were sold off at bargain basement prices.

31

Bat

1902 - 1926

The Bat Motor Manufacturing Company was based in Penge in southeast London, England. The name came from the first three letters of the name of the founder of the company, S.R. Batson. The three letters of Batson's name were also used as part of a new slogan, 'Best After Tests,' which may be why so many people refer to the company name in capital letters.

The first motorcycle was produced in 1902, but it was not a great success, prompting Batson to move on and start a company which produced office furniture. The Tessier Family bought the company in 1904, just two years after its founding.

The initial machines used 2 $^{1}/_{2}$hp De Dion engines which took the Chase brothers to many of their victories at Crystal Palace and other venues. The company received good publicity from these victories, but the most important race was undoubtably the Isle of Man TT. Bat sent two machines to the first meeting in 1907 and company owner T.H. Tessier rode one of them. Unfortunately, things did not go well and the machines were retired. It was good practice, however, and the following year, W.H. Bashall guided his Bat to second place behind a DOT machine in the Twin Cylinder race. (At the time, there were only two races at the TT, the Single Cylinder and the Twin Cylinder events.)

At the end of 1908, all machines were using JAP engines and Bat displayed several machines at the Olympia show in London. However, it was the sidecar model that caught the eye. The transmission on the sidecar had two wheels, making the machine a four-wheeler, and it could be completely removed, leaving the bike on its own as a single unit.

The years 1910 and 1911 were not great years for Bat as far as the TT was concerned.

By 1909, all Bat machines were using JAP engines. Note the springs below the rear of the fuel tank, part of the complicated, but effective rear suspension system.

Short, leading link forks were a Bat hallmark right from the early days. The principal was similar to that used by other makers half a century later.

The1913 Bat No2 Light Roadster was a sports touring machine and used a 770cc, JAP, side valve, V-twin engine.

The huge engine in the 1919 model Bat was a 990cc, JAP, V-twin unit. The power and speed was awesome.

Harold Brown recorded the fastest lap in the 1910 race and a seventh place was obtained in 1911 at the Senior TT, where two races per year were now being run, the Senior and the Junior. By 1912, Bat had produced only twin cylinder machines, using JAP engines of 6hp and 8hp. They had all chain transmissions and the clutch was housed in the rear wheel. Even in the early days, Bat had always taken great interest in the comfort of the rider. For the seat, a form of springing was adapted to the rear part of the frame, which was suspended by coil springs. These machines were very attractive to the public, who had to navigate some pretty bumpy terrain.

As with many motorcycle manufacturers, civilian production was halted during the First World War and military manufacturing took its place. After the war, production of civilian machines resumed, but sales were not good. Even the purchase of the Martynside Company in 1923 did not ameliorate the financial problem and although the company changed its name to Bat-Martynside, it was not enough to keep it in business. The company finally shut down in 1926.

Benelli

1911- to date

A Leoncino (lion cub) model.

In 1913, the five Benelli brothers of Pesaro, Italy, decided to start their extraordinary bicycle manufacturing venture. Their first design consisted of a single cylinder, 75cc engine fitted to a bicycle. This was followed up by a 98cc, two-speed version and a 147cc, two-stroke, a machine which was successfully raced until 1927 by the youngest of the brothers, Tonino. Yet now the Benelli brothers were looking into developing a four-stroke machine of 175cc, with ohc. Again Tonino raced the machine. It was hugely successful right until 1932, when it was replaced by an equally successful twin, ohc version.

The twin-cam layout became the standard of the day for Benelli until the outbreak of the Second World War. Machines were produced in 250cc and 500cc versions, for touring and racing models, and their new configuration had the engine tilted forward.

The small, two-stroke, 125cc engine of the Leoncino.

The Leoncino was the first machine produced after the Second World War and was ideal for the general public.

In 1935, Benelli produced one of its most famous machines. The 175cc Championship races had just been stopped and the company turned its attention to the larger capacity class and presented a 250cc, twin-cam single. Its first achievement was to beat the world record for the kilometer in the quarter liter category. It soon became the bike to beat. By 1938, the twin-cams from Pesaro had finished in the top three in the Grand Prix of Nations, obtaining better overall times than their English 350cc counterparts. But tragedy struck when Tonino Benelli, the racer of the family, was killed test-riding.

At the start of 1939, Ted Mellors rode a 250cc Benelli to victory in the Isle of Man Lightweight TT. Benelli looked to add a compressor to the machines while also developing a four-cylinder model. Unfortunately, these ideas could not be put into action before the war started.

Pesaro was situated on the Gothic Line in Italy, in an area the Germans bitterly defended against the Allied onslaught. Very little of the factory remained after the fighting. However, reconstruction started soon after the cessation of hostilities. And in 1950, just five years later, riding a modified and updated 250cc, twin-cam, Dario Ambrosini captured the 250cc class World Championship.

The first machine to come out of the factory after the war was a single cylinder, 125cc, two-stroke, the Leoncino. It remained in production for some 12 years and won several sporting events. It was followed by a four-stroke twin, the 250cc Leonessa, and by a 175cc, four-stroke. But this period also saw a change in corporate structure. In 1952, one of the Benelli's, Giuseppe, left to start up the Motobi factory, also located in Pesaro and later taken back under the Benelli family wing.

In 1959, Benelli presented a 250cc, single cam racer which the riders Grassetti, Duke and Dale put to good use, bringing home many trophies for the company. Overjoyed by this success, Benelli brought out a racing legend the following year. This was also a 250cc machine, but it had four cylinders. Riders such

The original Tornado of 1968 had a 650cc, twin cylinder engine. It was quite heavy and a little cumbersome, but had plenty of power

as Grassetti, Pasolini and Carruthers rode it in 250cc, 350cc and 500cc versions on the most important circuits of the world and the Australian Carruthers took the 250cc World title in 1969. In the meantime, the range of Benelli machines increased and a twin cylinder, 650cc machine was presented along with a 250cc two-stroke.

In the late 1960s, the motorcycle industry went into recession in Italy. Sales of motorcycles were down and the Benelli's were in difficulties. In 1971, the company in Pesaro was bought by an Argentinian entrepreneur, Alessando De Tomaso. Tomaso also bought the Moto Guzzi concern, subsequently owning the largest motorcycle concern in Europe.

Machines manufactured during the de Tomaso years were very different from those produced previously: a 250cc, two-stroke from 1977.

Facing the Japanese onslaught head on, Benelli produced the amazing 'sei.' A six-cylinder Italian beauty. This 113 mph machine used a Moto Guzzi manufactured single, ohc, 748cc, straight, six-cylinder engine. It was equipped with all the latest technology.

Everything about the Sei was beautifully designed, right down to the square clock housings. Warning lights separated the rev. counter from the speedometer.

With new management came new and extraordinary machines. The first presented after the take-over was no less than a two-stroke 250cc, rather surprisingly since the four-strokes seemed to have established themselves. De Tomaso, however, was going to beat the Japanese at their own game.

By now, the Japanese hold on the motorcycling world was phenomenal. So it was even more striking that Benelli should present a brand new, six-cylinder bike in 1974.

It had the typical Italian flare, six exhaust pipes split under the engine on either side of the rear of the machine in a trio of megaphone-style silencers. The 'Sei' was a beautiful 750cc four-stroke with five gears and a top speed of 112 mph. If this was not enough of a statement, the cylinder size of the 'Sei' increased to 900cc in 1978. The 900cc version had new styling and, although a good-looking machine, it lacked the charisma of the 750. Nevertheless, it was in production until 1988.

After all this excitement, Benelli seemed to get a little lost and faded into obscurity. The name remained on people's lips and rumors circulated that a new model was about to be presented.

In 1995, Andrea Merloni officially took over the company and promised a new machine. Benelli celebrated the 50th anniversary of Dario Ambrosini's win at the 1950 TT by officially taking part in the Tourist Trophy 2000 lap of honor. The parade was headed by the stunning new green and gray-liveried machines. The radical and eye-catching Tornado made its first public outing. Benelli was back with a bang and it will be fascinating to see what it brings out next.

The fuel tank and the fairing on this hand-crafted machine are made from carbon fiber. The two air extraction fans can be seen at the rear of the bike.

Instrumentation is a mix of analogue rev counter and liquid crystal display, which not only gives current speed, but will warn the rider of any malfunction.

The Benelli Tornado has a three-cylinder, 900cc motor cooled by the air passing through the under-side of the front fairing. After surrounding the engine, it is channelled out via two fans at the rear of the bike under the seat.

Bianchi

1897 – 1970's

The Bianchi motorcycle company made its mark between the two World Wars. The company began life in 1885 as a mechanical workshop on the Via Nirone, Milan, Italy. Five years later, it moved to the Via Borghetto, where production of a motorized tricycle started in 1897.

Just after the First World War, Bianchi produced a single cylinder machine with three gears. Originally designed for the military, it was adapted for civilian use after the war. Other machines were also produced at this time, some with large, V-twin engines, others with smaller, 175cc capacity engines.

In 1925, Bianchi had great success with a 350cc racer, its first twin-cam model and more than just a pretty bike. This was the 'Freccia Celeste' used by Nuvolari and Varzi. It was superseded by a similar 500cc machine which started racing in the mid-1930s, just as multi-cylinder machines were taking over. The company was spurred on to develop a four-cylinder, 500cc compressor model, tested by the young Alberto Ascari, in 1939. It met with little success.

During the Second World War, the factory was completely destroyed. Rebuilding started after the war and one of the first machines available was the 250cc, four-stroke Stelvio. The company concentrated on utilitarian models such as the 125cc, two-stroke Bianchina and the Aquilotto, a 45cc two-stroke. In the early 1950s, Bianchi, now on their new premises, designed and built mopeds and scooters like the

The Bianchi ES 250 model used a 248cc, single cylinder, four-stroke engine that produced 10hp at 4800rpm.

A fine example of a 1937 Bianchi ES 250. The machine had a top speed of approximately 65 mph and weighed 326 lbs.

Orsetto and other sporty little machines up to 250cc. Times were hard for the company, but they were still involved with racing. Between 1955 and 1956, they produced a 175cc machine and Lino Tonti was given the opportunity to design a 250cc, twin-cylinder Grand Prix machine, which appeared in 1960. It was a good racer, above all in its 350 version, although it was also produced in a 500cc version. The 350cc bike took Remo Venturi to his national title in 1964, after its promising results on the international stage. The effort to produce more models, as well as the poor state of the motorcycle market at the time, left the company in financial difficulties. At the start of the 1970s, the company was liquidated.

The Bianchina 125cc was produced to help people get around during the post-Second World War period. Cars were too expensive for normal people.

Bianchina fuel tank has instructions for refuelling: 1 part oil, 20 parts gas, which was equivalent to 1.7 oz of oil for every quart of gas.

Instrumentation for the Sila sport was limited, but simple.

Seen here is a 1962 Bianchi Sila 175cc sport version. These machines were often used quite successfully in sporting events.

Bimota

1973 to date

The first Bimota was HB1. This is the HB2 which used a Honda 900cc engine and had a top speed of 147 mph.

bimota In 2003, the Bimota Company celebrated its 30th anniversary. It was brought out of bankruptcy in the hope that it would make its mark on the world market once more.

Although Bimota was one of the world's smallest motorcycle companies, it still had a big name in motorcycling world, not just for local enthusiasts, but for the wider world. Based in the Romania region of central Italy, the company was known for its heating and air-conditioning systems until 1973.

The name Bimota is taken from the first two letters of each of the three founder's names: Bianchi, Morri and Tamburini. Their mission was to produce extremely advanced and refined limited edition motorcycles that would feature cutting-edge technology. These machines would be based on current Japanese and Italian superbike models.

The first bike, based on the Honda CB750 four, was called the HB1. Most of the models were designated in this way – H for Honda (or whatever company the engine came from) and B for Bimota. Clever engineering solutions, state-of-the-art technology and a great deal of attention to handling and weight factors contributed to some of the best machines the company produced.

It only took Bimota seven years to make its mark on the race circuits of the world and it won the 1980 World 350cc Grand Prix championship. The winning machine was based on the TTZ350cc Yamaha two-stroke twin. Then in 1987, Virginio Ferrari clinched the TT-F1 championship on a Bimota YB4, a machine based on the Yamaha FZ750cc.

The Bimota V was unreliable, but good looking. It used a 499cc, V-twin engine attached to a six-speed gearbox.

In 1977, Bimota presented their very first, complete road machine, the SB2, designed around a Suzuki GS750cc engine. Faster and much lighter than the original Suzuki, the machine used monoshock rear suspension and the fuel tank was placed under the engine to create a better center of gravity. After this, a Kawasaki-engined machine, the KB1, emerged.

At the Milan Show of 1982, Bimota presented another example of its innovative

cial difficulties in early 2000 and finally filed for bankruptcy. In 2002, it was taken over and renamed Bimota SpA, with a view to getting back to basics and producing what Bimota was good at: state-of-the-art technologies and material for specialist parts and bikes.

In 2004, Bimota is back with futuristic and hi-tech machines: the Ducati engined, 991cc, L twin cylinder, Desmodromic Tesi 2D.

engineering, the DB1. This machine was based on the Ducati V-twin engine. Making such innovative and hi-tech models is costly, which makes buying them expensive, thus limiting the market. Bimota found the market tough during the 1990s and with the failure of sales of its new Ducati-based machine with hub center steering, the Tesi, matters got worse. In 1998, Bimota launched its first bike with a Bimota engine, the 500cc V-Due. Unfortunately, there were severe problems with the fuel-injection system. The 'naked' style Mantra followed, as did the SB6 and YB9.

The company found itself in severe finan-

2004 brings the DB5 along with the twin cylinder Ducati 992ss engine.

BMW

1917 - date

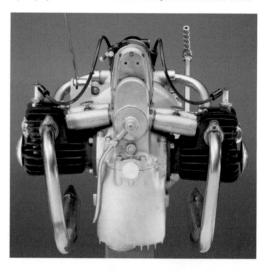

BMW, a company rooted in the production of aircraft engines, was not even two years old in June 1919 when the Peace Treaty of Versailles banned the production of aircraft engines in Germany. Accordingly, large displacement engines were replaced by 500-cc power units in 1920. These units, referred to as "Boxers" because of their two cylinders arranged opposite one other, powered the outstandingly successful motorcycles built by Victoria in Nuremberg in 1921. Taking over the Bayerische Flugzeug Werke, BMW became a motorcycle manufacturer itself in 1922. With Victoria developing their own models and with the Helios motorcycle suffering from technical problems, BMW's General Manager Franz-Josef Popp and his engineering colleagues decided that the best way to sustain the company's good repu-

tation as an engine manufacturer was to build their own modern motorcycle.

Max Friz joined BMW in 1917 and designed the Type IIIa aircraft engine, the most progressive power unit of its day. Taking up the challenge for the new machine, he completed his concept in full original size in December 1922. The idea was to fit the already existing engine into a position crosswise to the direc-

The BMW R32 engine: Four-stroke, flat twin, 494cc, 8.5hp, giving a 60 mph top speed. The machine was driven by a shaft to the rear wheel.

R32 was presented in 1923 at the German Motor Show, Berlin. The first Bayerische Motoren Werke (BMW) machine and designed by Max Friz.

tion of travel. The gearbox was driven directly by a friction clutch which was connected to a drive shaft providing the link between the gearbox and the rear wheel. Several horizontally opposed engines were already on the market and both FN and Pierce motorcycles had a drive shaft. Max Friz was the first engineer to combine all these features and incorporate them into the new BMW R32.

BMW proudly presented its first motorcycle on 28 September 1923 at the German Motor Show in the Kaiserdamm Fair Halls in Berlin. The BMW R32 entered series production before the end of the year and the first motorcycles went to customers at a price of 2,200 reichmarks each. BMW's new motorcycle stood out not only for its smoothly-clad engine/gearbox unit, but also for its frame structure featuring two fully enclosed steel tube hoops running parallel to one another. Fitted low down within the machine, the flat Boxer engine improved the center of gravity and the motorcycle's handling. Jet black, burnt-in paintwork and elaborate, white decal lines set high duality standards for the motorcycle's finish.

Success on the race track is the best way to promote a new motorcycle, especially a new brand entering the market. Aware of this important point, Rudolf Schleicher, a young engineer at BMW, started thinking about his young racing career. He had been working on the detailed design and engineering work for the R32. On 2 February 1924, he ended the day at the Mittenwalder Steig hill climb race on his BMW in record time and became the first winner in the long motorsport history of Bayerische Motoren Werke.

Using a cast light-alloy cylinder head designed and built by Rudolf Schleicher, together with overhead hanging valves encapsulated beneath a cover hood, three BMW works riders entered the Stuttgart Solitude race on 18 May 1924. Each of them won their individual categories. Winning other significant races throughout Germany and with Franz Bieber bringing home the first championship, BMW became a leading manufacturer and a champion on the race track in the

very first year of its motorcycle production. BMW's unusual Boxers with shaft drive also made headlines in Great Britain at the 1926 International Six Days Trial (ISDT) and with Paul Köppen and Ernst Henne winning the Targa Florio in Sicily, both the press and enthusiasts in Italy also started to take a very close look at BMW.

BMW quickly developed further innovations. The touring models, still featuring side-mounted valves, were joined by high-performance, expensive and exclusive sports machines with ohv power units. Despite the Depression, BMW successfully gained a strong foothold in 1931 in the 200cc entry level class with the R2. This single cylinder model again featured shaft drive and other components from BMW's larger models.

Stable, pressed-steel frames now replaced the former tubular frame technology. A 400cc, single-cylinder machine was introduced to plug the gap between the Boxers,

The frugal R2 was presented during the economic crisis in 1931. It used a single cylinder unit of 198cc, which could reach 59 mph.

The R47 was presented in 1927. This machine had the now familiar boxer engine with a capacity of 494cc and could achieve 68 mph.

now increased to 750 cc in size, and the small, single-cylinder bikes. BMW presented the first, telescopic, front wheel fork with hydraulic damping as a further milestone in motorcycle construction on the 1935 R12 and R17. One year later, an entirely new model entered the market, the R5, on which conically drawn steel tubes with an elliptical cross-section were connected by protective gas welding. The telescopic fork came with adjustable dampers while the new 500cc power unit featured two camshafts and a single piece tunnel/engine housing. The R51, with straight-travel, rear-wheel suspension, entered the market in 1938.

Ernst Henne was the man in the saddle to challenge the world speed record for motorcycles. In 1929, he set a new speed record of 134.39 mph, going on to break no less than 76 consecutive world records before finally achieving a phenomenal 173.29 mph on the 28 November 1937. This record was unbeatable for another 14 years. In 1935, BMW racing machines again featured a compressor, but also boasted racing engines with two overhead camshafts per cylinder (driven by side shafts) designed with all their elaborate features by Rudolf Schleicher. The first Grand Prix wins in 1936 were followed by the European Championship in 1938. Schorsch Meier, a new member of the BMW team, made the compressor BMWs almost unbeatable and even won the Senior TT in 1939. He brought home BMW's greatest racing victory so far, the Isle of Man Tourist Trophy.

The R11 was made from 1929 to 1935, starting with an 18hp, 745cc boxer engine, it then increased to 20hp for 1934. Ideal for sidecar work.

The military authorities were important customers for BMW in the 1930s. Single-cylinder R4 and R35 machines were used for training and the messenger services, while the R11 and R12 served as sidecar machines for rapid transportation of soldiers. Preparing for war, the German Wehrmacht replaced the cavalry on horseback with sidecar motorcycle riders. The Supreme Command of the German Army specified their design concepts and construction requirements. The BMW R75, an all-new machine, featured a 750cc, ohv engine. A limited-slip differential was added to the sidecar drive with its transverse shaft enabling it to tow more than 880 lb. Between 1941 and 1944, BMW built more

The R75 was prepared for the German Wermacht during 1940. It had a boxer 750cc engine, four forward and even one reverse gear as standard.

than 18,000 units of the R75 Wehrmacht sidecar motorcycle.

Both motorcycle components and production facilities were located at the Eisenach Car Plant, taken over by BMW in 1928. From 1947, Eisenach was considered part of the Soviet Zone in Germany. Production continued, while in Munich all the facilities had to be dismantled and the construction drawings were confiscated. The individual parts and components used by Alfred Böning to develop a new motorcycle came from BMW dealers, the 250cc, single-cylinder R24 entering production in 1948. In 1950, BMW brought back a two-cylinder Boxer, but the single-cylinder models still accounted for the majority of sales. It also brought home outstanding success in the racing arena. In sidecar racing, BMW's RS racing Boxers scored a series of victories, bringing home 19 World Championships between 1945

With the introduction of the R51/3 BMW launched a new generation of boxer engines for 1951, with more emphasis on reliability and smoothness.

and 1974 and Klaus Enders clinched the title six times. Unique technology was responsable.

With the introduction of the R51/3 in 1951, BMW launched a new generation of Boxer engines, placing even greater emphasis on reliability and running smoothness. The R68 followed in 1952 as BMW's first 100 mph machine. In 1955, full swinging arm suspension technology, front and rear, established a new benchmark in motorcycle construction. By the early 1960s, the motorcycle boom in Germany had come to an end. Continued demand from the authorities and from foreign markets nevertheless still justified BMW motorcycle production.

To the great surprise of both the competition and the public, BMW launched an all-new range of motorcycles in the fall of 1969. These were motorcycles developed from the ground up during the worst years of the market. The

The R75/5, 750cc boxer engine model was introduced in the late 1960s.

500 and 600cc machines with new engines as well as constant pressure carburettors and an electrical starter were joined by the top-of-the-range R75/5. As of September 1969, BMW's new motorcycles no longer came from Munich, but from Berlin-Spandau, a former BMW aircraft engine plant.

In 1973, BMW celebrated the 50th birthday of BMW motorcycles with the completion of the 500,000th unit. In the same year, the R90 S was upgraded in engine size and significant extra power and featured the first cockpit fairing on a production machine. Reg Pridmore subsequently won the American Superbike Championship in 1976 on a modified R90 S. The R100 RS sports tourer, launched in 1976, boasted a larger engine as well as the first full,

The R100RS was the sports version of the R series in the mid 1970s. The fairing was wind tunnel-honed and the engine was a 1000cc unit.

wind-tunnel tested fairing on a production machine. In 1978, the R45 and R65 were introduced.

BMW off-road machines participate in the long distance rally from Paris to Dakar in the West African country of Senegal. They had success at the third try in 1981, when French desert specialist Hubert Auriol won the motorcycle category. He repeated his success in 1983. Then in 1984 and 1985, Gaston Rahier, the former Moto Cross World Champion from Belgium, also left the competition in the dust.

BMW are regular participants in the desert races and in 1984 and 1985, Gaston Rahier won the gruelling Paris-Dakar race on his 1000cc machine.

The K100 RS was introduced in 1984 and had a completely new, four-cylinder, four-stroke, ohc engine. A high speed, long distance, comfortable machine.

Featuring electronic fuel injection, the BMW K100 entered the market with maximum output of 90 bhp. BMW engineer Josef Fritzenwenger succeeded in creating a new technical concept. The 987cc, straight-four power unit was fitted flat in a lengthwise arrangement. The "basic" model was soon joined by a sports tourer and touring model. The 740cc, three-cylinder version rounded off the range of in-line engines. As the top model in the range with its aerodynamic body including both front-wheel and rear-end fairing, the K1 was the first motorcycle in the world to feature a fully-controlled, three-way catalytic converter. Its 16 valve, four-cylinder power unit with digitally controlled electronic engine management offered ideal conditions for this technology.

The basic principle of the BMW Boxer remained unchanged, but everything else was new on the BMW R1100 RS launched in 1993. The drive unit formed a loadbearing element and there was no longer a frame in the conventional sense of the word and the front wheel ran on the Telelever. The rear wheel ran on the Paralever double-joint single swinging arm carried over from the K1.

Under the guidance of BMW, a European joint venture was established together with Ital-

The unmistakable K1 became BMW's fastest ever production machine with its four-valve, ohc engine and refined aerodynamic bodywork.

ian motorcycle manufacturer Aprilia and Austrian engine supplier Bombardier-Rotax to create the BMW F 650 Funduro, launched in 1993.

The old, two-valve Boxer generation was retired in the mid-1990s and the last R 80 GS Basic was built on 19 December 1996. The following sum-

The R 850 R, introduced in 1996, was the smaller stablemate of the R1100R roadster. The boxer engine now had four vales per cylinder.

mer, the 100,000th new Boxer, the R850R, set out on the road in the hands of an Italian lady rider.

On the highways of the United States of America, BMW presented an entirely new cruiser based on the Boxer philosophy. The R1200 C combined the progressive technology of BMW motorcycles with Digital Motor Electronics, a Telelever and highly effective brakes featuring optional ABS.

The C1 was introduced in 2000. This is the 2004 C1 200 which has a 175cc, single cylinder engine and can reach a top speed of 70 mph

In September 1998, BMW presented the K 1200 LT at the Intermot Motorcycle Show in Munich. This new luxury tourer was conceived and built for optimum safety and comfort with a reverse gear allowing superior manoeuvrability. A music system, cruise control and electric seat heating were just a few of the many options available.

More than just a "motorcycle with a roof," the BMW C1 is a sophisticated two-wheeler with elaborate technology allowing the rider to man-

A rider's view of the comprehensive and easy to read instrumentation of the C1. The C1 is probably the safest two-wheeler around.

The compact C1 200 engine produces 18hp and can reach 30 mph in just 3.9 seconds. Fuel consumption is 88.3 mpg at a steady 56 mph.

age without a helmet or protective wear. The BMW C1 entered the market in 2000.

The R1150 R naked bike, known as the "Roadster," made its appearance in 2001. The R1150 RS and the R1150 RT tourer, with its

The F650 uses an Austrian Rotax engine assembled by Aprilia in Italy but with the BMW name on the cases. This is a single cylinder, dohc, four-valve, four-stroke unit.

Boxer Cup 2003 made its debut in the United States, where the first of nine races took place at Daytona.

In 2002, BMW introduced a new type of road machine, launching the F650 S, which only shared the single cylinder power unit with its sister model and took the new name "Scarver." The range of BMW cruisers was also growing, the R1200 CL ranking as a luxury cruiser featuring four headlights. Comfort was also the primary feature of the new K1200 GT, a more

The R1100S, boxer 1085cc engine and an impressive 140 mph top speed.

1130cc power unit and six-speed gearbox, followed with the same improvements. The idea of staging a racing series with identical BMW R1100 S machines came from France. The BMW Motorrad Boxer Cup became truly international in 2001, with 30 riders from all over Europe competing in 7 races on production-based versions of the BMW R1100 S. In its third international year, the BMW Motorrad

The BMW Motorrad Boxer Cup races first took place in 1999 and now support the prestigious MotoGP championship. Replica machines are available.

This is the stunning R1200 C Montauk cruiser. It uses a 1200cc flat twin engine with dual-ignition system and can reach a top speed of 105 mph.

developed version of the sports tourer. The K1200 RS placed even greater emphasis on touring comfort. The R1150 R Rockster proved so popular as a design study at the Munich Intermot Show in September 2002 that BMW decided to make it a production model.

With a grand total of 93,010 motorcycles produced in the course of the last decade, BMW Motorrad has grown into the largest manufactur-

er in Europe. BMW are constantly looking to the future, continuing to focus on profitable growth with new models, ongoing expansion of the plant and highly efficient dealers and sales organization.

Anybody who has seen the movie, Paycheck, will recognize the R1150R Rockster. This machine is the sporty version of the R1150R boxer twin, where most of its components originate.

This is the K1200 RS, a sports tourer with comfort and plenty of high speed. The 1200cc engine can cruise happily all day.

Böhmerland RW

1925 - 1935

A 1928 model with four-stroke, single cylinder, 598cc engine.

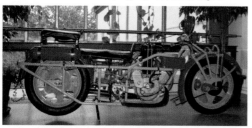

The Bohmerland motorcycle, or Böhmerland/Cechie as it could be known, was designed by Albin Liebisch and manufactured in Northern Bohemia at Krásná Lípa. Böhmerland is the German name for Bohemia, and Cechie is the local, colloquial equivalent for the same area. So either name might appear on the tank. The machine was first manufactured in 1925 and gained a reputation for being strong and reliable, albeit unconventional in its trademark red and yellow colors. The frame was a tubular steel construction, the front forks slightly unusual in that they were leading-link, and the suspension functioned through a spring under tension. The rear of the machine had no suspension at all.

The Bohmerland used a single cylinder 598cc, ohv engine, designed by Liebisch, with open-push rods and valve train. There is also one unique model, 10 $\frac{1}{2}$ ft long, which could seat up to four adults. Just before the Second World War, a new, 348cc two-stroke was made, but never saw production.

The leading link front forks and sprung suspension layout.

Bridgestone

1958 - 1971

BRIDGESTONE

The Bridgestone name is well-known as a tire manufacturer. But after 1946, it produced bicycles, clip-on type, powered bicycles in 1949 and moterbikes from 1958.

Bridgestone started as an automotive part trading company in Japan. It was run by Soichiro Ishibashi and the company name was taken from a literal translation of his name: ishi means 'stone' and bashi is 'bridge.'

Bridgestone began exporting to the American market in 1963. The American market was important and exports there began in 1963. The importer was Rockford Scooter Company of Rockford, Illinois, and its first model was the '7,' a fan-cooled, 50cc, two-stroke with three-speed rotary transmission. Dedicated dealerships were quickly established although the company never grew as large as the other manufacturers (the machines did not reach the British and Australian markets until about 1968). The vast majority of motorcycles were destined for the American market.

Bridgestone's best-known motorcycle series, presented in 1964, was based on rotary valve engines and ranged from 50cc to 350cc. The bikes were so advanced for the period that they were produced with little change until 1971. In the mid-1960s, the Bridgestone small capacity racers were a force to be reckoned with, dominating the circuits. Racing experience led to the presentation of the SR series, which were 90cc, 100cc and 175cc modified race-only versions of the road-going models. In 1970, the road version of the 175cc was enlarged to 200cc and the 350GTR was introduced. At $900 US dollars, it was an expensive machine especially considering that a Yamaha or Honda of similar size could be bought for less than $200 US dollars. It became obvious that corporate interest did not lie in motorcycle manufacture. Following the introduction of the 1971 model range, Bridgestone closed down its bike division.

Seen here is a rare example of the 350 GTO model of the late 1970s. It had devastating acceleration and top speed for the period.

The exhausts swept back from the engine either side of the machine

The 350 GTO twin cylinders – pollution laws contributed to its demise.

Brough Superior

1921 - 1940

William Brough, father of George, made motorcycles, but never as successfully as his son. The two had different ideas about the types of machines they preferred and when they started a business together, disagreements were inevitable. George planned to make top-quality, fast and extremely well-made machines to be sold in small quantities. William thought there was no market for theses bikes. George announced he would market and make his own machine under the name, Brough Superior, an aggressive declaration which did nothing to mend the strained relationship between father and son. William allegedly responded with the bitter quip that his product was now the 'Brough Inferior.'

George found himself some land in Haydn Road in Nottingham, England and a prefabricated, single storey building was built to accommodate the works. The first machines were built at his father's house with help from his friend, Ike Webb, who was to stay with Brough for many years. The first Brough Superior was available in early 1921. It had a specially designed, JAP, 986cc, ohv engine with Sturmey archer, three-speed gearbox and came fitted with number plates, horn, lamps and generator. The machine was heavily nickel-plated which helped prevent rust while enhancing its appearance. The machine was well-received by both press and buyers alike. When the first Brough Superior SS80 was tested by the Midlands editor of 'The Motorcycle,' he summed up its qualities, calling it the Rolls Royce of motorcycles. The name has stuck and George made great use of the compliment in his advertisements.

The first SS100 appeared at the 1924 Olympia show. It used a JAP, 1000cc, ohv, V-twin engine and was accompanied by a tag guaranteeing that it had obtained a speed in excess of 100 mph on the track. This machine was a direct descendant of the bike raced by the JAP development engineer, Bert le Vack, when he broke the speed record at Brooklands. The SS100 continued to be sold, as its designer requested, in small quantities. Quality rather than quantity was the watchword for the Brough Company.

At the 1927 show, the first four-cylinder Brough was unveiled to the public, but little was heard afterwards. (A price tag of £250

The huge, flat engine of the Brough Golden Dream: a machine that Brough was keen to build. It had a capacity of 996cc and was shaft-driven to the rear wheel.

Believed to be Lawrence of Arabia's fourth Brough, this is a 1925 SS100, which could exceed a speed of 108 mph. The engine was made by JAP of Tottenham, London.

might explain why people were slow to place orders, especially since the average house sold for around £300 at the time.) Also seen at the show was an overhead 680cc twin. Then came the Austin in 1932, a water-cooled, 800cc, four-cylinder-engined Brough, essentially made to pull a sidecar. It was a strange machine with twin rear wheels and a drive shaft and, of course, it had a reverse gear.

More machines followed, with larger and more powerful engines. But of all the models

The distinctive Brough SS 100 fuel tank.

George Brough wanted to build, the 'Golden Dream' occupied him most. The 'Golden Dream' was essentially a pair of flat twins mounted one on top of the other, transversely fitted to the frame. It had a shaft drive and Brough's usual high standard of finish. It was presented at the 1938 show and outshone all competitors. Customers put down deposits, but war loomed and production never started because the factory was mobilized for arms manufacturing.

T.E. Lawrence (Lawrence of Arabia) was probably Brough's most famous customer. He owned a succession of Broughs named for the English kings: George I to George VII. In 1935, he was killed while riding a Brough Superior.

The two cylinders of this four-stroke, JAP, V-twin, 998cc engine were fed via a Binks Mousetrap carburettor, fitted for high speed riding.

Although the company continued with precision engineering, production of motorcycles did not resume after the Second World War.

BSA

1906 - 1971

This is a 1949 SS100 that has been specially modified. It has a shortened frame, new rear plunger, Norton four-speed foot change and Rudge rear wheel with 8 in brakes.

The classic V-twin, four-stroke, JAP engine. Note the extremely well-finned exhaust manifolds, which help to disperse the hot air from the engine.

Quite capable of pulling a sidecar and two passengers: the Brough with Austin seven, 750cc engine of 1933.

In 1692, English king William lll was extremely worried that his army was poorly armed and that he would be obliged to buy all his armaments from Holland. So a contract was drawn up between His Majesty's Board of Ordinance and five Birmingham gunsmiths to supply firearms to the government of the day. Supply of firearms from Birmingham was not limited to England, but spread far and wide, even reaching many governments abroad. When the Crimean War began, a group of 14 gunsmiths from Birmingham formed the Birmingham Small Arms Trade Association. In 1861, the Birmingham Small Arms Company was created and a factory was opened at Small Heath in 1863. In 1880, the company moved into bicycle manufacture, making its own designs starting in 1881. The company concentrated on the production of a new magazine rifle between 1888 and 1893, but returned to bicycles in 1893, manufacturing hubs, frame lugs, pedals and many other components.

From 1903, whole machines were being built with BSA components and were powered by propriety engines, in particular those made by Belgian producer, Minerva. The first real BSA motorcycle, with its familiar green and cream tank, was introduced in 1909. It used a single-cylinder $3\frac{1}{2}$ hp engine with belt drive Soon this was joined by a 557cc machine and the two bikes were the mainstay of the BSA motorcycle range for some years.

As the First World War heightened, so did the production of military supplies. At its peak, the company was producing some 10,000 rifles per week and some 145,000 Lewis machine guns in total. The company was also making other mil-

1913 BSA 3 1/2hp model - the low handlebars, saddle and frame tube give a sense of sportiness. No pedalling gear was fitted to this racer.

itary supplies: staff cars and ambulances (made under the Daimler name which they bought in 1910), shells, fuses and aero components.

With the cessation of hostilities, the company once again returned to making motorcycles. By now it was under the control of BSA Cycles Ltd., a subsidiary of the original company. The two singles were still available, albeit under slightly different guise and a V-twin had been added to the range by 1920. This machine was seen as ideal for use with a fitted sidecar.

The little, 249cc, single cylinder, Round Tank model, named after the shape of its round fuel tank, was much loved as a utility machine.

The 1934 'Sloper' had a sloping engine (hence 'Sloper') and the fishtail silencers were very fashionable during the period.

In 1921, BSA challenged for the Senior TT and much work was done to produce a new machine. But it was a disaster: by the second lap, all six bikes had been retirád because of melted pistons.

Prior to the advent of the 1927 'sloper,' two smaller machines were produced. When the company acquired Daimler, they also acquired a designer by the name of Harold Briggs and his first machine was a small, but perky, 350cc, ohv machine capable of reaching 75 mph. The other was produced by Harry Pool and was a 250cc, side-valve model used by utility companies for their rounds. The model B, as it was designated, ended up with the nickname, 'round tank,' and sold some 35,000 examples. The Sloper, therefore, was introduced in 1927 as a 500cc, overhead-valve single, with its engine inclined forward. It was a firm favorite in the BSA range until the mid-1930s.

BSA's famous Star series started in the 1930s with the Blue Star singles in 250, 350 and 500cc versions. Featured is a 1934 348cc version.

Producing bikes for everyday use helped the company survive the Depression of the 1930s. The nippy, little, 150cc, ohv-engined model X was one such machine.

Following the Sloper was the sporty Blue Star range of machines, in 250cc, 350cc and 500cc versions, later superceded by the Empire Star, a more modern machine with foot gearchange and a chrome tank. The design came from the drawing board of a familiar name, Val Page, once of Ariel and Triumph. The M range earned quite a reputation, pulling the familiar AA sidecars for their patrol machines. It received even more

BSA was the largest supplier of motorcycles to the military in World War Two. This is the M20, which had a four-stroke, 469cc engine unit and special military fittings, such as panniers.

attention when used by the British Army during the Second World War.

Between 1940 and 1945, the BSA facilities were once again geared for military production. It now possessed 67 factories and was well-prepared to supply guns, fuses and other military items. A staggering 126,000 M20 military motorcycles were turned out for the Allied armies. The war took its toll, however, and the factory was heavily bombed by German bombers. 53 people on night-shift were killed. Much of the manufacturing equipment was also destroyed. But work continued.

When peace came and production of motorcycles for the general public was allowed once again, BSA's range consisted mainly of pre-war

Probably one of the most famous BSA's ever, the Bantam D1. They were produced between 1948 and 1963 and sold in their millions.

machines with the faithful M20 now making its appearance in civilian guise.

The first post-war machine presented was the B32 in 1946. Based on the B31, it was much improved and had better ground clearance, a high exhaust pipe and chrome mudguards.

The Bantam D1 engine was a single cylinder, piston port, two-stroke of 123cc. The cylinder was cast iron and topped with an aluminium

After this, the model A7 500cc machine made its debut at the Paris bike show.

In 1948, the original 125cc, two-stroke Bantam was introduced, its design taken from a DKW machine, the RT125. The Bantam became the best-selling British motorcycle of all time and over 500,000 machines were made over a period of 23 years.

BSA was also involved in trials and scrambling events and the B32 was given a 500cc engine and re-designated the B34. Riders John Draper, Bill Nicholson, Arthur Lampkin, John Burton and Brian Martin made names for themselves and brought a series of trophies to the BSA company. The 1949 ISDT alone saw 11 trophies go to BSA 500cc, Gold Star-mounted riders. For the first Isle of Man Clubman's TT, over thirty BSA machines were entered, with Harold Clarke taking the honors and the new Trophy on a Gold Star at a record speed of 75.18 mph.

Described as solid, dependable and economical, the 650cc A10 Golden Flash had four speed and plunger rear springing. It weighed 395 lbs.

The BSA A10 Golden Flash, designed by Bert Hopwood (originally of Norton), was announced in October 1949. It used a 650cc engine. It stayed in production until 1954 while higher performance models, the Super Flash and the Road Rocket, were introduced to export markets. The Gold Star was a versatile machine

The original Gold Star was a 500cc machine made in 1938. After the war, the name was given to the 350cc ZB32 model. This is a 1951 example.

and could be bought in several different versions: touring, trials, scrambles and, of course, racing. The DBD designation models of 1957 survived until the end of Gold Star production in 1963.

The 1960 C15T used a 247cc, single cylinder engine and produced 15hp. These were ridden with great success in trials competitions.

In 1958, a new series of unit-construction singles was developed which would remain in production until BSA ceased manufacturing. The ohv C15s with 250cc engines were increased to 350cc and even 450cc during their lifespan. This was a basic commuter bike manufactured as cheaply as possible and finally superseded by the B25 Barracuda.

In 1963, the sporty A65R was introduced, subsequently leading to the development of several sports machines based on the 500cc and 650cc engines: the Cyclone and Lightning as well as the Wasp and Hornet for the export market. The Spitfire Mk ll was introduced to the UK market in 1965 and upgraded to Mk lll and Mark lV status before finally being terminated in 1969.

The A65 was much more rounded than its predecessors. The 654cc twin was coupled to a four-speed gearbox.

By the mid-1960s, Japanese machines were starting to get a foothold on the world motorcycle market and BSA knew that they had to 'keep up or go under.' Doug Hopwood came up with the Rocket 3, a development of the Triumph twin which had quite radical styling for its time. Examples were sent to the United States, where they were warmly received. Several were entered in the Daytona race of 1970 and, although beaten by a Honda, they performed well. In 1971, the company returned to Daytona and won first, second and third places. The publicity was amazing – 'BSA takes Daytona.'

which subsequently continued motorcycle engineering and spares distribution. The BSA name was still used and machines like the Tracker and Bushman were produced with foreign engines. Buy-outs and mergers have resulted in the BSA name mutating into the BSA-Regal group. A 50cc mini bike entered production in 1996, followed by a limited edition, 400cc machine. In 1999, a hand-built 500cc, the Gold SR, was introduced. Although the die-hard BSA enthusiast will refuse to recognize this as a genuine BSA, the name lives on and the BSA roots are still there.

The Rocket 3 was designed with America in mind. Styling was different, to say the least, but the power of the 740cc, triple-cylinder engine was awesome.

These triumphs, however, were short-lived. Problems were building up at home. Following a rescue plan initiated by the Department of Industry, BSA, one of the major companies in Britain, was absorbed into Manganese Bronze in 1972. The plan to rescue the combined Norton, BSA and Triumph motorcycle factories ran into trouble. Triumph workers were unhappy and formed a workers' union, occupying the factory with a sit-in. The result was that 7,000 workers lost their jobs and the Norton Wolverhampton and BSA Small Heath factories closed. The union survived for four years before being rescued by the hastily assembled NVT motorcyles,

The Rocket 3 had a top speed of 120 mph.

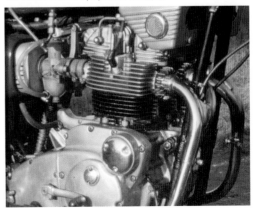

Buell

1988 to date

On 19 February 1998, Erik Buell announced that he had sold almost all of his interest in the Buell Motorcycle Company to his business partner, Harley-Davidson, Inc., a minority partner in the company since 1993. Buell raced bikes and worked as an apprentice engineer for the Harley-Davidson concern in Milwaukee. In 1982, he left Harley-Davidson to pursue the dream of creating his own race bike. The machine was the square-four, two-stroke RW750, a bike made to compete in the AMA Formula One road race series in America. A prototype was rolled out in the summer of 1983 at the Pocono Speedway. There was further development of the bike, and when tested later that year at Talladega, Alabama, it reached a phenomenal speed of 178 mph.

In 1984, a production version was released, but only one example was sold! Unfortunately, the AMA decided to scrap the 1985 Formula One racing series and the RW750 was rendered ineligible for the class.

Buell was determined not to be affected by this setback and returned to his project of building the first world class sportbike designed and made in America. Using his knowledge as a Harley-Davidson engineer and his experiences on the race track, he created his first sportbike, the Harley-Davidson-powered, single-seater RR1000. The bike used the Harley XR1000 engine and 50 examples were finished between 1987 and 1988. This was not a totally conventional machine: the engine was used as a fully stressed part of the frame and the rear suspension was mounted underneath the engine. The Buell-patented 'Uniplanar' system of rubber mountings was also introduced on the model. Being fully faired on both the front and rear wheels, the RR1000 was totally unique.

The RR1000 went through many development changes, especially when the Harley-Davidson 1203cc Evolution engine was added. Buell modified the frame and adjusted the mechanical parts to suit the upgrade and the RR1200 came about, introduced in 1988. 65 examples of this machine were made for sale in 1989. The RS model, a two-seater version of which 100 examples were made, was introduced in 1990. The machine was the first production bike to use 'upside down' front forks, stainless steel, braided brake pipes and six piston front calipers. A single-seater version of the RS was introduced in 1991 and named the RSS1200.

By 1993, Harley-Davidson had decided to expand its business by attracting new customers in new market segments. Harley had been keeping a close eye on Erik's work and naturally turned to him at this time. In February 1994, the new Buell Motorcycle Company was born, 49 percent owned by Harley-Davidson.

In 1994, the Thunderbolt S2, the first model made under the new partnership, was introduced, followed in 1996 by the Lightning S1. Classed as a 'street fighter,' the Lightning S1 had minimal bodywork and a 1203 engine. The Thunderbolt and the Lightening were continually upgraded. They were followed by the Cyclone M2. The new Thunderstorm engine was introduced to the Buell line-up in 1998. In 1999, the machines were given new bodywork, new frames and new suspension, along with new paintwork.

In 2000, a completely new machine, the Blast, represented a move away from twins to a single cylinder with a 492cc engine. The Firebolt

A rare RR1000 Battletwin. Fully enclosed bodywork included the front wheel. There is a 998cc Harley-Davidson engine tucked inside.

This is a 1999 version of the S1 White Lightning. It uses an air-cooled, ohv, V-twin, 1203cc engine. The top speed is rated at over 140 mph.

Bultaco

1958 to date

This Spanish company was founded in 1958 by Francisco Bulto, a designer at the Montesa motorcycle company in Spain. His decision to form his own company started with a disagreement with his employer, who wanted to stop competing. Unable to persuade the company hierarchy to continue competition, Bulto left and started his own company from a farmhouse in the village of Adrian de Besos, on the outskirts of Barcelona, his home city.

The early road machines were small capacity. The original, a single cylinder, two-stroke, was designated TTS. Water-cooled versions followed, available in 125cc and 250cc. They were made until 1969, when an air-cooled, 350cc model was produced. In 1965, a talented rider, Ramon Torres, crashed a Bultaco and was killed, which nearly made Bulto pull out of the sport. Fortunately, he was dissuaded. It was at this point that the 125cc and 250cc road racing bikes were starting to perform. A highlight for the company came in 1967: a one-two-three finish in the Isle of Man Production TT by three factory-entered Mantrillas in the 250cc class.

In 1962, a very welcome surprise came with Don Rickman's victory, riding at Bultaco Mat-

XBR9R was introduced the following year and went on to become the XB12R. Today, Buell is well-established around the world and boasts a mouthwatering array of machines. The company has clearly made its mark on the bike world and is sure to develop exciting models in the future.

Like its predecessors, the 2004 Buell XB 12 R Firebolt is full of technology and innovation. It has a 1203cc motor and a five-speed gearbox.

The 2004 Buell XB 12 R belt drive system features an additional idler pulley that ensures a constant path length for the belt.

In between races: a 1960s Bultaco 125 TSS race bike.

jese, at the 250cc Spanish motocross Grand Prix. The Matisse used a Rickman frame and the two Rickman brothers were well-known in the scrambling world.

The first Bultaco entered a motocross race in 1965. The machine was the Pursang Mark 1, a 250cc machine with four-speed gearbox, upgraded to five-speed in 1966. The model was produced into the 1970s, increasing to 370cc in size.

One legendary name in the Bultaco story is Sammy Miller. The Irishman made his mark with his superb riding. In 1964, Bulto approached Miller with a clean sheet of paper and asked him to design a winning machine. From this came the Sherpa which, so the story goes, was completed within a month. The all-conquering Sherpa trail bike achieved five straight wins in the World Trials Championship between 1975 and 1979.

In 1976, Bultaco returned to the Grand Prix scene, winning the 50cc championship. The feat was repeated in 1978 and 1981. By 1978, a new, two-stroke machine was on the Bultaco books, the Frontera, available in 250cc and 370cc versions. However, all was not well with the company and due to industrial unrest and market pressures, Bultaco production closed in 1979.

The factory reopened in 1980, but closed again in 1983.

In 1998, however, Bultaco hit the motorcycle scene once again with the Sherco, a 250

Probably the best known Bultaco model: a 1970s 325cc Sherpa.

trials bike and even after a 20 year absence, they could still make an impact. Graham Jarvis won the Scottish Six Days Trial on his lightweight machine. The Bultaco name was used under license and the actual factory bought out by the Derby concern, but the real thing was not seen since the factory closed in the 1980s.

The launch of the 250 Sherco in 1999 was also the return of Bultaco. It used a single-cylinder, two-stroke engine.

Cagiva

1978 – date

 In 1950, Giovanni Castiglioni founded CAGIVA, a company producing small metal components. The name of the company refers both to the founder's initials and to the name of the city where Cagiva bought the factory in Schiranna, Varese, Italy on 17 October 1978. In 1978, Cagiva entered the motorcycle business and the small family concern quickly became one of the most dynamic motorcycle industries in Europe. The factory in Varese was once the home of the Aermacchi motorcycle business.

Cagiva are no strangers to the scooter world. The Cucciolo has been around for some time now and continues to serve the commuter well.

With an area of 5 square miles, the site hosted skilled technicians and engineers inherited from Aermacchi aeronautics and from the nearby MV Agusta Company. With such rich human potential, the Castiglioni brothers revamped motercycle production by investing in technology and founding a new technical office.

From its oblong front headlight to the baby rack on the rear, the 1993 W12 was an ideal off-road machine.

Just one year later, the company could boast more than 150 employees, an annual production of 40,000 motorbikes and a brochure showing 8 models with two-stroke engines ranging from 125cc to 350cc. All were sold under the HD Cagiva brand. By 1980, the entire production was sold under the Cagiva name and the company had made its mark as a fully operational factory capable of designing and building its own engines, frames and accessories.

Between 1981 and 1982, as a result of sound marketing policies, much success was obtained and innovative ideas were implemented by the Castiglioni brothers. Good quality products outshone the competition, prices were fixed at moderate levels and a good level of servicing was assured.

It was such self-confidence that made Cagiva the only Italian manufacturer able to fight the invasion of the mighty Japanese brands. The

A 600cc engine gave the W16 power to tackle all types of terrain.

Cagiva models were innovative, developing new segments on the market and continuing to dominate the small displacement sector. The range spanned from cross to enduro to street bikes with international sales distribution. In 1983, the company entered the large displacement sector. An exclusive deal with Ducati enabled Cagiva to use the Ducati 350cc to 1000cc, four-stroke engines.

Between 1985 and 1986, the expansion continued to buy-out competitors who either faced difficult times or were not yet fully developed. Thus Ducati, Moto Morini and Husqvarna came into the Cagiva fold. A new

commercial company was subsequently founded in Bologna in 1986, Cagiva Commerciale S.P.A. The company was now selling in more than 50 countries. In 1987, in the Republic of San Marino, the Cagiva Research Center (CRC) was founded. It became a leader in technology and style research for the entire motorbike sector, partially brought about thanks to the friendship between Claudio Castiglioni and Massimo Tamburini, director of the Center.

In 1990, a new factory was built at Morazzone (Varese) to produce both steel and aluminium frames. The factory subsequently housed the Crimson Design Center, directed by the Argentinian Miguel Galluzzi. In 1991, Cagiva bought out the MV Agusta brand, a company with a great history and a long list of racing victories. The buy-out initiated a radical plan of investments aimed at revitalizing and renewing the myth of the MV mark.

In 1996, for strategic reasons, Cagiva decide to sell the Ducati and Moto Morini brands. A year later, the official presentation of the new MV Agusta was held at the Milan International Salon. The motorcyling world was completely overwhelmed by the fabulous new F4 Serie Oro.

First launched in 1991, the Mito (which means "myth" in Italian), is a small capacity replica road racer. It uses a very lively 125cc, two-stroke engine.

A new factory in Cassinetta di Biandronno (Varese) opened in 1999 with the company now comprising:

Schiranna - top management, mechanical production of strategic parts, engine production and assembly, painting of frames and components, research and development.

Looking like something from the film Jurassic Park, *the Raptor Xtra has its own unique styling. Power is via a Suzuki 1000cc, V-twin unit.*

The 2004 Navigator: Cagiva put the Suzuki TL1000 V-twin engine into the Grand Canyon frame to produce this muscular machine.

Morazzon - frame production, Crimson style center.

Cassinett - full assembly line, parts warehouse, technical assistance.

San Marino - Cagiva Research Center (CRC).

The employees now numbered 500, with 150 designated solely for research and development. In 1999, the group was also restructured so that MV Agusta Motor now became the main brand, comprising Cagiva and Husqvarna. At the Milan

The Cagiva 500cc GP racing machine used by Eddie Lawson and Alex Barros in 1992. Lawson gained Cagiva's first victory in Hungary.

International Salon, the new Cagiva models, including the Raptor, V-Raptor and Navigátor were presented. All the models were well-received, both in Italy and worldwide.

RACING HISTORY
500 GP

1980 The Cagiva name appeared for the first time in the 500 World Championships at Nürburgring, Germany, where Virginio Ferrari qualified with the first Cagiva racing motorbike.

1981 The Cagiva 2C2 was introduced to the grand prix circuit. It developed 118hp from a 4-cylinder, in-line engine with rotary disc distribution.

1982 Cagiva gained points for the first time in the GP series.

1987 Randy Mamola (runner up for the World Championship) raced for Cagiva.

1988 Spa Grand Prix (Belgium) - Cagiva gained their first podium with the C588. The bike used a new aluminium frame with a curved rear fork and a sealed fairing, a first in racing.

1988-1990 Cagiva gained points as well as experience in the GP series.

Another American who raced for the Cagiva team, Randy Mamola, won the company's first podium finish in Belgium in 1988.

1991 Eddie Lawson, three-time world champion, joined Cagiva and immediately clinched a podium at Le Castelet (France) and an overall 6th place in the championship.

1992 In Hungary, Cagiva won their first race, a just reward for the dedication the Italian team had put in throughout all these years of competition with the big Japanese teams.

1993 Doug Chandler was on the podium in the first race of the season and John Kocinski, enrolled by the team manager Giacomo Agostini at the end of the season, won at Laguna Seca.

1994 Cagiva had its most exiting season yet with Kocinski on the podium seven times. It won the Australia GP and was classified 3rd overall.

1995 New strategies pushed Cagiva to retire from racing. The MV Agusta project became more and more important.

MOTOCROSS

In 1979, the 'Reds,' as they were known, from Schiranna, started racing in the international series and with Renato Zocchi in the world championship. Cagiva immediately obtained results in the 125cc class.

Cagiva's best period, however, was between 1984 and 1988 when they halted the Suzuki monopoly. Victory came in the Finnish with Pekka Vehkonen in 1985 and the Dutch in 1986 with Dave Strijbos. In the last race of 1984 in Luxembourg, Corrado Maddii broke his tibia while 30 points in the lead and in the last race of 1987, Strijbos lost the championship against Bayle.

In 1987 and 1988, Vehkonen came in second overall in the 250cc series. In 1988, Cagiva raced its last Motocross. During this season, the transition to the new brand, Husqvarna, was gradually carried out, using the new blue and white colors.

RALLY

In 1985, Cagiva made their first appearance in the Paris-Dakar. Hubert Auriol, Giles Picard and Giampaolo Marinoni, who finished 8th overall, made up the team. Over the following years, Cagiva showed themselves to be exciting contenders. Ciro De Petri and Edy Orioli won. The courageous Hubert Auriol broke both ankles. These results all helped to market the machines around the world. Using the Dakar experience, Cagiva promoted the Elefant model in various displacements over a period of 10 years. Other rallies were contested and some victories gained. Cagiva won the Pharaohs' Rally three times and the Tunisia Rally twice.

The Desmodromic, Lucky Explorer, Paris-Dakar desert racer.

Racing in the sand not only takes a good machine, but incredible riding skills as well.

Calthorpe

1909 - 1938

George Hands, manu-facturer of bicycles in Birmingham, England during the Victorian era, was no stranger to the world of two wheels. His company went through several name changes, but the first Calthorpe motor-cycle was exhibited at the Stanley Show in Islington in 1909. This machine used a belt drive and a 3hp White & Poppe engine. In 1910, at the Olympia show, Calthorpe exhib-ited no less than six machines including a sidecar model. The following year, there was more choice: a 2hp, lightweight model was available accompanied by a larger 4hp model, to which the company would supply a sidecar if required. In 1912, the first V-twin was introduced, equipped with a Precision 750cc engine with a kick start.

After the First World War, at the 1919 Olympia show, the company exhibited only two lightweight machines. One used a JAP 2hp and the other a 2hp, Peco, two-stroke engine. The following year, the JAP-engined machine

Exposed valve springs were often a problem.

A 1938 Calthorpe made in the last year they were in business.

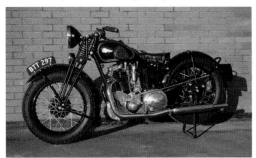

This 1938 model had a 250cc engine and no springing. A Burman gearbox was used.

remained almost the same, but the Peco-engined machine was upgraded to a 350cc engine with 3hp. In 1921, there was a substantial reduction in the price of most of the machines and a new V-twin Calthorpe made its debut at the end of the year: a 4hp, JAP-engined machine with Sturmey Archer three-speed hub gear and side-car. By 1924, all the bikes were fitted with chain-drive, clutch and a kick-start.

In 1926, Calthorpe introduced a new sporting 500cc with ohc, a single cylinder engine made by Calthorpe itself. Then came the 'Ivory,' in 1928: a completely new machine with a duplex frame and saddle tank. It had a beautiful ivory color scheme, hence the name. This machine went through many upgrades and was with the company to the end when both the company car and cycle business were crippled by financial difficulties. The company was finally liquidated in 1938. The outbreak of the Second World War destroyed any plans the new owner, Bruce Douglas, had to revive the mark.

Chater Lea

1900 - 1937

The company was established in 1900 as the Chater Lea Manufacturing Company Limited and produced components for frames from its

In 1903, Chater Lea produced their first complete machine. The one featured is a 1907 model with belt drive.

More than a dozen different engines were fitted into Chater Lea frames – the one here is a 1907 Peugeot V-twin unit of 800cc.

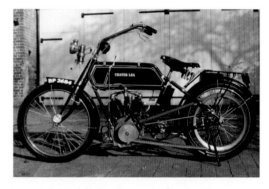

Equipped with a horn and a speedometer, like a police machine.

The popular 1930 Calthorpe Ivory, which used a 348cc engine.

Chater Lea became well-known for supplying machines to the English Automobile Association. This 1936 machine is in everyday livery.

Golden Lane Works in London, England, where it remained until 1912, when it moved to the Banner Street premises. Full frames and then motorcycles in 1903, following component manufacture.

In 1908, the first Chater Lea at the Isle of Man TT finished a respectable sixth. Many different engines such as JAP, Blackburne, Villiers and even Peugeot were used during the lifespan of the company. Chater Lea machines also broke many records, and W.D. Marchant produced an ohc engine which made its debut in March 1925, attaining 100 mph, making it the world's fastest 350cc machine at the time. During the 1920s and 1930s, Chater Lea was famous for the machines it supplied to the Automobile Association, with their distinctive yellow paintwork. From 1930, the motorcycle side of the company deteriorated, even though it exhibited up to 1934. By 1936, shadowed by war, Chater Lea motorcycle production ended and the company produced munitions during the Second World War. After 1945, motorcycle production recommenced.

Although only single cylinder, this 1936 machine used a 545cc power unit and was quite capable of pulling a sidecar.

Gearchange was still carried out by moving this lever either backwards or forwards, depending on the desired gear.

Clyno

1909 - 1916

The Clyno Engineering Company was formed by two cousins, A.P. Smith and F.W.A. Smith, to make adjustable belt pulleys for motorcycles. A small workshop was rented in Thrapstone, England and orders soon began to pour in.

The two cousins were now thinking about producing their own motorcycle and soon a prototype, a 350cc machine of simple construction, featuring a Chater Lea frame and a Stevens engine, was produced. A few were sold locally. Later, a V-twin was made, again with a Stevens engine. Stevens were now in voluntary liquidation and negotiations were carried out to purchase it. The Clyno Company moved to Wolverhampton.

A new, chain-drive, two-speed model was developed and was used successfully by Frank Smith, not only in trials, but on hill climbs. A

A view from the top of the 1914 Clyno V-twin, four-stroke, 744cc engine. The Amac carburettor is positioned between the barrels.

The transmission was all chain with three-speed countershaft gearbox, operated via the lever situated on the right of the fuel tank.

Everything was well-engineered, robust and reliable on the Clyno. Many machines were sent to the front during the First World War.

This beautifully restored 1921 Clyno model B has a 261cc, two-stroke engine producing 2.75hp. The drive belt is enclosed at the engine end.

great deal of work was put into making the side-car a stable accessory.

The Clyno Motor Cycle Detachable and Interchangeable wheel, an influential invention in motorcycle history, was introduced.

The trials was intensified. Well-known riders such as Hugh Gibson and Archie Cocks joined the team. A 250cc, single cylinder two-stroke was manufactured and equipped with lamps, horn and number plate.

The machines remained little changed and at the end of the year, the First World War dealt a blow to the company, already suffering from financial problems. But war contracts helped the financial situation slightly and the company began manufacturing combinations with attached machine guns known as the Vickers-Clyno machine gun/motorcycle outfit.

Disagreements arose between the two cousins and it was eventually agreed that A.P. Smith would retire from the company, after which very few motorcycles were made and the company concentrated on motor cars.

Comfort was always a prime objective for Clyno as is demonstrated clearly here.

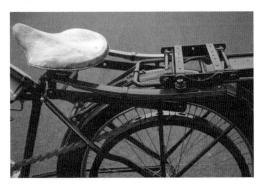

This early Clyno has an outside flywheel and high handlebars. The machine is one of the exhibits at the Moray Motor Museum in Scotland.

Cotton

1920 - 1980

Francis Willoughby Cotton patented his first design before the First World War. After the war, he decided to carry on with his project and acquired a small building at 11a Bristol Street in Gloucester where he set about developing the now familiar Cotton frames. The Cotton motorcycle company based in Gloucester, England, began manufacturing motorcycles proper in 1920. The company was noted for its triangulated, lightweight and rigid frame design.

The first Cotton was announced in 1919 for the 1920 season. It was a modestly powered machine with a 269cc, Villiers, two-stroke engine, with a two-speed gearbox and the final drive was via a belt. By 1922, a 350cc, side-valve model was added and sales began to increase for the little company. The engine used in this machine was a Blackburne linked to a three-speed Burman gearbox. However, side-valve engines were seen as old-fashioned and when Blackburne announced they were changing to ohv engines, Cotton took full advantage. It was not enough, however, to have good-looking machines with good specifications. What was needed was a good result in a major tournament. None was bigger than the Isle of Man TT and Cotton entered three machines for the Junior event in 1922.

While the name, Stanley Woods, is now well-known in motorcycling history, he was just a boy from the West Country. Along with two others, however, he secured a ride on one of the Cotton bikes for the TT, which turned

The 1927 Cotton TT racer had a 490cc, single cylinder, ohv, JAP four-stroke unit with three-speed close ratio gearbox and weighed about 285 lbs.

The straight, triangulated frame tubes, running from head stock to the rear wheel spindle was the principle on which Cotton was established.

out to be quite an experience. At one stage, the machine ignited while refuelling, but after a gritty ride, he finished a respectable fifth with the other two following in eleventh and fifteenth places.

In 1923, Cotton kept the same riders and Woods, at the tender age of 19, won the first of his many TTs, despite hitting a wall and finishing with almost totally decimated brakes. From this point on, the Cotton started to make its mark in other races, even finishing second in the French Grand Prix. There was a new category for the TT in 1924, the 175cc, Ultra-Lightweight TT, and the Cottons came in second, third and fifth, even though Woods had moved on by now. Armed with so much success, the Cotton Company began to reap the rewards and sales started to pick up. The little factory was not big enough for so much production and a new site was found in Quay Street, also in Gloucester.

In 1926, Cotton achieved their best TT result ever, by default. The three machines came in first, third and fourth, the lone Moto Guzzi of Pietro Gherzi splitting the first two. But it was later declared that the Moto Guzzi was using a different make of spark plug from the one specified on the entry form. So Gherzi and his Guzzi were disqualified for technical reasons, bikes three and four were moved up one place each and Cotton had the first, second and third places.

In 1927, the frames were modified to accommodate new engines from Blackburne

Seen here is a rare 350 Cotton machine from 1926. The triangulated frame is very evident.

and JAP. Following the Depression years of 1930 and 1931, which hit everyone's pocket, the company also sold a small, 150cc model alongside its other larger capacity machines. Like many other motorcycle firms, Cotton kept the company busy making military machines during the Second World War. After the war, it produced a rather unsuccessful, JAP, V-twin-engined machine with a rear-sprung frame.

Cotton seemed doomed until two experts came to the rescue. Monty Denley and Pat Onions renamed the company E. Cotton Motorcycles and produced a range of Villiers-engined roadsters. The famous Cotton triangulated frame was shelved.

The Cotton Telstar was made between 1963 and 1967 and featured a 247cc, single cylinder, two-stroke engine which could reach 110 mph. This is a replica machine.

The Cotton Telstar, as it was known, was raced by Bill Ivy, Derek Minter and Peter Inchley among others and a Cotton won the British Road Race Championship in 1965. Disaster struck when Villiers closed down. Engines had to be obtained from Italy via the Minarelli Company. The company was now involved with trials and enduro racing, initially using 175cc and later 220cc engines. There was another move to Stratton Road, still in Gloucester and another new machine was developed which used a Rotax engine, the Cotton 250cc model LCRS. In 1980, Armstrong took over the company, but there is still some dispute as to who actually owns what.

Coventry Eagle

1909 - 1939

The company's origins date back to the Victorian era of bicycles. Under the 'Royal Eagle' name, Coventry had a workshop in Lincoln Street, Coventry, England. From bicycles, it progressed to motorcycles, producing what was simply a bicycle with an MMC engine fitted to the front in the early 1900s. By 1903, however, a better frame was made, along with a choice of engine make and size. The Trimo, a three-wheeler with a steering wheel and a passenger seat placed in the middle of the two front wheels, was presented. It was powered by a 2¼hp De Dion engine. Then the company disappeared from the scene, re-emerging after the First World War. Two new sidecar models were offered in 1921, each with a 500cc single and a 680cc, V-twin, JAP engine. They were followed by two new sporting models, designed by Percy Mayo, using Sturmey Archer gearboxes and equipped with kick-starters.

By 1922, the Coventry range had become comprehensive. There was the TS1, a 2½hp two-stroke, the S29 with a 293cc, JAP engine, the S35 with a 350cc, JAP engine, the sporting S50 with a 500cc, JAP engine, and the C68, a 680cc-engined V-twin used for pulling sidecars.

In 1923, a new ultra lightweight model, the S15, was introduced. There was also a new 348cc model, the S34 with its Blackburne engine and a big single, the C55, with a 500cc, JAP engine. At the top of the range was a big, twin, 8hp, Super Sports Solo with a 960cc, JAP engine. The following year, a new sport model, the Flying-8, made its debut.

This range of machines changed little over the next few years. A two-stroke with a pressed steel frame (a feature that would distinguish the company for some time) was shown in 1927. By 1928, there were four pressed steel frame bikes on show, alongside a good selection of engine sizes and other models. Among these were the Flying-350, Flying 500 and the two Flying-8 models. As the Depression hit, the company slimmed down. Smaller capacity machines were exhibited and, although bicycle production continued after the Second World War, the motorcycle wing shut down.

Two engine sizes available in 1933, 250cc and this 150cc unit.

The 1927 Coventry Eagle Flying Six with 674cc, V-twin engine. Note that both exhaust pipes came out the same side of the machine.

By 1933, low-priced uniformity was the order of the day and only two engine sizes were available. Featured is a 1934 150cc model.

Curtiss

1901 - 1913

Glenn Hammond Curtiss was born in Hammondsport, New York State, in 1878. His names were chosen both in honor of the town founder and of the glen which graces the head waters of Lake Keuka. In this way, he was forever linked to his birthplace.

As a boy, he worked as a bicycle messenger for Western Union and soon realized his love of speed. He purchased an engine kit from E.R. Thomas and fitted it to a bicycle, giving the machine the nickname, Happy Hooligan.

But Curtiss was convinced he could produce a better engine and his first single cylinder engine came out in 1901. He built up a sporting goods and bicycle business, including motorbikes, under the Hercules name. He

The first single cylinder Curtis machine came in 1901, but V-twins were also produced for racing.

went on to build a V-twin for racing, using it to break several records. In 1905, on the horse track at Syracuse, New York fairgrounds, Curtiss set three new records. He went on to win major dirt-track events and broke two more speed records at Ormond Beach, Florida.

In 1907, the New Yorker set a new world record for the mile at 76 mph. The excitement,

however, was only just beginning. With the help of two friends, he rolled out the most outrageous machine, a 7 ft long motorcycle with a V-8 engine. The machine had shaft drive to the rear wheel and weighed 275 lbs. Following a two-mile run to build speed, Glen Curtiss crossed the line at 136.36 mph to become the fastest man on earth.

Following the bike speed record of 1907, Curtiss, also an aviation pioneer, concentrated on the aviation side of his talents and formed his own aviation company. The two wheel business lasted a further six years, headed by his racing friend Tank Waters, who did business under the Marvel name. Glenn Hammond Curtiss died in 1930 and was buried in Hammondsport's Pleasant Valley Cemetery.

The Curtiss V8 engine, initially designed for use in an aircraft. The engine in this record breaker was 4000cc and had a top speed of 136 mph.

The machine that Curtiss rolled out at Ormond Beach, Florida, USA, in 1907. It became the fastest machine on earth after reaching 136 mph.

Cyklon

1900 - 1905

Not the best place to have an engine: this unit was a 300cc, four-stroke which could reach 22 mph.

Based in Berlin, Germany, the Cyklon works was a pioneer of the German motorcycle industry. Owned by Paul Schauer, the company used a variety of propriety engines, including De Dion and Werner. Its early 1900 model had the engine fitted on the front of the machine, above the front wheel and mudguard. Weight distribution would, no doubt, have been a problem especially when turning or braking. The machine was equipped with a belt-drive to the front wheel. The usual pedals and chain were affixed to the rear wheel to help it to start and climb hills.

The machine was evaluated by the German Army in 1902, but there were problems with the carburettor and the electrics and the tests came to nothing. Cyklon also built a three-wheeler called the Cyklonette, but production was short-lived.

The 1900 Cyclon was not the most stable of machines because the position of its engine tended to make it unstable, in particular when cornering, braking or doing both at the same time.

CZ - Jawa

1929 - to date

Seen here is a rare 1958 CZ 250cc Grand prix racer. The company was successful both in road racing and off-road events.

CZ – The Factory, known as Ceska Zbrojov-ka, was built in 1918 to manufacture arma-ments in Czechoslovakia. It was only in 1930 that an interest was shown in motorcycles. Like many others, the company started by making bicycles and its first machine, a rather ungainly two-stroke, was based on a man's bicycle. 1933, however, saw the introduction of a new model with many improvements, but still based on a bicycle frame. It was desig-nated CZ76 with sprung forks and a 76cc, two-stroke engine mounted in the frame below the seat.

By 1934, the CZ98 was in production, a simple machine with a two-stroke engine, but lessons still needed to be learned. 1935 intro-duced new 250cc and 175cc models. The CZ175 had a pressed steel frame, single cylinder, two-stroke engine and a foot-con-trolled, three-speed gearbox. The CZ 250 sold in Touring and Sport versions. In 1934, CZ entered competition with the CZ175. They introduced a 500cc model in 1937, fol-lowed by the introduction of sidecars for that model in 1938.

The outbreak of war stopped production and the Germans appropriated the factory for arms and munitions manufacuring. It did not open again until 1946.

The first machine to herald its new era was the CZ125 A, a twin port single, with hand change and a rigid frame. People wanted small, reliable machines and the 125 sold well. 1947 saw the introduction of the CZ125B. The only real change was the engine, a new, two-stroke, twin port single with foot gearchange. CZ returned to competition at the ISDT and won

the Silver Vase. In 1949, Jawa amalgamated with CZ under the control of the Czech Auto Industry (CSAZ).

JAWA –
The factory was situated in Prague and also produced armaments. However, it was found-ed by Frantisek Janecek in 1928 to produce

When Jawa first started production, they used a Wanderer engine, as featured in this 1929, 18hp, 500cc model.

motorcycles. Janecek did not want to develop his own machines, but wanted to produce a current machine under licence. He chose the Wanderer 498cc, four-stroke model, which was expensive to make and only about 1000 were produced. The name JAWA comes from the fist two letters of the founder's name: JA and first two letters from the Wanderer machine. When the Wanderer failed to sell, a reappraisal of the situation was carried out and he decid-ed to make his own machine, which did not sell well either.

An Englishman, G.W. Patchett, showed the way forward. In 1932, a machine with a Villiers, 175cc, two-stroke engine and Albion three-speed gearbox was produced with great success, followed by a 250cc machine and JAWA become the most popular mark in Czechoslovakia, even bigger than the imported brands. During this period, a four-stroke, 350cc was presented with a new duplex frame and more models were added to the line-up

1955 saw this twin cylinder, 500cc model which could produce 28hp. The pressed steel frame was still evident.

A fine example of a 1935 350cc, four-stroke Jawa. The machine had no rear suspension and gears were selected with a lever.

The engine for the 350 produced 14hp. Note the spring for the rider's seat and the kickstart lever.

during the 1930s, the two-strokes remaining best sellers.

An attempt to produce a scooter, the Robot, followed in 1937, alongside a 98cc, two-stroke and the 175cc and 250cc, Villiers engines were replaced by Jawa's in 1938.

1949 saw a new 250cc two-stroke, an advanced machine that became the basis of Jawa roadster design for years to come. Then, in 1949, Jawa joined forces with CZ.

CZ/JAWA –

Production continued, a strange situation for two former rivals now competing together.

In 1951, Jawa produced a 500cc, ohc twin while CZ put out a 150cc, commuter class model. And Jawa built a 350cc, two-stroke twin in 1954. By 1956, the 350cc Jawa was catalogued as the Jawa-CZ 350cc and a similar 250cc came on stream.

In 1959, a scooter, the 175cc Cezeta, later also produced as a three-wheeler delivery truck, was presented and the Jawa-CZ Motokov range unveiled the Manet S100 scooter. Two new mopeds appeared: the Stadion S22 and S32, using 50cc, two-stroke engines and produced under the Jawa banner. As a rule, the CZ machines were small capacity bikes and larger capacity machines were labeled Jawa.

The company was still entering competitions such as the ISDT, although the machines were of fairly simple design. Off-road racing was their main concern, but track racing was undertaken as well. Two racing machines of interest in the mid 1960s were the 175cc and 250cc ohc singles, closely followed by a 125cc also. 1963 saw a 250cc CZ come in second at the World Motocross Championships and when the 360cc came out in 1964, ridden by Joel Robert, he seized the championship. A second championship was gained in 1965 with rider Viktor Arbekov and the 500cc championship was won in 1966 while rider Paul Friedrichs was equally successful in 1967 and 1968. Gold medals were also won in the ISDT.

A little known company, ESO, was also part of the CSAZ operation. They had been around

This 1970s CZ is fitted with special touring screen and top-box.

Jawa have always been well-known for their speedway machines. Seen here are bikes at the start of a typical race.

since 1949 and, although successful, lacked the publicity of CZ and Jawa. They produced a 498cc speedway machine called the ESO DT5, later the Jawa DT type 680. In road racing, the 250cc, 350cc and 385cc machines succeeded, but there was a new machine, the 125cc, R67, a V-twin, two-stroke and a V4, 350cc version following. Bill Ivy used the V4 with great success.

In 1967, the CZ360 was introduced to the motocross and trials scene. By 1968, a new range of machines, from 50cc to 350cc, were available. As the 1970s dawned, the company continued to be successful and Jawa won the World Trophy in the ISDT from 1970 through 1974.

The largest machine in the Jawa range in 1977 was the 350 twin De Luxe tourer and two CZ developments by the UK importers were the CZ MX 250 RV and the MX 400 RV fitted with reed valves.

Cagiva bought out CZ for their nuts and bolts facility and the last CZ machines, now with the Cagiva logo, were produced between 1988 and 1989. They still used the CZ emblem in Eastern Europe.

In 1997, JAWA Moto spol. s r.o. was established as the successor authorized to use the registered trademark, JAWA, and 2004 saw new machines emerging from the Czech Republic.

The Jawa 650 Classic was launched in 2004, powered by a single cylinder, four-stroke, water-cooled Rotax engine.

Daimler

1885

Reutlingen, Germany, 1865. Thirty-one year-old engineer, Gottlieb Daimler, was workshop manager of the 'Bruderhaus,' a social institute with adjoining production facilities built and run by orphans. (Daimler himself was tragically orphaned at the age of ten.) His attention was caught by Wilhelm Maybach, a 19-year-old with a talent for drawing. The two formed a close bond.

In 1872, the Deutz Gasmotorenfabrik was looking for a technical director. Daimler seized the opportunity, both for himself and Maybach. One of the factory's founders in Deutz was Nikolaus August Otto, whose atmospheric gas

engines had already drawn attention. Maybach was charged with optimizing these designs and preparing them for series production. Otto and Daimler made no secret of their mutual animosity and Daimler returned to Southern Germany in 1882. He purchased a large property in Cannstatt, near Stuttgart, Daimler set up a workshop in a glassed-in outhouse with plenty of light. He appointed Maybach chief designer. The objective: to give the four-stroke engine a helping hand. Gas, previously used mainly for removing stains and available exclusively from the pharmacist, fuelled the engine.

A major breakthrough came at the end of 1883 when the pair succeeded in running a single cylinder, four-stroke engine, which was far lighter than the Deutz engines. In 1884, it reached the 600 rpm mark, a sensational speed for the time. The high speed was made possible by the curve groove mechanism, invented by Daimler and Maybach, as well as by the hot-tube ignition process, which was another revolutionary step forward. In his patent application dated 16 December 1883, Daimler described the ignition mechanism as "a metal

The wooden frame test bed for the 1883 Daimler engine. The two smaller wheels at the side helped to keep it upright when at a standstill.

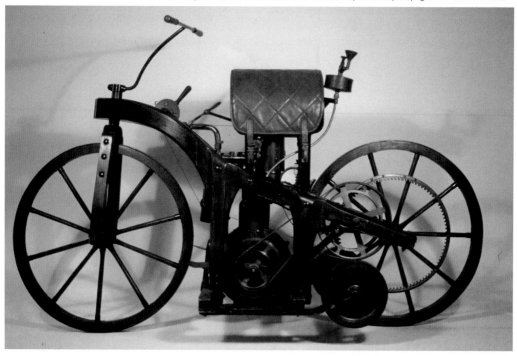

ignition cap, the inside of which has a constantly open connection to the combustion chamber," which then ignited the fuel/air mixture.

In 1884, the first fast-running engine followed, equipped with a vertical cylinder and capable of running on gas, thanks to Maybach's float carburettor. The first test engine of this type went down in engineering history as the 'Grandfather Clock,' a reference to its striking arrangement with the vertical cylinder. It generated about one horsepower at a speed of 600 rpm.

Daimler and Maybach initially focused on two-wheel, motorized transport. In 1885, a 'grandfather clock' with a displacement of 0.264 quarts powered what became the first motorcycle: "a gas or petroleum engine positioned underneath the seat and between the two vehicle axles of a single-track chassis," to quote the original patent issued on 29 August 1885. Three months later, Maybach tested the so-called 'Reitwagen' (riding carriage) from Cannstatt to Untertürkheim (a two mile route), without experiencing problems and reaching a top speed of 7.5 mph.

De Dion

1885

Albert Comte de Dion was born in France in 1856. While still in his twenties, he met Georges Bouton, a steam engine maker. The two men became partners, creating the De Dion-Bouton Company. They produced a selection of steam-powered tricycles, one of which won the Paris – Rouen race of 1894. It is said that after seeing all the oily machines at the end of the race, the Count instructed Bouton to forget steam and develop a gas engine. The engine was a 120cc unit initially using the hot tube ignition system and later replaced by electrical ignition. 1885 saw it fitted to a tricycle behind the rear axle. Examples of the machine were entered in long distance races. Engine capacity was increased and soon $1^1/_4$, $1^3/_4$ and $2^2/_3$hp units were available, followed by water cooling.

1901 was the last year of the De Dion-Bouton tricycle, after the quadricycle and forecar were developed. Engines were later fitted to two-wheel bicycles.

The Daimler engine was housed in the wooden frame. It was a four-stroke, single cylinder, 264cc unit and could reach a speed of 7 mph.

This is the engine of a 1904 model de Dion, single cylinder machine. De Dion engines were used by many different manufacturers at the time.

DKW

1919 - late 1970's

Company founder Jörgen Skafte Rasmussen was born in Nakskow, Denmark in 1898. He moved to Dusseldorf, Germany in 1904 and then to Zschopau, Saxony in 1907. Rasmussen began to experiment with a steam-driven motor vehicle in 1916, registering DKW as a trademark. In 1919, the company, now renamed Zschopauer Motorenwerke, switched to the manufacture of small, two-stroke engines, then marketed under the DKW name.

Rasmussen's first year of trading came in 1920 and he added the Hugo Rupp-designed, 122cc, two-stroke engine in 1921. This could be clipped to a conventional bicycle. The rear wheel was driven via a leather belt. The Golem scooter was also marketed and the following year, the Lamos scooter with a 142cc engine was presented.

The 175cc, single cylinder, two-stroke engine of the little 1925 racer. Note the rather strange finning on the exhaust downtube.

Weighing a mere 154 lbs and with the number 3 still on the side, a DKW racing machine. Belt-driven and able to top 60 mph.

The Z 500 model of 1926 was the first DKW motorcycle with a twin-cylinder engine. Here is a 1927 model Z 500 with water cooling.

The 497cc, water cooled, two-stroke engine of the Z 500, which could produce 15hp at 4000 rpm. It was an extremely heavy machine.

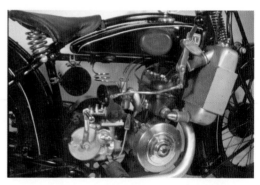

In 1924, the SM (Steel Model) machine, a 173cc, single with pressed steel frame was introduced. Armed with workforce of 15,000 after absorbing several competitors, DKW became the world's largest motorcycle manufacturer in 1930. But sudden growth created bank debts and losses which forced restructuring.

On 29 June 1932, Audiwerke, Horchwerke and Zschopauer Motorenwerke – DKW merged to form the Auto Union AG on the initiative of the State Bank of Saxony. A purchase and leasing agreement was concluded with Wanderer at the same time for the takeover of its automobile division. The new company head offices were in Chemnitz and the emblem was four interlinked rings symbolizing the inseparable unity of the founder companies. Each was assigned a specific market, DKW assuming responsibility for motorcycles and small cars.

DKW entered motorcycle racing in 1929 with 175cc and 250cc machines using inter-cooling and supercharged engines. It enjoyed

Depicted here is a 1936 DKW, 9hp, sport 250cc model.

success in 1931, however, thanks to the Hermann-Weber split single layout. The first was a 0.25 liter machine, the basis for future engines and often faster than the 350s used at the time. Riders at this time included such talents as Fleischmann, Herz, Steinbach, Klein, Muller, Ley. Rosemeyer, Wunsche, Kluge and Winkler.

At the 1935 Berlin show, DKW presented the SS250, based on the factory water-cooled, two-stroke racer, along with a full range of two-stroke roadsters up to 350cc. In 1938, Ewald Kluge became the first German to win the Isle of Man TT, even though he had to make an extra stop due to bad fuel consumption. Many other medals were also won at the ISDT. Riders such as Hermann, Schertzer, Demelbauer, Fahler, Leppin and Beckhausen used machines between 100 and 500cc.

By 1939, DKW had the biggest racing department in the world, making some awesome machines such as the 250US super-

charged, double piston twin and the similar 350cc machine. For the TT, DKW entered machines for the 250 and 350 class. In the lightweight class, both Britain and Italy had competitive machines, but in the end, Mellors won on his Benelli. Kluge on the DKW was second, after the Guzzis dropped out. At the Dutch TT, DKWs took all three categories, but not easily after challenges from Motor Guzzi and Gilera. This was an all-conquering time for the Deeks, as they were known. The ISDT represented a clash between the German teams and the British, each having had a string of three year wins. Unfortunately, the shadow of war deterred many foreign competitors, including Britain.

Between 1939 and 1945, military machines were made, including the NZ250 and 350 and some NZ500s. The most significant machine to come out of the war was the RT125. It used a 122.2cc engine, three-speed gearbox and became the most copied motorcycle of all

A wonderfully colorful advertising poster, showing how fun biking could be on your RT 125/200, with your special lady, of course!

time. The BSA Bantam, Harley-Davidson Hummer, Moska 125 and even the Yamaha YA1 were all influenced by the RT125. DKW, like many other factories, was severely damaged during the war and found itself on the Russian side of a divided Germany. The old plant went on to make machines for the Warsaw Pact under the names of Ifa and later MZ (Motorrad Zschopau).

Auto Union AG was expropriated by the occupying Soviet forces at the end of the war. The company's leading figures moved to Bavaria and a new company, Auto Union GmbH was formed at Ingolstadt in 1949. This also used the same ringed emblem. The first motorcycle project to come out of the new Auto Union Group, re-entering production in 1949, was the RT125.

German machines were not allowed to race after the war. The pre-war machines were very fast and still used superchargers. Unfortunately, superchargers were banned by the FIM in 1946. Recovery was in full swing by 1950, however, with 24,000 machines produced. In the years following, the RT 125 went through major upgrading and in 1950, DKW announced it would start racing again in the 125cc World Championships, having been re-admitted into the FIM.

In 1951, a Tele-fork model of the RT 125 was introduced, along with the first of two new models, the RT200. Looking much like the R125, it had a four-speed gearbox and telescopic front forks. The racing 250cc twins did not do well, even though Erik Wolf joined DKW. He was unable to give the machines the increased power needed to overcome the Guzzi, Benelli and Parilla rivals.

In 1952, the machines were improved by replacing the megaphones with a pair of expansion chambers. Then a three-cylinder DKW, with two near-vertical cylinders and a horizontal one at 75 degrees as well as a four-speed gearbox, were all fitted. The 350cc race saw high drama, but no results, the 250cc race was won by newcomer Rudi Flegenheier on the penultimate lap, giving DKW their first post-war victory. The ISDT also provided great results with several medals won.

The next few years were disappointing for DKW, with many retirements and accidents. At the post-war German International Motorcycle Exhibition (1954) in Frankfurt, the line-up for DKW introduced two new machines: the RT175cc and RT350cc roadster twin. There was also a new technical director for the racing department, Robert Eberan von Eberhorst. Hellmut Georg was employed to look after the day-to-day running of the competition shop with a view to making the 350 competitive. Many changes were made and at the first outing in May at the Nurburgring, DKW took the first three places in the 350 class. However, it failed to produce a race or lap speed to match the 250 NSU Renmax models. The company withdrew from racing for further development. The same year also saw the introduction of the Hobby, a two-stroke, single cylinder scooter with automatic transmission.

Over the winter of 1954, much work was carried out on the racing 'three' machines and a much-improved bike was available for the new 1955 season. Streamlining was now the order of the day, even though some riders did

Not the prettiest of machines, the 1957 RT 175 VS, a single cylinder, two-stroke machine that weighed 287 lbs and could reach 62 mph.

The ringed Auto Union emblem, of which DKW was now part, can clearly be seen on the headlight housing of this 1957 RT model.

The 1964 DKW Violetta was typical of the type of moped produced at the time. It had a 48cc, 3hp engine and could speed along at 40 mph.

Fitted on the side of the Violetta's engine is the Zweirad Union badge. A group created to amalgamate Victoria, DKW and Express in 1958.

not like the idea. At the Eifelrennen, the streamlined, 350cc machines ridden by Hobl and Hofmann finished first and second. The year saw Hobl acclaimed as German 350cc champion, finishing third overall in the World Championships. He managed to be runner-up in the 1956 World Championships, but sadly this turned out to be the last time the screaming 'Deeks' would race – a similar situation also for the off-road machines. A new moped, the Hummel, was launched mid-year, but motorcycle sales were bad and the whole German industry was feeling the pinch. Three revised models were presented at the Frank-

furt show with Earls forks and designated 'VS.'

In 1958, there was a huge shake-up as three major German motorcycle producers amalgamated. On 1 January 1958, Daimler Benz AG gained control of Auto Union by share purchase and the decision was made to abandon independent motorcycle production. The new grouping, known as the Zweirad Union, included Victoria, Express and DKW. In 1966, the Zweirad Union joined forces with Sachs-Hercules and remained the largest German producer through the 1970s. The DKW name was quietly relegated to the history books.

By the time the Hummel was presented, DKW were struggling. This is a 1965 type 155, which used a 48cc engine and had a top speed of 44 mph.

DOT

1903 - late 1973

In 1903, Harry Reed acquired premises at Ellesmere Street, Hulme, Manchester, England where he set up business as H. Reed and Co., changing later to Dot.

Initially, Fafnir engines were used, then the V-twin Peugeot. In 1908, Dot prepared a V-twin machine for the TT and won the two-cylinder class race.

By 1923, all machines were all JAP-powered, but later that year, a brand new Bradshaw engine, a 350cc ohv was used. A Dot with torpedo sidecar came second in the 1924 sidecar TT, a Dot-Bradshaw came second in the Jumior TT with a Dot-JAP finishing second in the 250cc race.

Financial problems caused a change of name to Dot Motors (1926) Ltd., and Harry Reed retired. Machines with Villiers engines continued even with a horizontal model.

A military three-wheeler delivery truck saved the company and was produced through the 1950s. DOT participated in trials and scrambling, Bill Barugh at the forefront, but was affected by the Villiers withdrawal. Other engines were tried, but nothing caught the public's eye and production soon ceased.

The 349cc, 11hp, single cylinder, Bradshaw engine was an air-cooled unit, fitted with either an Amac or Binks carburettor. It weighed 245 lbs and was capable of 65 mph.

The Dot of 1923 had a low, rakish, diamond design frame, like a real race-bike. The frame was a Dot design and made at the factory.

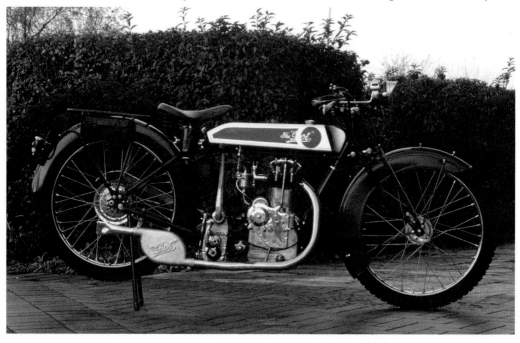

Douglas

1902 - 1957

Douglas The Douglas motorcycle goes back to a man called W.J. Barter, who built an unpopular, single cylinder engine between 1902 and 1904. The next engine he designed was a horizontally opposed unit which he called 'Fée,' or 'fairy' in French. A company, Light Motors Ltd, was formed in 1905 to take over the design and the first machine produced had a 200cc engine. This was followed by a 300cc twin and a prototype of around 800cc. The company never achieved the necessary sales and after it failed, Barter joined the Douglas brothers.

A beautifully restored 1913 Douglas model P. It uses the familiar Douglas flat twin engine, which, in this case, is a 348cc, 2 3/4hp unit.

Barter's design was produced as a 350cc flat twin and powered in 1907. By 1910, the machine was upgraded with a two-speed gearbox. The following year was the first time that the mountain course was used at The Isle of Man TT. Douglas entered four machines, two of which finished sixth and twelfth. The following year, the company did better when it entered six machines and finished first, second and third in the Junior race. The company also won the Six Day Trial, with a 350cc, three-speed machine.

War was looming and the company went into full production, building some 25,000 machines for the military, including a new 600cc model. When the war was over, the company indulged in breaking speed records and, by the end of 1922, five Douglas riders held over-100 mph records and Cyril Pullin was timed at over the 'ton' on a 500cc machine at Brooklands.

By 1922, the Douglas model range included a 500cc, ohv, a 733cc, ohv and a 350cc side-valve as well as a 585cc, side-valve machine. The following year, Tom Sheard won the Senior TT on an RA (Research Association Brakes) model and Freddie Dixon won the

This is a Douglas model W, made between 1914 and 1925. The engine is a flat, twin, 348cc unit with two-speed gearbox and belt final drive.

sidecar TT. The RA model was introduced at the 1923 motorcycle show and a detuned 500cc racing model, the RA/25, was shown at the 1924 show. The EW range was worked on by Cyril Pullin to be introduced at the 1925 show. The machines were developed further over the next two years. In 1928, models included a 350cc, ohv model derived from the EW models and Freddie Dixon worked on the ST and S6 models, adding dry sump lubrication. In 1930, the 350cc A31 was introduced and in 1931, the K32 and M32 models.

As another investor was found to help the company finances, the company once again changed its name to Douglas Motors (1932) Ltd. Unfortunately, the change was temporary and the company folded again within the year after disappointing sales. The company resumed production again and there was an attempt to use Villiers engines in 1933. However, it was dropped. In 1934, the 5Y2 model, known as the Blue Chief, a 500cc, side-valve machine, was

The 1934 Douglas Endeavour: although still a flat twin, the engine was positioned transversely and drive to the rear wheel worked through a shaft.

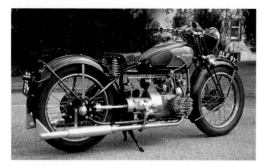

The transversely mounted Endeavour engine was a 494cc flat twin unit.

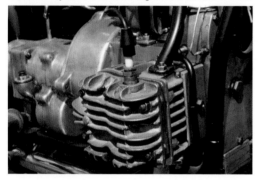

introduced. But sales remained slow and the company went into a slump. There was another sale, this time to the British Aircraft Company, and another new start in 1937 under the name

of Aero Engine Ltd. The Second World War helped to keep the company alive. It produced aircraft parts, light industrial trucks, generators and industrial engines, but few motorcycles.

This is a 1951 Douglas 348cc, 90 Plus, of which only 218 were made.

After the war, a revolutionary, transverse, 350cc twin was announced: the T35. In 1946, there was a change of name to Douglas (Kingswood) Ltd. The 80 plus and the 90 plus were introduced in 1949, but by 1951, the production of Vespa scooters was proving more important. In 1954, the Dragonfly series was introduced, but the final blow came in 1953 when Westinghouse bought shares in the company. Vespa and Douglas motorcycle production ceased in 1957.

The Douglas Dragonfly was the last production machine made at the Bristol factory. It used a four-stroke, ohv, 348cc flat twin engine.

Dresch

1923 - 1939

Henry Desch was one of France's more important motorcycle manufacturers and built a large number of machines, fitting proprietary power units from French and other European makers into his own frames. They used two-stroke engines for the smaller models of 98cc to 246cc and four-stroke engines for larger motorcycles up to 748cc. In 1930, they launched a model with a 498cc, in-line, side-valve twin engine with pressed steel frame and shaft drive. The company also made 498cc and 748cc versions of the design. Production ceased with the onset of World War II.

Dresch were based in Paris, France. This is a 1930 500cc parallel twin.

The engine's 18hp was transmitted to the rear wheel via a shaft.

Comprehensive instrumentation was neatly inlaid into the fuel tank.

Ducati

1923 - 1939

In 1926, the Ducati family, along with other investors in Bologna, Italy, founded the Società Radio Brevetti Ducati. Their aim was the production of industrial components for the growing field of radio transmissions, based on Adriano Ducati's patents. The first product, the Manens condenser for radio equipment, was rapidly followed by others. Success throughout the world allowed the company to expand and on 1 June 1935, the cornerstone was laid for a new factory in Borgo Panigale. The new complex was an extremely modern project which sought to establish an industrial and technological center in Bologna.

During the Second World War, Italy saw much combat and the Borgo Panigale factories were razed to the ground. The Ducati brothers, however, spent the war studying and planning new products to introduce to world markets when peace came. After the war, the Italian people went about trying to put their lives back together. Italy had been devastated by the retreating German armies as well as by Allied bombing. Ducati pushed ahead, nonetheless, and at the Milan Fair in September 1946, it introduced the Cucciolo, a small auxiliary motor for bicycles destined to become world famous. Initially, it was sold in an assembly box which could be attached to a bicycle. It was not long before it actually acquired a frame of its own. Thanks to the Cucciolo's success, and that of its descendants, Ducati became an affirmed trademark in the mechanical sector of the world.

In 1952, the futuristic Cruiser 175cc, with electric starter and automatic transmission, emerged. The following year, the company unveiled a 98 cc, economy model which was subsequently increased to 125 cc.

Without doubt, 1954 was a very significant year for Ducati, although few knew it at the time. Joining the company was a person destined to become a legend in the motorcycle world. Engineer Fabio Taglioni was a teacher at the 'Tecniche' (Technical College) of Imola and had already built motorcycles characterized by original technical character and exceptional performance.

The Taglioni design, both avant-garde and non-conformist, was tested during races. From his debut at Ducati, the engineer demonstrated the quality of his ideas and his machines participated in long-distance races such as the Milano-Taranto and Giro d'Italia. By the end of 1956, Ducati production included a four-stroke Tourer of 174cc with Special and Sport models, capable of 68, 75 and 84 mph.

In 1958, Ducati produced the 200 cc 'Elite.' 1958 also marked the triumph of the desmodromic system, which engineer Taglioni had been developing since 1955. This project resulted in the famous twin-cylinder, 250cc of 1960. One was ordered from Ducati by racing legend Mike Hailwood, who specifically requested a machine of "superior" performance. In the meantime, the 250cc model was added to the prestigious roster of commercial

single cylinders in the Diana, Monza, Aurea and later G.P types were capable of around 93 mph – an exceptional performance for the time. This model directly influenced all subsequent single cylinders until the famous 250, 350 and 450cc 'Scrambler.' The 1964 Mach 250, which could exceed 93 mph, won the hearts of sports fans everywhere.

Then Ducati bewitched bike aficionados with the fabulous performance of the 450 Mark 3D in 1968, the first production Ducati with desmodromic distribution capable of more than 106 mph. In 1972, after the success attained with the Scramblers in America at the beginning of the 1960s, Ducati proposed using the same formula on the Italian market. It was incredibly successful, particularly the desmodromic 450.

The end of the 1960s coincided with the boom of the maxibikes. Once again, engineer Taglioni provided Ducati with the winning weapon. On 23 April 1972, Ducati returned to racing, participating in the Imola 200 Miles with a new twin cylinder, desmodromic 750cc. The awesome machine was entrusted to

The Darmah SD900 of 1978 had an 864cc, V-twin, desmodromic engine.

Yet to be restored, this is a rare model TL100 with 98cc engine.

Ducati produced the 160 Monza Junior in 1965. This machine used a 156cc, single cylinder engine and had a top speed of 65 mph.

The 1973 350cc scrambler had a tubular-steel frame.

The Ducati 900SS is a classic collectors' machine. This is a pre-production model from 1977 with duel seats which varies little from the final production model.

Paul Smart and Bruno Spaggiari who finished first and second in the race. In response to this spectacular race result, the exceptional 750 Super Sport was created.

In 1978, Mike Hailwood, who had grown up racing Ducati singles, got back on a bike for the Isle of Man Tourist Trophy. He absolutely astonished the public and fans by winning the Formula 1 TT on that magic and mythical Mountain circuit. The bike was a Super Sport elevated to 900cc and, in recognition of his exceptional effort, Ducati created the splendid limited edition 900 SS Mike Hailwood Replica.

Not all was well at the company, however, and it was purchased by Claudio and Gianfranco Cas-

The Mike Hailwood replica of his 1978 TT winning machine.

The beautiful, 864cc, desmodromic, four-stroke engine.

tiglioni in 1983 and incorporated into the now expanding Cagiva Group. With this change of management, Ducati came into the hands of two motorcycle enthusiasts. From that point on, the mark was destined to move aggressively forward.

Now the triumphs of the Superbike era began to unfold. New legends were made, concerning both machines and riders. The adventure began in 1988 with Marco

Lucchinelli on his superb 851, constructed by engineer Massimo Bordi. Under the management of the Castiglioni brothers, Ducati expanded its share of the motorcycle market, introducing new models, increasing the supply of large displacement motorcycles and intensifying the company's commitment to racing.

In 1993, the Argentine Miguel Galluzzi conceived the idea of the Monster, which represented a whole new approach to motorcycles. The bike was stripped of all unnecessary clutter and aptly described as 'naked.'

But who could forget 1994 when Ducati stunned the world with the amazing 916? It was another Ducati-inspired revolution in the high-performance sports motorcycle category. With the 916, technology and style, performance and symmetry reached maximum levels. Ducati once again managed to create the perfect harmony of form and function, logic and emotion. From the world's most prestigious bike magazines, the 916 received the title "Motorcycle of the year" and many other well-deserved compliments.

Unfortunately, 1995 was not a good year. Despite product innovation and racing suc-cesses, Ducati entered a deep financial crisis. Its cash was drained by unsuccessful ventures of the sister companies within the Castiglioni group. Ducati was on the brink, but this time there was someone waiting to save them.

In 1996, the company was taken over by the Texas Pacific Group, an American investment fund which brought in much needed cash and a new group of international managers.

Simultaneously, the launch of the ST family allowed Ducati to enter the Sport Touring segment of the market. But if anything turned the company around it was the Monster Dark, the best-selling motorcycle in Italy in 1998

The naked design of the Monster Dark helped to keep the company alive. Thousands were sold.

Unmistakably a Ducati - the trelis frame gives it away. This is a 1994 900 Supersport.

For many, the most exciting machines to come from Ducati. The front end of a 916. Elegant, fast and furious, it won many people's hearts.

The 1995 748 biposto was always overshadowed by its bigger brother, the 916. It was a fast and elegant machine which handled well.

and 1999. The huge success contributed to a reversal of fortune for the Ducati Company, culminating with the listing of Ducati Motor Holding on the New York and Milan Stock Exchange on 24 March 1999.

In 2000, the MH900e became the first motorcycle ever to be sold exclusively on the internet. Just a few weeks after the eve of the new millennium, 2,000 enthusiasts had already booked the new bike, designed by Pierre Terblanche in homage to Mike Hailwood.

With the new millenium came a staggering selection of new bikes, and the Superbike championship belonged to Ducati with year-after-year successes. By 2003, the success of the 916 and Carl Foggerty had turned into the success of Neil Hodgson, claiming the super-

The amazing MH900e, a machine which could be bought only over the internet. It is now a sought-after collector's item.

Pierre Terblanche's 900cc Super Sport of 1998 used a 90-degree, V-twin, desmo, ohc, four-stroke engine and was capable of 140 mph.

name Ducati was now as well-known as the Japanese Big Four.

Multistrada is a good name for this versatile machine. Best ridden on twisty mountain roads, it uses the 992cc, L twin-cylinder Ducati engine.

bike championship once again, but this time on a 999. The monster that had saved the company a few years earlier was beefed up to a 900cc and looked more monster-like than ever. There was also a new kid on the block, the Multistrada, a bike that could tackle any terrain and which was as quick as anybody could desire. Middle-of-the-road was the 748, which looked good in red, but was also very cute in yellow… and no slouch either! The company had spread its wings, ventured into areas it could never have imagined and the

One of the most exciting machines of its time. The 999 used a 4-valve, L twin-cylinder, testastretta, desmodromic engine.

Durkopp

1901 - 1960

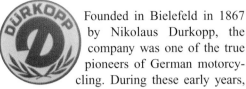

Founded in Bielefeld in 1867 by Nikolaus Durkopp, the company was one of the true pioneers of German motorcy-cling. During these early years, they made only bicycles, but by 1901, had produced a motorcycle and had both singles and V-twins in production by 1905. Production stopped prior to WWl and did not start again until the 1930s when clip-on type engines of 60cc, 75cc and 98cc were produced. 1949 saw machines powered by Sachs and Ardie engines and they produced a 150cc machine with their own engine, 175 cc and 200cc versions followed in 1951.

The 1953 MD150. Single cylinder, two-stroke engine with three speeds.

Durkopp is best remembered for its post-war scooters. In 1954, the Diana appeared and remained in production into the 1960s when motorcycle production ceased.

The 1957 Fratz moped used a 48cc engine and could reach 25 mph.

Excelsior (UK)

1896 - 1965

Excelsior Motorcycles started life on Lower Ford Street, Coventry, in 1874, under the name of Bayliss, Thomas and Co, as part of their range of penny farthing bicycles.

In 1896, the company started making motor-cycles using Minerva engines and became one of the earliest British motercycle manufacturers.

In 1910, the company was renamed The Excelsior Motor Company Co Ltd. After World War One, it was taken over by one of its major suppliers, R.Walker & Son, and production was

Leaving little room for the front wheel to move, this 1903 Excelsior has a 211cc engine strapped to the front downtube.

transferred to the Walker's site at Tyseley, Birmingham. Machines used varying engine makes: Blackburne, Villiers, JAP and others, ranging in capacity from 98cc to 1000cc.

Racing success on the Isle of Man brought popularity and they introduced what was to become their most famous model, the Manx-man, in 1935. It was available with either a 246cc or 349cc, single cylinder, shaft-driven, single, ohc engine. The bevel box cover had the Isle of Man symbol engraved on it, even though it never actually won the TT. The Manxman was produced until the Second World War when the company changed to war-related work. During wartime, they manufacturing the 98cc, Villiers-engined 'Wellbike,' a small motorcycle used by the Allied Paratroopers.

Civilian motorcycle manufacture resumed after the war, but was confined to lightweights. One of the better known models was the Talisman, which used a 243cc, Excelsior, two-stroke engine and four-speed gearbox.

They introduced the 'Skutabike' in 1957, followed by the Monarch, which used the same panels as the DKR scooter, but employed Excelsior's own 147cc engine. In 1965, the company ceased motorcycle manufacture and continued making car and motor cycle accessories.

The 1935 lightweight, 250cc, Manxman racer. It used a single cylinder, four-stroke engine, attached to a three-speed close ratio gearbox.

The Excelsior welbike could be folded into a container and dropped from an aircraft. It was used during the Second World War.

Excelsior (USA)

1905 - 1931

The story of the Excelsior really begins in 1876, with the founding of the Excelsior Supply Company. By the time Excelsior built its first motorcycle in 1905, the company already had 30 years of experience, engineering bicycle frames and parts. Their first motorcycle was a single-speed machine, featuring a single-cylinder "F-head" engine with a flat leather belt to the rear wheel.

Excelsior offered its first two-cylinder model with a 1000 cc engine in 1910. The two-cylinder Excelsior Auto-Cycle Models F and G were single-speed.

In August 1911, Excelsior rider Joe Wolters set an unofficial, two-mile record and later in the same month, he set a new, one-mile record at a speed of 88.9 mph. In September, Excelsior rider Jake DeRoiser set an unofficial world record at 94 mph.

In 1911, the Schwinn Company entered the motorcycle industry. Although initially drafting plans to build their own motorcycle, it eventually decided to purchase Excelsior on 1 February 1912.

On 3 December 1912, an Excelsior became the first motorcycle to officially reach 100 mph. At the one-mile track in Playa del Ray, California, Excelsior rider Lee Humiston "turned a ton," becoming the first motorcyclist officially timed at 100 mph by a sanctioning organization. On the same track a few days later, Humiston set every record for the distances between 2 and 100 miles.

In 1913, Excelsior was advertised as the only motorcycle with "complete control in the handlebars" because the right-hand grip controled the throttle and the left, the clutch. It offered its first two-speed model and also returned to the single cylinder market in 1914, offering the Lightweight, its first two-stroke machine with a 250 cc engine. The following year, a new model, the "Big Valve X" with Excelsior's first three-speed transmission, was introduced. It was advertised as "The Fastest Motorcycle Ever Built."

1917 saw the Henderson Motorcycle Company in serious financial difficulty and on November 15, Schwinn bought them out. Excelsior-Henderson produced the legendary Super X for the first time in 1925. It weighed about 100 lbs less than a comparable machine and had a much lower seat height. The three-speed transmission and the engine were of unit

motorcycles at a brisk pace and dealers continued to prosper in spite of the economy.

In 1931, Schwinn made a trip to Washington, DC and came away realizing that the Depression was going to worsen considerably. On 31 March 1931, he assembled his chief motorcycle management and announced: "Gentlemen, today we stop." Production ended immediately and the process of dismantling the motorcycle operation started at once. Dealers and owners were shocked at the sudden disappearance of Excelsior-Henderson.

Early Excelsior's came in a variety of colors, but were painted olive drab, even for civilians, after the United States joined the Great War.

construction and the sport version, the Super Sport X, came with high compression pistons. In 1930, the United States and entire world were in the grips of the Great Depression, but Excelsior-Henderson continued to sell its

An example of a 1925 Super X, which used a 750cc, V-twin engine.

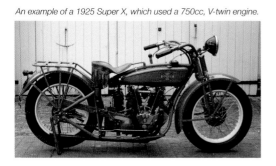

The 1918 Excelsior came with a speedometer, which was driven using a gear on the rear wheel.

FB Mondial

1948 - 1979

The engine of the 1956 Mondial had a 175cc, four-stroke unit producing 10hp and able to propel the machine to 68 mph.

The initials FB stand for Fratelli Boselli, (the brothers Boselli) who owned the Mondial Company, in Milan, Italy. During the late 1930s, they were making three-wheeled vans, but in 1948, they decided to diversify into producing sporting motorcycles. At the end of that same year, they introduced a 125cc four-stroke with double

The Mondial name is well-known for its racing machines, ridden by such riders as Ubbiali, Hailwood, Tarquini and Provini. This is a 1956 model.

overhead cam. Road machines and a four-stroke, 125cc model were introduced in 1949, followed by 200cc, single cylinder machines. The 1950s were the most productive for the company.

In 1956, Mondial went back to Grand Prix racing and introduced a 125cc and a 250cc machine, which would win both the 125cc and 250cc world titles one year later. The riders were Provini on the 125cc and Sandford on the 250cc.

Having reached the peak of their success, the company announced their retirement from racing. The Mondial engines were still competitive, however, and through privateers such as Francesco Villa, more titles were won: the Italian 125cc title in 1961, 1962 and 1963. The following year, the Villa brothers raced a new 125cc bike with a horizontal cylinder, cooled partly by air and partly by water. It was their own design and distantly related to the Mondial machines.

The range of models at the start of the 1970s comprised a 75cc two-stroke, a 98cc, 125cc and a 175cc four-stroke. By the end of the 1970s, the majority of machines were two-strokes and mopeds were produced with 49cc engines in 1975. These were offered also in motocross versions with 125cc Sachs engines. Suffering now from financial problems, the company was obliged to shut up shop in 1979. An unsuccessful attempt by the Villa brothers to reopen the gates was made in the 1980s.

FN

1901 - 1957

FN started producing bicycles in 1898. Their first motorcycle came in 1900 when FN mounted a 'clip-on' type engine onto a bicycle frame. The first FN motorcycle was produced in December 1901. It had a 133cc engine and acquired the nickname "Little Donkey."

By 1903, the engine capacity had grown to 188cc and used either battery or magneto igni-tron. The machine was also shaft-driven. A 2 1/2hp with 300cc engine followed and a 3hp,

This early design FN machine inspired American makers to develop their four-cylinder machines. This is a 1910 model.

The Mondial Piega is a hand-built, liquid-cooled, 999cc, V-twin machine. It has a Honda-based engine and great looks.

362cc engine was available by 1905, the first four-cylinder, shaft-driven, motorcycle built by FN. Engine capacity continued to grow by 1912 and the Fours were equipped with a new Bosch Type "Z" magneto. A new 285 model was introduced with a single cylinder 247cc 2 1/2hp engine, a two-speed gearbox, a clutch and a shaft drive.

1913 saw the Fours emerge with new frames, fuel tanks, clutches and innovative two-speed gearboxes on the rear of the shaft drive. The model designation changed in 1914 for the Fours. The Type 700 came with a 748cc engine and rear-mounted gearbox.

The First World War took its toll and not many parts remained in the FN workshops afterward since many FN machines saw action on the battlefields. A letter 'T' was added to the model designations in 1921, and the single cylinder became the 285T with a new frame, a different fuel tank and footboards. The four-cylinder model now became the 700T with an 8hp engine and a three-speed gearbox.

Between 1923 and 1925, a new Four, the M.50, was introduced. This featured a chain, instead of the more expensive shaft-drive, a new AMAC carburettor, new front fork design and front brakes. Another new model, the M.60 was available in a 'Sports' or 'Comfort' edition. In 1927, one of the most successful FN models of all time, the 350cc side-valve M.70, appeared. It was nicknamed 'Moulin Rouge' because of its red flywheel. Three military officers crossed the Sahara Desert on one and the motorcycle was soon known as 'Sahara.' FN's reply to the Depression in 1933 was the introduction of an affordable, new two-stroke, the M.200 model, which came with a two-speed gearbox.

In 1934, the powerful M.86 'Super Sport' was introduced, with its 500cc, ohv engine, four-speed gearbox and dual exhaust pipes. FN also broke the world speed record at 139 mph with a modified supercharged M.86. A new model introduced in 1937, the M.11, which featured a new and advanced all-aluminium engine. It was available with a 350c, ohv, 500cc SV or 600cc SV engine. The M.14 racer with Roots Compressor was also introduced in 1937.

The M.12, introduced in 1938, was a powerful motorcycle with twin cylinder 1000cc engine and shaft drive, available only to the military. Between 1939 and 1940, there were no new models, the M.XIII being in prototype stages at the time of the German invasion in May 1940.

After the Second World War, FN revamped their motorcycle production with the introduction of the popular FN M.XIII, available in a variety of configurations: 250, 350 and 450 OHV and with a 350 and 450 SV engine. In 1953, FN introduced the M.22, a two-stroke twin and 1955 saw the introduction of Moped sales. The first machines were manufactured by Royal Nord for FN and sold under the FN name and logo. Another model, the 'Type S,' was manufactured in a cooperation with Sarolea. It was a 125 or 200cc, single cylinder, two-stroke machine.

In 1959, FN produced its own line of 49cc mopeds: Utilitaire, Luxe, Fabrina, Princess and a sport model, the 'Rocket.' However, all production ceased in 1966. FN was last seen at a motorcycle show in 1965 and the last moped left FN in May 1967.

The M13 model, with its slightly strange front suspension set-up, had a 449cc, single cylinder, four-stroke engine.

Francis-Barnett

1919 - 1964

 Gordon Francis, son of Graham Francis of the Lea Francis Company, combined his talents with Arthur Barnett in 1919 to create a new lightweight motorcycle. Barnett was already making motorcycles under the Invicta name.

In the post-war era, economical transportation was at a premium and they designed the new machine not only for the motorcycle enthusiasts, but also for people who needed a reasonably priced mode of transportation. The Great War had taken a toll

Archer gearbox and its red and black gas tank was a very pleasing sight to a prospective buyer.

The price of the machine was a problem, however, and did not comply with their original idea of a reasonably priced transportation since manufacturing costs were high. In the army, Francis observed with alarm the frequency of motorcycle frame fracture. He therefore worked on ideas for overcoming the problem at the Francis-Barnett workshop and came up with a revolutionary plan to make manufacture cheaper and give the buyer a stronger, fighter and more reasonably priced machine.

In 1923, he designed a system of tubes, in triangular format, to make up the framework of the motorcycle. The wheels of the new Francis-Barnett were on spindles which could be easily removed. The machine was powered by a 147cc, Villiers, two-stroke engine with a flywheel mag-

The 1937 cruiser had a pressed steel frame and used a Villiers engine. The combination provided the possibility of low-budget transport. It was a clean, comfortable machine.

and although the motorcycle was not cheap, it was more practical for those for whom everyday transportation was a necessity rather than a pleasure, although, of course, it could also be used for pleasure trips.

Barnett and Francis started their business in Coventry, England and their first machine was constructed in the same workshop as the first English motorcycle, the Bayliss-Thomas Excelsior.

The first Francis-Barnett used a 292cc, side-valve, JAP engine with a two-speed Sturmey

The cruiser had all the mechanical parts enclosed in a casing.

The pretty, little 1953 Francis Barnett Falcon.

The Falcon used a Villiers Two-stroke, 197cc engine.

A large speedometer helps the rider keep within the law.

neto, Albion two-speed gearbox and belt final drive. The cost finally corresponded with the company's original ideas and was not too hard on the average person's pocket. The new machine was claimed to be "built like a bridge" because its innovative tubular construction and frame were, in fact, forever guaranteed against breakage.

In 1923, 250cc and 350cc machines with sidecars were also available. Next, Francis-Barnett produced the Pullman, which used a vertical, in-line, 344cc, Villiers, two-stroke engine. It was available to the public in 1928.

The 250cc Cruiser followed in 1933, a virtually totally enclosed bike whose production continued until the Second World War. At this time, there was also a model called the 'Stag,' a 248cc, Blackburn-engined machine with overhead valves, first introduced in 1935. Another pre-war machine was the 125cc "Snipe" and an even smaller machine, an autocycle named, "Powerbike," which used a 98cc engine.

Both of these machines made a come-back immediately after the end of the war.

Although the company continued to produce under the name Francis-Barnett, they amalgamated with Associated Motor Cycles Ltd, the London-based Matchless concern, in 1947.

Models like the "Plover," "Falcon" and "Cruiser" sold well in the 1950s. The color changed from the rather drab black finish of the earlier years "Arden Green." A full range of factory-designed accessories was also available to ensure rider comfort and convenience.

The off-road rider was also catered for a range of competition models such as the Trials 85, although they were plagued with problems from the AMC engine.

The market place was changing, however, and production was transferred to the Birmingham-based James Company (also part of the AMC Group) in the early 1960s. All individuality disappeared and both James and Francis-Barnett models were now virtually identical, apart from the badges and color, until 1966 when production ceased and the Francis-Barnett name was laid to rest in the history books.

Garelli

1919 - 1964

Adalberto Garelli was born in Turin, Italy in 1886. Unlike his father, who graduated with a degrese in law, he studied industrial engineering. Like many other Italians in the field, he went to work for Fiat.

In 1911, he designed a split cylinder, 500cc, two-stroke engine, which was patented in 1912. He moved to the Bianchi concern in Milan in 1912, where he also designed a highly regarded gearchange for motorcycles later adopted by Bianchi. Garelli was well-regarded, not just as a passionate sporting motorcyclist, but also as a technician. It was obvious that he was no longer content to use machines made by others or to simply contribute to their projects.

In 1912, therefore, he decided to produce his own machine: a two-stroke, split cylinder 350cc model, rather than a 500cc as originally presented. The machine became a legend and many records and races were won with it after the First World War. Once the machine was built, however, Garelli wanted to test it and there is confirmation in the Garelli archives of a feat of such daring that it is scarcely credible. The story was recounted by Captain Carlo Contrada at the Ospizio barracks at Moncenisio and translated something like this: 'Today, 10 January 1914, I saw approaching the barracks at Moncenisio, the engineer Garelli on a Garelli motorcycle...' This account was signed by the Commander of the barracks. It does not sound like much until the date, the time of year and the altitude of 1.2 miles are taken into account. Unfortu-

nately, this particular machine was never put into production because of the war. When the 350cc did go into production in 1919, it was changed considerably.

In 1915, Garelli moved to the Stucchi concern where he stayed until 1918, when he joined the Italian army. While in the Italian forces, he won a competition for designing a small motorcycle based on the 1913 model. Only one example was made. At the time, he encountered Ettore Girardi, head of testing at the Parma barracks. The opportunity to make the motorcycle for the military disappeared after the war and Garelli decided to produce it for himself.

The prototype machine appeared in the first Marcia Motociclistica Militare on 2 July 1919 – a timed event whose route was Genova-Trento-Trieste-Verona-Genova and whose distance of 810 miles had to be completed in four stages. The little machine, ridden by Ettore Girardi, saw off 56 of the 63 entrants including machines of larger capacity. Production of the machine started in June and was based at the De Vecchi establishment in Milan. With the success in the Marcia Motociclistica, the machine was entered in many more races, including the longest speed trial of them all – the Milan to Naples. The race took place in October 1919 and of the 44 who were expected to turn up, only 29 did. A mixture of 16 Italian and foreign machines reached Rome. Several more retired on their way to Naples. Astonishingly, the Garelli 350 ridden by Ettore Girardi won in 21 hours and 56 minutes.

Garelli 'mosquito' engine. This is a 1940 version and has a cylinder size of 38cc.

In the early 1920s, the Garelli machines were victorious at international events. In 1922, they won at the Grand Prix of Strasbourg, then at the Gran Premio delle Nazioni at the Autodromo of Monza, Italy. Famous riders such as Varzi and even Nuvolari rode for Garelli. Successful record-breaking attempts were also carried out between the wars.

In 1924, however, the factory pulled out of road racing, although the machines were still raced by privateers. As war clouds gathered in the 1930s, the company began to concentrate on other projects and the last motorcycle left the factory in 1935.

After the war, however, people looked for a cheap mode of transport. Garelli returned to motorcycle production with a 38cc Mosquito engine which could be strapped to a bicycle.

A wonderfully economical machine, the 1974 Garelli Katia automatic, was aimed at the thriving commuter market.

This engine was developed and produced for many years at the Garelli factory at Sesto San Giovanni. The company later merged with the Agrati concern, Italy's largest maker of bicycle parts, becoming one of Italy's largest producers of mopeds in 1977.

In 2000, the company could boast of a series of innovative, well-priced, good quality scooters. It was apparently on a mission to build new franchises and revamp a reputation once legendary in the Italian motorcycling world.

Gilera

1909 - date

In 1887, in a small agricultural town, Zelo Buon Persico, halfway between Milan and Crema in Italy, a baby was born to a farming family. His name was Giuseppe Gilera. As a boy, he decided that he did not want to work in the fields. He loved mechanical things and he wanted to be in a workshop. His enthusiasm at the tender age of 15 got him a job as an apprentice in a small workshop. He subsequently gained experience in all three of the principal motorcycle companies of the period: Moto RevelItalia, Bianchi and BucherZenda.

Although Giuseppe worked in a workshop, he also enjoyed racing on the old machines of the day, soon establishing himself on the local racing scene. For example, riding a Buchet in 1908, he set a new overall time in the Como to Brunate Classic. As an expert mechanic, he modified and worked his own machines. The move from 'working on' to 'constructing' was fast and in 1909, at only 22 years old, Giuseppe started his own company. In a workshop on the Corso XXII Marzo in Milan, Moto Gilera opened for business. The first machine was no more than a bicycle, strong and simple, using a 317cc, overhead-valve engine which had a belt-drive and proved good for racing as well. The company grew fast and started to outgrow its premises as the First World War got underway.

When hostilities ended, the company moved to Arcore to concentrate on producing a four-stroke, 500cc single. By now, there were three more people involved, the brothers of Giuseppe's wife, Ida Granata – Angelo, Valentino and Rosolino. They would go on to open Gilera franchises in Rome, Genoa and Milan.

The director of the racing department was Giuseppe's younger brother, Luigi, who went down in history as the mythical Luisin. The infamous Luisin, along with Rosolino and Miro Maffeis, won the Six and repeated the victory at Merano the following year.

In 1936, Gilera acquired the rights to the Rondine engine, a supercharged, four-cylinder, 500cc racing engine designed by the engineer, Remor. The Rondine (swallow) – now a Gilera and much improved in performance – made its debut in 1937 and immediately broke world records when Piero Taruffi took the 500cc world speed record away from Ernst Henne of BMW. The machine was encased in a streamlined body, and looked like a stubby little aircraft with no wings. Over the next three years – 1937,

The ventilation duct for the front brake is seen clearly here.

The beautifully finished, 6500cc engine of the Saturno.

The Gilera Saturno is one of the best-known Gilera models. Depicted is one of the first competition models of 1947.

A beautifully restored, four-stroke, single cylinder, 249cc engine of the Gilera Nettuno Sport. It could propel the machine to 78 mph.

The 1949 Gilera Nettuno 250 Sport, had a four-speed gearbox, chain final drive, and cost around $217 US dollars today.

championship was back with Gilera and they signed Geoff Duke in 1953. He became champion three times. Apart from 1956, Gilera held on to the championship until the company retired from racing in 1957. Besides road racing, Gilera's championship victories included the Tourist Trophy, Italian titles and the Milano to Taranto race, Bruno

1938 and 1939 – the machine was raced with great success and gave Dorino Serafini the European Championship.

The bikes became a dominating force in motorcycle sport. The Saturno 500 was presented in 1939 and became the basis for the production models. Unfortunately, the Second World War disrupted the domination achieved and enjoyed by the Gileras.

After the war, the company was faced with a dilemma. Superchargers had been banned and the Rondine had to be fitted with carburettors, which proved unsatisfactory. The solution was there, however, in the form of the single cylinder Saturno. Over the next five years, it achieved considerable victories, including the 1947 Italian Grand Prix and the 1950 Spanish Grand Prix. Riders of the period were Bandirola, Pagani, Masetti and Liberati.

The long-anticipated machine that followed was a development carried out by Remor on the old Rondine engine. It was much changed, however, and became an instant winner, outshining its main rival, Norton.

In 1950, Umberto Masetti took the 500cc World Motorcycle championship, although Gilera lost the following year. In 1952, the

The 1958 single cylinder, 175cc Gilera Rosso extra. With the Italian economy in trouble a small capacity machine was necessary.

A fine example of a Gilera 300cc twin of 1959.

By the mid-1970s, Gilera were making small capacity machines, like this 50cc trial machine, for example. It could reach 40 mph and returned 92 miles per gallon.

Francisci's great achievement. The company won 44 world championships in all.

By the 1960s, the company was relying on its single cylinder, four-stroke machines, which ranged from 98cc through 175cc. They even produced a 50cc scooter. By the end of the 1960s, however, the Italian market was in trouble. The company was in dire financial straits and the Piaggio group bought it out in 1969. Only a couple years later, Giuseppe Gilera passed away at the grand old age of 84.

During the 1970s, the usual four-stroke machines were replaced with two-strokers of 50, 100 and 125cc, which also did well in racing. In the 1980s, a new, single cylinder four-stroke with dual cam distribution was produced, initially in 350cc and 500cc versions to be followed by a 600cc version. It won its class twice in the Paris-Dakar rally and was overall winner in the Pharaoh's Rally. Other machines of the time were the avant-garde SP-02 and CX-125. In the 1992 and 1993 season, Gilera returned to world championship status in the 250cc class. In 1993, production was transferred to Ponted-

era and the successful 'Runner' scooter was introduced. Then the revolutionary DNA, a 'naked' motorcycle with an automatic engine, was launched in 2000.

In 2001, Gilera returned to Grand Prix racing in the 125cc class with rider Manuel Poggiali. It was 38 years since the company attained a victory and now, at the Le Mans circuit in France, Poggiali became 125cc World Champion.

Today the Gilera line-up ranges from the Nexus 500, the first Maxi Supersport scoot-

A combination of the normal moped and a scooter, the odd-looking DNA is the best of both worlds. It has a 50cc engine and weighs 223 lbs with a seat height of 2½ ft.

er, to the superb all-terrain Gilera RCR 50cc and the amazingly futuristic Ice. Keep watching because there's a lot more to come!

Gnome-Rhone

1919 - 1959

The Nexus is a true Maxi-scooter and a real sporting machine. The engine is a sophisticated, 500cc unit with electronic injection capable of producing over 40hp and reaching 99 mph.

GNOME RHONE This French concern started out as an aircraft engine manufacturer during World War I and started producing motorcycles in 1919. They began by building British-designed motorcycles under license. From the early 1920s, they produced machines of their own design. A range of different displacement engines of both side valve and overhead-valve configurations were produced and later, a number of flat twins were mounted in pressed steel frames.

Originally aircraft engine manufacturers, Gnome et Rhone also produced a variety of motorcycles. This is a 1939 boxer engine model.

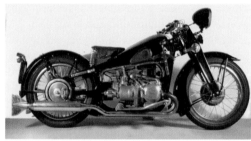

With a market flooded with scooters, the Gilera ICE stands out from the rest. The main constructive and design characteristic is the molded steel chassis. The power comes from the 250cc engine.

The company collaborated closely with ABC, England before producing their own flat twin which, as seen here, was shaft driven to the rear wheel.

The 1939 model had a 749cc, horizontally opposed, twin cylinder engine and a 4-speed gearbox, propelling it to a top speed of 81 mph.

Greeves

1952 - 1977

These BMW-style machines were available with both 495 and 745cc engines. Before World War II Gnome et Rhone had six motorcycles in production: the Junior, Major and Super Major, as well as the D5, CV2 and Type X. The first three were 250cc and 350cc, four-speed machines while the latter three were a 500cc single, a 500cc twin and a 750cc flat-twin. The flat-twin was enlarged to 800cc when produced for the French Army prior to World War II.

The company resumed production after the war and continued making motorcycles until 1959, mostly two-strokes of less than 200cc.

During the Second World War, the company produced machines for the French military. These were fitted with sidecars, had flat twin engines and shaft drive.

The story goes that Bert Greeves was mowing his lawn one lovely summer evening. He was watched by his cousin, Derry Preston-Cobb, in Worcestershire, England. Preston-Cobb was paralyzed from birth and sat in his wheelchair as Greeves maneuvered the mower up and down the lawn. At some point, Preston-Cobb challenged his cousin to fit a lawn mower engine to his wheelchair. Without too much thought, Greeves took on the challenge and after a short time, he had removed the engine from the mower and fitted it to the wheelchair. Admittedly not the most sophisticated adaptation, but the design went on to become the foundation of Invacar Ltd., a company that supplied three-wheelers for invalids to the government.

The company moved from its origins in Worcester, finally ending up in Thundersley, Essex. Bert Greeves started making plans to produce a new motorcycle. A Villiers-engined prototype was seen coming and going from the Invacar works and the name Greeves was stamped on the tank. Frank Byford, works manager of the Invacar works, regularly used an experimental Greeves scrambles machine in local events. In 1953, however, the Greeves bike finally made its official debut. It had changed quite considerably from the prototype seen a couple of years earlier.

There were three models: a scrambler, a three speed roadster and a four-speed roadster. All were powered by the Villiers, 197cc, Mk 8E engine. In 1954, the complete Greeves line-up was displayed at the Earls Court show in London. There was a surprise at the show in the form of a twin by the name of Fleetwing, which used a British Anzani 242cc, two-stroke engine.

The British public took time to come round to this new mark, but shortly after, Greeves assembled an official trials team including Peter Hammond, Jack Simpson and Norman Stoper.

Brian Stonebridge was employed in 1956 as development engineer and competitions manager. Stonebridge convinced Greeves to fit an engine test-bed in the works. He challenged the scrambles stars of the period to a race at Hawkstone Park, winning the 350cc race and coming in a handsome second in the 500cc race on a 197cc machine! Naturally, the next Greeves machine took the name Hawkstone. Dave Bickers joined Greeves and, at the first round of the 1960 250cc championships, he completed the course first, the first of many wins before walking off with the title at the end of the year. The scrambles machine was modified and changed and Bickers won more and more competitions. Orders started to come in, not just from Britain, but from America and other countries too. Bickers won his second 250cc championship with Greeves the following year and Alan Clough joined the team. At the end of the season, however, Bickers moved to Husqvarna.

In 1962, Greeves moved into 250cc road racing, using a prototype machine named the Silverstone. In the hands of Gordon Keith, it won the Manx 250cc Grand Prix in 1964, the same year that an all-Greeves scrambler, the Challenger, was announced. It was to be ridden by the returning Dave Bickers in the 250cc Motocross championships. The first experimental model, ridden by Garth Wheldon, won the Terry Cups Trial.

By 1967, the Challenger had a larger stablemate, the 346cc, twin port model and a corresponding road-racing machine named the Oulton. A special machine for the United

The top-end of the Greeves 32DC engine, a 342cc, air-cooled, parallel twin, Villiers unit. The carburettor is a .1 cm Villiers item.

The Greeves 32DC Sport Twin of which only 184 were built. It used a championship winning frame and short, leading link front forks.

This is a 1963 version of the Greeves 24MDS ISDT machine produced between 1962 and 1969. This machine achieved a gold medal in the 1963 ISDT.

Probably better known for their off-road machines, but Greeves also produced road racers. This is the 1965 250cc Silverstone model.

The single cylinder, 246cc engine was made by Villiers of Wolverhampton, England. It had a four-speed gearbox and chain final drive.

States, known as the Ranger, was also developed. By 1968, Villiers was on the verge of withdrawing its engine production and Greeves pulled out of trials, although the company did return later with the Puch-engined Pathfinder.

In 1968 came the introduction of a 390cc motocross model, making its debut at Thirsk. Two-stroke specialist Dr Gordon Blair was employed to assist with the design of the new Griffon machine in 1977, but the company had diversified its production into wholesaling of accessories. Bert Greeves was retired and Derry Preston-Cobb did the same in 1977. The company ceased trading soon after.

Harley-Davidson

1903 - date

The popular Modelo 9 was available in two versions, the 9A with belt drive and the 9B with chain drive. This is a 1913 model A.

The model 9A engine was an air-cooled, single-cylinder, four-stroke unit, using a single Schebler carburettor and could reach 55 mph.

The Harley-Davidson motorcycle company reached the grand old age of 100 in 2003. Celebrations took place all over the world, starting in their headquarters in Milwaukee, Illinois, USA. Meetings, run-outs and rides took place in many cities to pay tribute to the largest manufacturer of motorcycles in the United States.

William S Harley, only 21 years old, completed the design for an engine that could be fitted to a bicycle. He teamed up with Arthur Davidson and so the Harley-Davidson Company was created. The birthplace of the machine was a 10 x 15 ft wooden shed which had the words 'Harley-Davidson Motor Company' marked crudely on the door. Two years later, Harley-Davidson introduced its first production motorcycle in 1903. It was built to be a racer and had a 3 1/8 in bore and $3^1/_2$ in stroke engine.

The first dealership opened in Chicago. By 1906, a new factory was built on Chestnut Street (later renamed Juneau Avenue) and a staff of six set to work. A catalogue was produced in which the nickname 'Silent Gray' was used for the first time.

On 17 September 1906, the Harley Davidson Motor Company was incorporated. The numbers of staff increased, as did the size of the factory. Harley-Davidson machines were ridden by the founder members and won all types of races, spreading the company name around the country.

In 1909, the Company introduced its first V-twin machine, a configuration that would become synonymous with the company for years to come. The engine was a 7hp unit and had a displacement of 2 pints. The following year, the famous Harley Davidson badge was patented and used for the first time. More endurance and hillclimb events were won by Harley Davidson machines and 1911 saw the 'F-Head' engine introduced as the company's main powerplant. It would remain so right up until 1929.

By 1912, the dealer network had grown to over 200 nationwide. Machines were shipped to Japan, which constituted the first sales outside the United States. The following year, an official racing department was established with William Harley as main race engineer, backed up by his new assistant, William Ottaway. The company officially entered the racing fraternity in 1914 and, dubbed 'The Wrecking Crew' by rivals, it soon dominated proceedings. In 1916, the Eight-Valve racer was introduced and helped the Harley-Davidson Racing Team win every single national championship race of the 1921 season.

When America became involved in the First World War in 1917, Harley-Davidson became the main supplier of bikes to the US military. The so-called Quartermaster School was set up specifically to train military mechanics on these motorcycles.

Following the war in 1919, the company produced the opposed twin cylinder Sport model, which was appreciated for its lack of vibration, but never widely sold in the United States. It used a 584cc, 6hp engine which sat in the frame facing front to rear. With 2000 dealers in 67 different countries, Harley-Davidson became the largest motorcycle manufacturer in the world in 1920. The following year, the JD and FD models were equipped with a new 3 pint motor and the fuel tanks took on the distinctive teardrop shape in 1925.

In 1925, Joe Petrali, not only one of the most famous dirt track racers for Harley-Davidson, but one of the most famous racers of all time, started racing for the company. In 1932, he took his dirt track Harley-Davidson machine on a five-year consecutive winning streak of the AMA Grand National Championships. Not satisfied with that, he also won the National Hill-Climb Championships from 1932 to 1935. And this was only the beginning.

This is a 350cc Peashooter class machine, designed to be slower than its larger capacity stablemates, but ended up almost as fast in the end.

In 1926, the Harley-Davidson single cylinder machines, the models A, AA, B and BA available in sv and ohv versions, made a comeback. In 1928, the first twin cam was introduced for the JD series and the machine was able to reach the magic 100 mph mark. The following year the 2 gallon, V-twin engine (later known as the 'flathead') was introduced on the D models. This engine remained in production until 1972.

By 1931, Harley-Davidson faced only one competitor, Indian. It would remain the dominant force until 1953, when Indian also went out of business.

The EL model, an ohv, 2 pint-engined machine promptly nicknamed 'knucklehead' because of the shape of its rocker boxes, was introduced in 1936. It was followed the same year by an 2½ pint, sv engine and the first

A beautifully restored 1938 Knucklehead model EL. The name came from the shape of the rocker covers.

The peashooter was used for dirt track racing. The engine was an ohv, single cylinder unit with dual port exhaust.

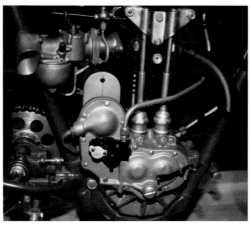

WL model was introduced the following year. In 1937, Ben Campanale, on a Harley-Davidson WLDR, won the first of two consecutive victories at the Daytona 200. He was followed on the same model in 1940 by Babe Tancrede.

America entered the Second World War late, but Harley-Davidson was called upon to supply the US Army. Civilian machines were neglected while the factory geared up to supply the military, the Quartermaster's School once again giving lessons to the soldiers who had to maintain the machines. In 1941, the

This is a 1947 1200cc FL model and was used by Western Union as a local delivery machine in Asheboro, North Carolina, USA.

new 1200cc, ohv FL series was introduced, although fewer than 2500 were made. The US Army requested a BMW style machine for some time and Harley presented them with the XA series, a virtual copy of the BMW with horizontally opposed twin cylinders, shaft drive, hand-operated clutch and a foot-operated gearchange. The cost of the machine drove the military to choose the WLA series

An alternative to the WLA model was the XA flat twin model, a near replica of the BMW engine used by the Wermacht. Expensive to produce, it was soon dropped.

instead, which could do everything the XA series could (only 1011 XAs were built) at a cheaper price per unit. By the end of the war, some 90,000 WLA machines had been produced for the military. It did not take long for the factory to resume production of civilian machines. In 1946, it introduced the stripped WR racing machine.

The appropriation of Germany's DKW manufacturing rights was divided between BSA in

Harley was the main supplier of military machines to the US Armed Forces in World War Two. This is a well-equipped WLA model.

the UK and Harley-Davidson. Harley introduced its 125cc, DKW-engine, lightweight 'S' series, an oddity to Americans which never broke sales records. Dealers did not like it and the only people who bought it were youngsters, subsequently inspired to move to the larger machines once they had mastered the hand clutch and foot gearchange. Larger engines followed at 165cc and 175cc and the machine acquired the name Hummer.

In 1949, hydraulic front forks first appeared on the new Hydra-Glide models and the side valve K model was introduced in 1952. It used a unit construction engine and had four single lobe camshafts working the valves. It was not an especially fast machine, but it was the first Harley with suspension at the rear as well as the front.

Used by the Wilmington Police Department in North Carolina, USA, a 1954 Hydra-Glide WPD1 anniversary edition model.

British Nortons were stealing the show at Daytona during the period, a fact which did not go down well at the Halley-Davidson head office in Milwaukee. So it was up to Paul Goldsmith to get the record straight, which he did when he took a 37 hp K series to victory in 1953, at the same time increasing the average speed by some 7 mph. The K eventually evolved into the Sportster.

1953 was an important year. The company celebrated its fiftieth anniversary with an attractive new logo depicting a 'V' in honor of the engine with a bar reading 'Harley-Davidson.' Above were the words '50 years' and below, 'American made.' A medallion version of this logo was placed on the front mudguard of all the 1954 models.

There was much excitement in 1953 when the new Sportster was announced. Although more a sports tourer, it was produced to combat the British twins. The V-twin XL engine was 883cc and produced 40 bhp at 5500 rpm.

On the racing scene, dirt track racer Joe Leonard won the AMA Grand National Championship in 1954 and the Championship was consistently won by Harley-Davidson racers. A seven-year run of consecutive victories at the Daytona 200 began in 1955 with riders Brad Andres, Johnny Gibson, Joe Leonard and Roger Reiman.

In 1960, Harley-Davidson bought half shares in the Aermacchi motorcycle company in Varese, Italy. The bikes sat beside the larger capacity machines, enhancing the lightweight range now that the Hummer-derived machines had dropped out of the competition. In 1961, the 250cc Sprint was born. It was basically an Aermacchi, distinguishable by its single, ohv, horizontal cylinder engine. It acquired the H desig-

The 1964 Harley-Davidson Sprint H 250 was based on Aermacchi machines and was built at their Schiranna factory.

nation in 1962 and was given a street-scrambler look with a small tank and high exhaust. Several other variations also appeared. The company was keen to get onto the scooter bandwagon alongside Vespa and Lembretta and the Topper scooter, which made its debut in 1960, should not be overlooked.

In 1965, the Duo-Glide was replaced by the Electra-Glide, which was the first FL equipped with an electric starter. Then the 'shovelhead' engine was introduced for the Electra-Glide models in 1966, replacing the Panhead. At the end of the 1960s, Harley-

This 1965 'Big Twin' Electra-Glide is one of the first and also the last of the pan head models. It uses a five gallon fuel tank.

Looking very American in its red, white and blue colors, this is a 1971 AMF 1200cc, special edition, FLH, shovelhead model.

Davidson merged with the American Machine and Foundry Company (AMF).

In 1970, on the Bonneville Salt Flats in Utah, Carl Rayborn smashed the motorcycle World Land Speed Record. The all-enclosed, cigar-shaped vehicle with a Sportster engine managed a staggering average speed of just over 265 mph. In 1972, a new, more powerful and reliable aluminum alloy XR-750 made its debut, proceeding to become the dominant dirt track racer for the next three decades. The following year, production was moved to a new plant in York, Pennsylvania, while the rest of production remained in Milwaukee and Tomahawk.

At Daytona Beach in 1977, the new FXS Low Rider was presented to the public. It had a long, low, laid-back aura and lived up to its name. Later that year, a special version Sportster, the Café Racer, was introduced and the FXEF Fat Bob appeared in 1979. Why Fat Bob? "Fat" because of the large, twin-style fuel tank and "Bob" because of the bobbed mudguards.

In 1980, the FLT was introduced. Designed to combine long-distance touring comfort with sport bike handling, it absorbed annoying vibration using its new rubber engine mounting system. The drive chain was also replaced by a kevlar belt, later added to the whole range. The same year, the FXWG Wide Glide was introduced to the range.

The following year, a buy-out of Harley-Davidson by thirteen of its executives was completed.

In 1981, Scott Parker joined Harley-Davidson for the racing season. He became the most successful racer for Harley-Davidson, winning 93 victories and 9 Grand National Championships 9 times in 10 years.

The Evolution 1340cc engine took seven years to appear, but when it did in 1984, it was worth the wait. It produced more power, ran cooler and did not leak oil. It was fitted to the new Softail model along with other older models, including the Sportster.

As 1988 rolled around, Harley-Davidson celebrated its 85th Anniversary with a 'Homecoming' in Milwaukee attended by over 60,000 enthusiasts.

The early 1990s saw the debut of the Dyna

range of machines, the first of which was FXDB Dyna Glide Sturgis. In 1992, Harley-Davidson bought a minority stake in the Buell Motorcycle Company.

The following year was the 90th anniversary of the Harley-Davidson company. There was a family reunion in Milwaukee and some 100,000 people paraded the streets on motorcycles. In 1995, the classically-styled FLHR Road King was introduced. A new assembly plant, the first outside the United States, opened in Brazil and Harley acquired another 40 percent of Buell, leaving Erik Buell as Chairman of Buell operations and a one percent share. In 1999, all big twin models received the new Twin Cam 88 engine and fuel-injection was unveiled as a feature in 2000.

The VRSCA V-Rod, inspired by the VR-1000 racing motorcycle, was introduced for the 2002 model year. It was the first Harley-Davidson motorcycle to combine fuel-injection, overhead cams and liquid cooling. The engine delivered 115 hp and Halley-Davidson continues proudly into the new millennium.

This is a rear view of a 1977 1200cc FLH Electra-Glide Classic.

The 2005 VRSCA V-Rod has a liquid-cooled, 1130cc, Revolution V-twin engine and features a silver-leaf aluminium frame.

Heinkel

1951 - 1965

Heinkel became an important aircraft manufacturer, supplying innovative designs to Germany's civil and military departments along with other well-known German manufacturers of the period, such as Dornier and Junkers.

The company was started by Ernst Heinkel in 1922. Since the need for aircraft was desperate during the Second World War, the company prospered. After the war, however, German aircraft manufacture was banned and the company was forced to diversify. They turned to building mopeds, scooters and three-wheeled bubble-cars.

The Tourist scooter, powered by a 149cc, four-stroke engine, was launched in 1953. It was followed a year later by the Perle 49cc moped. The Tourist engine increased to 174cc in size and gained a reputation for high quality and comfort, with substantial bodywork protecting the rider. Over 100,000 were made.

This same engine was also used to power the 1956 Kabinen bubble-car, later made in Southern Ireland and was sold as Trojans in Britain in the 1960s.

In 1957, Heinkel launched the Roller 112, an unsuccessful, 125cc scooter. The Tourist was updated in 1960 and joined by the Heinkel 150 two years later. Both went out of production in 1965 when Heinkel returned to volume aircraft manufacture.

A large, single headlight was fitted to the Tourist.

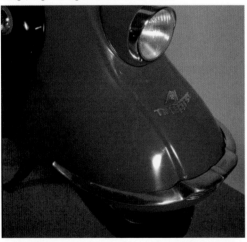

The Perle engine was a 50cc unit and could be started by pedalling.

A fine example of a 1956 Heinkel Tourist 103 A1. There was room for two and the spare wheel fitted to the rear of the machine.

The engine of the Perle produced 1.5hp and could propel the little machine along at 25 mph. An ideal mode of inexpensive transport.

Henderson

1911 - 1917

In October 1911, the Henderson Motorcycle Co., based at 268 Jefferson Ave., Detroit, Michigan, USA, announced a new 4-cylinder motorcycle. The machine was the brainchild of William G. Henderson, in partnership with his brother Tom W. Henderson, and was the third 4 cylinder motorcycle to be manufactured in America. One of its most innovative features was the folding hand crank for easy starting.

The 1914 Model C – the first to have gears – was given a two-speed gearbox incorporated in the rear hub. In 1916, the Model F included a 'mechanical oiler' driven from the cam gears as well as a kick-starter.

Significant advancements were made with the 1917 Model G. The oil was now held in the crankcase and a three-speed gearbox was included. This new Henderson was an elegant machine and sales rocketed.

In spite of many endurance successes, the company experienced severe financial difficulties caused by spiralling material and labor costs, combined with irregular supplies due to the First World War. Therefore, on 17 November 1917, Ignaz Schwinn bought Henderson. The manufacture of the 1918 Model H was moved from Detroit and the Chicago-built models were distinguished by a serial number beginning with Z rather than H.

The 1919 Model Z improvements included a GE generator on the Z 2 electric model and a new Henderson logo incorporating the red Excelsior 'X.'

On 2 December 1918, Tom Henderson left the company. Arthur O. Lemon, credited with the revolutionary design of the 1920 Model K, joined Henderson as a salesman in 1915. The Model K engine's 3 pint capacity was rated at 18hp. It was the first motorcycle to use full pressure lubrication. The cylinders were redesigned to use side valves for both intake and exhaust.

William Henderson was unhappy with the changes and he left Excelsior in 1920 to form the Ace Motor Company. Schwinn consequently placed Arthur Lemon in charge of engineering for all Excelsior and Henderson motorcycles.

1922 proved the apogee of the Henderson mark with the introduction of the Arthur O. Lemon-inspired 28hp. De Luxe. There were many improvements in durability and perform-

One of the first rare Schwinn built machines under Henderson

The unique 1918 engine has valve enclosures.

ance. Excelsior was keen to demonstrate the new model and Paul Anderson reached 98 mph on the Roosevelt Highway on a fully laden PD Henderson in front of the Chicago Police in February 1922. The performance was repeated at 100 mph for the San Diego Police Department later and both departments placed large fleet orders.

The frame was redesigned for the 1925 De Luxe, sloping downward at the rear to give a lower center of gravity and consequently a shorter, wider, 4 gallon fuel tank. The excellent 1927 De Luxe had polished 'Ricardo' cylinder heads as standard. There was a new instrument panel on the gas tank incorporating speedometer, ammeter, oil gauge and ignition switch.

In June 1928, Schwinn lured the highly respected Arthur Constantine, lured away from Harley-Davidson, hiring him as Chief Engineer. 'Connie' studied the old De Luxe and decided there was only one possible course of action: to start a new design. The 'Streamline' Henderson KJ, his resulting masterpiece, appeared in March 1929 boasting 57 new features and developing 40hp at 4000 rpm.

On Tuesday, 29 October 1929, the Wall Street stock market crashed, heralding the Great Depression. Nevertheless, Henderson sales remained strong. On 29 April 1930, Excelsior demonstrated the new Henderson 'Special' KL high speed 'solo job' on the new smooth highway concrete of St. Charles Road, Illinois. Joe Petrali took the Henderson to 116.12 and 109.09 mph on the two recorded runs averaging 112.61 mph. The KL had a remarkable top gear range capable of going smoothly from 8 to 110 mph. This outstanding machine quickly became a standard of US Police Departments.

In the summer of 1931, Schwinn called his department heads at Excelsior to a meeting and simply told them "Gentlemen, today we stop." He was convinced that the Depression

would worsen and he was not prepared to take the risk.

A special manifold and carburettor were fitted to the racer.

Maldwyn Jones attempted the 24 hour endurance record in October 1917 on this machine.

The 4-cylinder engine of the record-breaking Henderson.

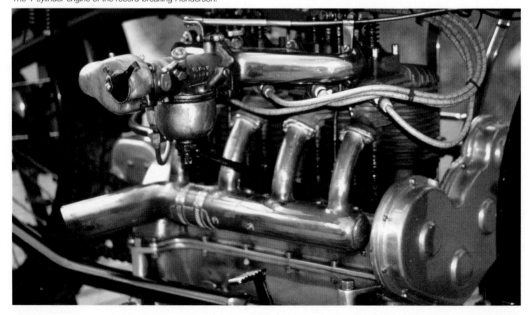

Hercules

1904 - 1992

Like so many motorcycle manufacturers, Hercules began as a bicycle maker. But by 1904, it was offering a heavyweight bicycle fitted with an accessory engine and a direct belt drive to the rear wheel.

In the years that followed, the company prospered by producing a wide range of motorcycles using many different makes of engine – Bark, Columbus, Fafnir, JAP, Ilo, Kuchen, Moser, Sachs, Sturmey-Archer and Villiers – and by the 1930s, it was making machines from 73 to 498cc and winning many trials and races.

The Hercules factory was badly damaged during the Second World War and motorcycle production did not resume until 1950, initially with a pair of lightweight two-strokes of 98cc and 123ccc.

Within two years, the range had increased by five new models. Hercules then entered a period of consolidation, which helped to see them through the mid-1950s when German motorcycle sales fell dramatically. It was able, therefore, to participate in the 1956 Frankfurt Motorcycle show, where two of the main exhibits were the K100 and the K175 (both with Sachs engines). There was also a Hercules Scooter, designated the R200, which remained on the books until 1960. The company also participated in the ISDT, where Walter Bromsamle rode a K175.

In the 1960s, Hercules continued to make a range of lightweights, many powered by Sachs or Ilo engines. In 1966, Hercules joined the Zweirad Union, which was swallowed up by the huge Fichtel Sachs Industrial empire in 1969. The following year, it began developing the unconventional rotary engined W2000, sold as a DKW in some markets. The power unit used the Wankel technology owned by Sachs, which was developed from a snowmobile engine. Although it dominated the headlines, the machine sold in tiny numbers and suffered from controversy over what capacity class its unorthodox engine belonged to. The company sold

lightweights and off-road singles with more success, and the Wankel was discontinued in 1975.

The Sachs Company was taken over by GKN (Gust, Keen and Nettlefold) in 1976. Herkules then concentrated on making small two-strokes, mostly either mopeds or lightweight motorcycles like the Ultra LC water-cooled, 50cc machine and the K50LR LC of 1978. All the machines were upgraded and supplemented. Some were as big as 125cc. By the early 1980s, all was not well and even Hercules was starting to feel the pressure of the Japanese invasion.

In 1982, distribution of the Yamaha-scooters CV 50 and CV 80 was carried out under the brand-name Hercules and Hercules built a motorcycle for the German Federal Armed Forces in 1992.

In 1995, there was shareholder restructuring and the bicycle department was sold to the Dutch ATAG-group. The motoring department

The Fichtel & Sachs, single rotor, 249cc per chamber, rotary engine.

was renamed SACHS Fahrzeug- und Motorentechnik GmbH.

The Hercules Wankel 2000 machine was also sold under the DKW banner. This is a 1977 model with a top speed of around 100 mph.

Hesketh

1980 - 1982

As the British motorcycle industry floundered and finally gave up, one man attempted to revive the industry in Britain by producing a new, all-British bike. The Hesketh V1000 was inspired by Lord Hesketh, who had a background in F1 racing at the time. The machine was developed on the Easton Neston estate in England in the spring of 1980. The heart of the Hesketh was its 90 degree, V-twin engine.

Research, development and road-testing continued and after two years, the bike was announced to the press. The City of London invested in the venture and Hesketh motorcycles PLC was formed. In 1981, a modern factory was set up in Daventry. The problems noted by the press regarding the bike's presentation were confronted and rectified. Unfortunately, so much money had been spent that the company collapsed with a mere 100 bikes sold.

A prototype ran in 1980 and the real machine was presented to the press two years later. This is an original V1000 machine.

The Hesketh Vampire, the V1000 touring version. It did little to help the company survive, closing for a second time in the 1980s.

The development team, which continued its work on the machine, offered support and modifications to the bike owners. This venture expanded into the manufacture of machines, starting 1982, under the name of Hesleydon Ltd., which went on to develop the Vampire after requests for a touring version of the V1000. But with the general downturn in the motorcycle market, the decision was made to cease general manufacture.

Since 1984, Broom Development Engineering has retained the capacity to assemble a limited number of bikes (to order) and has continued to develop aspects of the machine. While retaining the looks of the first V1000 model made over 18 years ago, the contemporary model possesses many 21st century innovations.

The heart and soul of the Hesketh was a huge, 90 degree, V-twin engine of 992cc. It used a five-speed, constant mesh gearbox.

Hilderbrand and Wolfmuller

1894 - 1896

The potentially lethal ignition box was situated below the fuel tank. It was basically a burner sending heat to the ignition tube.

The world's first production motorcycle was made by Hildebrand and Wolfmuller of Munich and patented by Alois Wolfmuller and Hans Geisenhof in 1894. The machine was fitted with a 1428 cc, water-cooled, four-stroke engine which produced 2.5 bhp. The frame was formed of four horizontal tubes between which the two-cylinder engine was mounted. The downtubes of the frame served as lubricating oil reserves. The machine weighed 115 lbs and had a maximum speed of approximately 24 mph.

Made in France under license – under the name Petrolette – many were built in Germany and France up to 1896.

The Hilderbrand & Wolfmuller - later also named Petrolette - machine was the world's first ever mass-produced motor cycle.

Suitable tires were a problem, which was resolved by a tire maker named Veith, who provided large section pneumatics for the two unequally sized wheels.

Honda

1948 - date.

The eldest son of a black-smith, Soichiro Honda was born in November 1906 in Komyo, near Hamamatsu, Japan. His interest in all forms of machinery was kindled at his father's small

workshop where he helped with bicycle repairs. As a young man, Honda built a series of racing cars. He was lucky to escape serious injury when he crashed spectacularly in 1936. The following year, he set up a piston ring factory, responding to technical snags he encountered by studying metallurgy.

In 1946, he set up the Honda Technical Research Institute which, despite its grand name, was only a wooden hut. Seeing a desperate need for basic transport all around him in war-scarred Japan, he hit on a scheme. Buying a batch of 500 surplus engines designed to power military radio sets, he assembled a team to help him attach them to pedal cycles.

Produced in 1947, the rather spindly Model A – progenitor of the entire Honda line – proved popular. Simply an air-cooled, 50cc, two-stroke engine bolted onto a pedal cycle frame, it drove the rear wheel via a long, flexible belt. Like Honda's earlier bikes with bought-in engines, the Model A's fuel tank was based on a hot water bottle. Unfortunately, the model gave off black exhaust fumes, earning the first engine its nickname, 'the chimney.'

Honda's own products duly followed and the Honda Motor Co. was established in 1948. Soichiro Honda was undoubtedly the driving force behind the company, but Takeo Fujisawa, who joined Honda in 1949, complemented Honda's imaginative genius with a hard-headed

grasp of finance. Fujisawa nursed Honda through a difficult patch in the mid-1950s, masterminding an unprecedented expansion of sales and service networks in Japan. His astute understanding of marketing initiated Honda's phenomenal world expansion beginning in 1959, the same year the company first contested an Isle of Man TT race.

Knowing that racing success was the key to global sales, Soichiro Honda came away from his visit to the Isle of Man TT in 1954 determined to match — and surpass — the high standards of engineering he had seen in action. Therefore, in 1959, the Honda team competed in its first TT and the first victory was completed in 1961 when Honda swept into the first three places in both the 125 and 250cc races.

In 1966, Honda conquered all five solo capacity classes. Finally, after winning 18 TT races and 17 manufacturer's world championships, they withdrew from Grand Prix racing in 1967 to concentrate on a new challenge: the automobile.

There was a return to the Grand Prix scene in 1979, but to a very different racing world, which now included changes in the rules, limits on the number of cylinders and gear ratios and penalized four-stroke machines. In spite of the overwhelming odds, Honda engineers opted for the greater challenge of a competitive four-stroke, devising the unique NR500. Countless technical difficulties had to be overcome before the NR500 achieved 11th place in the 1982 championship.

The company's first true motorcycle, the 1950 Type D, or the first chain-driven Honda, had a

This is a CB 92 Benley, parallel twin cylinder, four-stroke machine of 1963. It used a 125cc engine producing 15hp at 10,500rpm and could reach a top speed of 87 mph.

two-stroke engine. It had a two-speed transmission and a sturdy, pressed-steel frame with the latest type of telescopic fork front suspension. Then came Honda's twin-cylinder machine, the lively 125cc C92 Benly tourer, an advanced machine with two cylinders and overhead camshaft, a refinement most makers reserved purely for their racing machines. It was also equipped with an electric starter, very rare on a motorcycle.

In 1958, Honda produced what would become the world's biggest seller. Manufacturers had dreamed of creating a two-wheeler with genuine mass appeal. Honda was the first to make it reality with the C100 Super Cub series of scooterettes.

Not a lightweight at 350 lbs, the 1967 CB72 could, nevertheless, reach 100 mph. It had a twin cylinder, 250cc engine and a four-speed gearbox.

The Super Cub was introduced in 1958 and achieved phenomenal popularity. It was a step-through, single cylinder, 50cc run-about.

There were two models around at this time, the CB72, featured here, and the CB77. Both similar except the 77 was more powerful.

The engine provided enough power to carry both its rider and various loads (from luggage to live farm animals) and the 'step-thru' design created a fun two-wheeler easily ridden by people of all ages and sexes.

The impact of Honda's 1960 250cc, twin-cylinder CB72 made it the most controversial motorcycle in the major markets of Europe and the United States. The power of its free-revving engine was a revelation to riders who had only experienced such performance from big, heavy, often awkward, oily and unreliable machines. It was a superb introduction to motorcycling for the masses of young novices who learned to ride on the CB72, known in the United States as the Hawk.

Output from Honda's Japanese plants reached an industry record of 100,000 per month in 1961. Manufacturing started in Europe in 1963, with production of mopeds at the Honda Benelux facility set up in Belgium.

The first model to be manufactured was the 49cc C310. Although not initially a success, modifications and improvements produced the subsequent C320 and C311 mopeds. By 1965, Honda surpassed every other make in both production and exports. A succession of new products was in progress.

In the world of leisure, the 1965 P25 was designed to cater to the highly influential moped market. It featured rear engine location with an overhead camshaft unit neatly built into the wheel.

When unveiled at the 1968 Tokyo Motor Show, the CB750 astonished the motorcycling world. Probably the single most dramatic expression of Honda's desire to offer the customer consistently innovative products, the four-cylinder machine represented one of the greatest technical leaps since motorcycling began. Not only did it boast a potent overhead camshaft engine, but also a disc front brake, a five-speed

Probably the best-known Honda of all, the CB750 Four, often quoted as the first real Superbike, certainly deserves the title.

gearbox and electric starting as well. It showed its mettle by winning France's 24-hour Bol d'Or race in 1969 and the 1970 Daytona 200-mile event in the United States.

Miniaturized versions followed, including the CB500F, CB350F and CB400F.

The range covered everything from mopeds to 125 mph superbikes by 1970, and by setting up local production facilities, Honda was able meet particular demands in different regions.

Having stunned the world with six-cylinder Grand Prix racers in the 1960s, Honda dropped a bombshell by announcing its road-going six in 1978. Possessing a magnificent bank of air-cooled cylinders and a row of six exhaust downpipes, the CBX delivered colossal power. Originally conceived as a sport bike, the big six became a grand tourer in the form of the CBX1000FII Pro-Link of 1981, with a fairing, luggage boxes, and an important new Honda feature, Pro-Link single shock rear suspension.

At the other end of the scale for 1979 (looking speedy even when standing still!), the sleek,

The engine is an in-line, four cylinder unit of 736cc and could develop 67hp at 8000 rpm, giving the machine a top speed of 120 mph.

racy, little MB was perfect for a novice with sporting instincts to take on the road safely. Its light and lively, 50cc, two-stroke engine provided an ideal mix of performance, easy maintenance and economy.

The concept of the trail bike, a street-legal motorcycle with realistic, off-road capability, was born in the 1970s. The first really effective,

The Gold Wing was announced to the public in the early 1970s. It had a flat, four-cylinder, 999cc, water-cooled engine.

The incomparable Gold Wing, with its six-cylinder, 1520cc engine, celebrates 30 years of first-class motorcycle touring.

dual-purpose Honda machine was the lightweight SL350 twin, powered by Honda's new generation, twin cylinder engine. It was followed by XL singles with four-valve cylinder heads.

The original 1974 liquid-cooled, four-cylinder, 1000cc GL1000 heavyweight tourer impressed the motorcycle world with its sheer size and incredible de luxe specification. When launched as a four, the Gold Wing surpassed all previous standards for comfort while offering a high cruising speed. The GL was improved in

The 1978 CBX 1000 outshone every other machine on the market. Producing 105 hp, it could top 135 mph.

1980 by a redesigned 1100cc engine with ample horsepower for long distance work. The subsequent GL1200 Wing De Luxe (Aspencade in the United States) of 1984 featured a voluminous fairing and spacious luggage capacity as standard equipment.

The punishing trans-Africa Paris-Dakar Rally and its escalating popularity in the 1980s inspired the XL600LM, a high-built trail bike offering lusty performance from its single cylinder 'thumper' engine. The first Honda to win the Rally in 1982 was a near-standard XL500 trail machine with its engine enlarged to 550cc. Evolving out of the XL600R came a more refined and usable, desert racer-inspired single. The Dominator NX650 became a highly respected and enduring favorite with European riders.

Accepted as king of the big singles, the NX650 Dominator was at home both on city streets and in the arid wastes of North Africa.

Introduced in 1981, the CX500 looked unlike any previous motorcycle. It introduced four-valve heads, liquid cooling, shaft final drive and tubeless tires. The basic CX500 design incorporated Honda's advanced turbo-charging technology. The CX500/CX650 Turbo was the world's first turbocharged production motorcycle and Honda's first fuel-injected production vehicle.

In 1982, Honda took an entirely new approach in choosing the V-four layout for high performance engines. The format first appeared on the ground-breaking VF750S, known in some countries as Sabre. Even in its first incarnation, the 90-degree, V-four engine churned out 82ps from its liquid-cooled, 16-valve configuration and its final drive was by shaft.

Honda found fault with the V-four and it was only in later models that the format truly surpassed itself, gaining power alongside rock-solid reliability. The VFR750F of 1985 took the V-four layout to new heights, but then came the legendary VFR750R/RC30 of 1987, a racer for the road which thrilled high-performance riders. It featured the single-sided rear suspension arm of the RVF factory racers, derived from the French Elf-sponsored project. Its engine was hand-assembled to provide sensational performance. Its scintillating results in Superbike and TT Formula 1 competition spoke for themselves.

Mighty V-four potency and state-of-the-art chassis technology summed up the stunning

The VFR750/RC30. 1988 saw the inauguration of the World Superbike championship. Fred Merkel rode one to victory in 1988 and 1989.

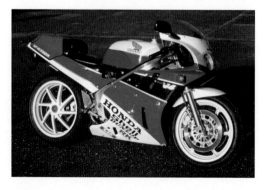

RC45. John Kocinski took his Honda to victory in the 1997 World Superbike series.

Hard on the heels of victory in the 1983 500cc World Championship was a sports roadster closely modelled on the factory racer. The NS400R's track-style aluminium frame was the first seen on a Honda roadster and with a fairing shaped and decorated like Freddie Spencer's 1985 Rothmans Honda, it really looked the part. Most importantly for a middleweight sportster, the V-three offered fantastic handling thanks to its stiff chassis, superb suspension and reliable braking.

On another level, incorporating all the aggression of a racing machine, while conforming to capacity restrictions on learner riders, the 1984 NS125 offered younger riders a zippy, two-stroke lightweight. The benefits of Honda's enormous investment in Grand Prix racing paid off with the stunning NSR125, a miniaturized version of the hottest super sports bikes in the range.

Honda took an entirely fresh approach to the trail concept in 1986 with the civilized Transalp, powered by a 600cc version of the liquid-cooled, six-valve, V-twin engine first seen on the VT500 tourer. In April 1997, Honda celebrated the tenth anniversary of the model, coinciding with Transalp production and reaching 100,000 units.

Never shy to enter new markets, scooters too were abundant in the Honda camp. The CN250 initiated a new breed of easy-rider two-wheelers originally aimed at the American market. Long and sleek, Honda took the enclosed, small-wheeler scooter format and reshaped it into an armchair-style cruiser with ultra-modern overtones. In 1987, Honda first launched the liquid-cooled CBR600F, the 600cc super sport category now a red hot zone. By 1995, the CBR600F had developed into a mind-blowingly powerful sports machine that amazed even the most hardened high performance riders.

The CBR900RR FireBlade was Honda's super sports sensation of the 1990s. Originally conceived as an extreme specialist machine with a limited market, the CBR900RR was almost as light and compact as a 600. Through race track experience, imagination and ingenuity, Honda

The CBR600F gives cutting edge power and performance from its four-stroke, 16-valve, in-line, four cylinder 599cc, liquid-cooled engine.

1992 saw the introduction of the CBR900RR Fireblade. In 2004, it is quicker, faster and cleaner, with a thoroughly managed, 998cc, liquid cooled, 16-valve powerplant.

engineers ensured that every detail on the machine was refined for maximum effectiveness, minimum weight and optimal aerodynamics. The latest generation 'Blade' is even lighter and more powerful. The 1990 ST1100 Pan European offers an alternative to the Gold Wing for long distance, two-person travel with luggage,

As the name suggests – Pan European – this is a long range tourer. Powered by a 90 degree V4 engine, it has a top speed of 130 mph.

cruising effortlessly at motorway speeds and returning reasonable fuel consumption with a range of approximately 224 miles between refills.

Another positive result was the NR750 road machine, dramatically unveiled in 1992

Often described as the ultimate machine, NR750 was the first production bike with oval pistons and used programmed fuel injection.

as a high-cost, limited edition motorcycle, and now highly sought-after by collectors. As well as being the first production motorcycle with oval pistons, the NR750 introduced many other innovations, from programmed fuel injection and a novel cooling system to a race-style cassette gearbox. The chassis and bodywork were designed using computer analysis and testing to create superb aerodynamics, luxuriant comfort and stunning, aggressive looks.

The magnificent Honda 1996 F6C blends rocketship power with an authentic, hot-rod style. The F6C has a traditionally simple, but bold, color scheme, complemented by a wealth of gleaming chromium plate emphasizing the flat engine and its distinctive exhaust system.

The CR250R racer of 1997 represents two-stroke technology at its sharpest, featuring Power Jet Control and state-of-the-art digital ignition. But this machine's biggest surprise is not the engine, but the chassis along with the alloy swinging arm for the delta Pro-Link rear suspension to which motocross will subject it. Proof that it works well came with Stefan Everts' 1997 250cc motocross world championship, won on a CR250R.

In the early 1970s, the first of Honda's hugely successful, two-stroke motocross racers stormed the sporting world and the company has since shown its mastery of Grand

Happy on rough or normal terrain, the little CR125R has a liquid-cooled, two-stroke engine. The frame is a semi-double cradle, aluminium, twin-spar type.

Prix road racing technology. With environmental friendliness at the top of Honda's agenda as we enter the new century, the achievement of cleaner burning from a two-stroke by Activated Radical Combustion (ARC) marks a significant step forward. The years ahead present new technical challenges to be overcome, especially with regard to the environment.

After 50 years of progress and expansion, the spirit of innovation at Honda is stronger than ever. You only have to look at the line-up of machines and the stream of new technology that rolls out each year to see why Honda is the largest motorcycle company in the world.

Soichiro Honda retired in 1973, leaving the company in the capable hands of Kiyoshi Kawashima. Soichiro then devoted himself to the Honda Foundation, seeking harmony between technology and the environment. Having fulfilled countless dreams for over half a century, he died in 1991 leaving his wife, Sachi, a son and two daughters.

HRD

1924 – 1928

The initials HRD are those of the founder, Howard Raymond Davies, a well-respected motorcycle racer for both Sunbeam and AJS. Shaky reliability prompted him to make his own machines.

Premises were bought in Heath Town in the West Midlands, England, in September 1924. The first priority was to have some machines to exhibit at the forthcoming Olympia show in London. There was little time, but a team was assembled and four models were exhibited when it opened on 3 November 1924.

All bikes were designated HD. The HD 90 was fitted with a special 500cc, JAP racing engine, the HD80 used a 350cc, ohv, double port, JAP engine and the HD70 also had a 350cc engine. Lastly, the HD70/S, which could be purchased with or without sidecar, used a 500cc sports, side-valve, JAP engine.

The machines were well-received, but the logistical and technical problems of setting up

The JAP logo, whose engine was used, can be spotted at the bottom of the crankcase, the HRD logo is also present on the casing.

workshops manifested themselves after the show. Things settled down, however, and by May, about 60 bikes were produced.

It was now TT time and five machines were ready. The riders were Harry Harris and Howard Davies. Three 350cc machines and two 500cc machines, all slightly modified standard bikes, were present on the Isle of Man. It proved to be a good outing, with Howard Davies coming second in the Junior race and Harris finishing fifth. Howard Davies won the Senior race in three hours, 25 minutes and 35 seconds. There were big celebrations on their return to Wolverhampton.

New orders now came thick and fast and the cramped, old premises could not accomodate them. A new site was chosen on Fryer Street and the move was completed in October. Just prior to the Olympia show, there was some more good news. H. Le Vack entered an HD90 at Brooklands and set a world speed record of 104.41 mph for the classes C and D as well as a British record for the flying mile.

The 1925 Olympia show opened a month earlier than usual and HRD displayed five models, all fairly similar to the bikes of the previous year with the exception of the HD70, which had been dropped. There was now an HD super 90 fitted with a new 500cc, twin port engine. It could achieve a top speed of about 100 mph. Sales continued to be good, but the company never made a profit.

TT time came round again, but 1926 was not a good year. HRD entered three bikes, two factory and one private, in the Junior Race. There were five factory entrants and three privateers in the Senior Race with Howard Davies leading the

factory team. As the teams went out to practice, it was obvious that the HRDs were not as fast as the other bikes. The average speed was now topping more than 80 mph and the HRDs were struggling with 77 mph. In spite of low morale and bickering, the team did what they could to improve the performance of the machines. Between crashes and broken engines, the race was not one to write home about. It was a great disappointment to Davies, who had hoped to repeat his victory of the previous year.

But the Olympia Show was approaching fast and a mixture of old favorites and completely new machines was presented. The HD90 was replaced by the HD75, which used a 500cc ohv engine, while the new HD 600 was powered by a 600cc sports, side-valve JAP engine. The HD65 was a new model, based on the HD 60,

Depicted is the cylinder of the model HD70, which used a 490cc, side-valve engine. The machine could also be bought for sidecar use.

Possibly the oldest HRD in existence, this is a 1925 Model HD70, currently on display at the Black Country Museum, Dudley, England.

but fitted with a standard 350cc, ohv, single port, JAP engine. In 1926, there was another increase in sales, but somehow the company remained stalemated.

In 1927, the HRD machines continued their competitive successes. Sales were affected, however, by the General Strike of 1926, and the market was hit hard by the recession. HRD machines sold at a high price, reflecting their high end finish and quality. Unfortunately, it was exactly this market that was hit hardest. The company entered the TT and performed somewhat better than the previous year since Freddie Dixon won the Junior with an average record speed of 67.19 mph. Again, there were big celebrations upon the team's return to Wolverhampton.

As Olympia approached once more, six machines were prepared and prices were reduced to help sales. Unfortunately, the price reduction was not enough. By 1928, the company was in voluntary liquidation. It was purchased by Ernest Humphries, owner of OK Supreme Motors. It was subsequently sold to Phillip Vincent, who moved production to Stevenage.

A rare HRD with JAP engine is seen exhibited at a show in England.

Husqvarna

1903 - date

HUSQVARNA

For most people, the Husqvarna motorcycle history is closely associated with the long series of World Championship victories in motocross that the company captured in the 1960s, 1970s and 1980s. But Husqvarna's motorcycle history actually goes back much further. Like many other motorcycle manufacturers, Husqvarna began by making ordinary bicycles.

In 1903, the company built its first motercycle. Again, like other manufacturers of the period, the company started by fitting the Husqvarna bicycle frames with engines from makers such as FN, Moto-RZve and NSU. Some of the early machines also used 250cc and 500 cc engines from Sturmey-Archer and JAP.

By 1920, Husqvarna had established its own engine factory. The first engine designed was a 550cc, four-stroke, side valve, V-twin similar to those made by companies such as Harley-Davidson and Indian. It was not long before Husqvarna decided to enter the world of competition, developing racing motorcycles in classes up to 1000cc. At the end of the 1920s and into the 1930s, Husqvarna enjoyed great success in Sweden and at numerous European events. It faced tough competition from manufacturers such as BMW, DKW, Excelsior, FN, Harley Davidson, Indian, Norton and Velocette. Husqvarna gained a great deal of success in the enduro class (like the International Six Days), the speed races (like the international Grand Prix) and the TT. Much of this success was due to the designer Folke Mannerstedt, a pioneer in the use of light alloys, not just for the engine parts, but also in the rest of the motorcycle, resulting in an outstanding power-to-weight ratio.

A 1935 racing Husqvarna. These machines were successful racers during the 1930s with such riders as Stanley Woods on board.

The engine of the 1935 Husqvarna was a V-twin, 496cc unit, producing 41hp at 6700 rpm and could power it to a top speed of 119 mph.

In the mid-1930s, Husqvarna pulled out of the racing scene, partly because of the shrinking civilian market for large motorcycles. By 1936, the production of large motorcycle engines had stopped. Nevertheless, these engines reappeared later in modified form. Albin, the engine manufacturer, used the Husqvarna engine as a basis for a single cylinder, 500 cc army motorcycle it built in conjunction with Monark.

Husqvarna produced its first two-stroke motorcycle in 1935. The lightweight motorcycle had pedals like a traditional bicycle, a 98 cc engine and soon became very popular.

During the years before the Second World War, thousands of machines were produced, putting many ordinary Swedish people on the road.

In 1946, the legendary 'Svartkvarna' machine was introduced and soon became the archetypal light, reliable and hard-wearing motorcycle. It was an attractive alternative to the automobile. The 'Svartkvarna' was built according to what the Swedish regulations called a 'light motorcycle' – meaning that it should not weigh more than 165 lbs. The early 120cc, lightweight bikes, originally painted black, were nicknamed 'Blackqvarnas.'

A completely new, powerful and sporty 175 cc motorcycle, the now legendary Silver Arrow (Silverpilen), capable of 62 mph, also weighing less than 165 lbs, was presented in 1957, followed a year or so later by the Golden Arrow (a 200 cc version). Unfortunately, the Golden Arrow was considered too fast for the Swedish roads and the Swedish authorities asked Husqvarna to restrict its production to the 75 cc machine. However, both the Silver and the Golden Arrow proved the perfect foundation for further development of motocross machines, beginning Husqvarna's long and successful motocross era with victories at both the European and the World Championship levels. Rolf Tibblin, Bill Nilsson, Torsten Hallman, Bengt Aberg, Heikki Mikkola and Haken Carlqvist all become winners in the 250cc and 500cc classes. It is worth noting that starting in 1969, Husqvarna's 360cc and 400cc, two-stroke machines ended the dominance enjoyed by four-stroke motorcycles in the 500 cc class.

In the early 1970s, Husqvarna motocross and enduro bikes became wildly sucessful exports, particularly in the United States. High power and a low weight were combined with reliability, a winning formula for many American champion riders in dirt track, enduro or even desert races. In the United States, Husqvarna machines became classics: prototypical, modern, off-road motorcycles.

Oddly enough, the Husqvarna motorcycle enterprise was taken over by Elektrolux in 1979, producer of sewing machines, washing machines and lawn mowers.

In 1982, a lightweight, powerful, 500cc, single cylinder, four-stroke was introduced which would develop into today's modern, 610cc, water-cooled unit. Elektrolux, however, decided that motorcycles were not for them and the Italian company, Cagiva, took over production in 1986, continuing motorcycle development under the Husqvarna name.

In 1993, Husqvarna celebrated its grand old age of 90 with the 500cc world title. The company's four-stroke machine was pitched against the traditional two-strokes. At the Cologne show in 1996, the company presented a new single cylinder, four-stroke, all-terrain machine, the TE 610E, with electric starter. The same year, it captured the European Cross Country title in the 125cc series. In 1998, Chicco Chiodi won his first title in the 125cc class and repeated it in 1999.

In the new millenium, Husqvarna won the Six Days' Enduro for the first time, using a four-stroke machine ridden by Merriman. Later that year, the 'NOX' super racer was sold exclusively over the internet. In 2001, a new 250/400cc, four-stroke engine was introduced and Husqvarna became 100 years old in 2003. It was a triumphant year, during

which they won four world titles and launched the centenary TE 510. The future looks bright for a now well-established company.

Standing high on its box: a Husqvarna of the Cagiva days.

The 2005 4-stroke bike shares body style with the TE 510 Centennial, created to celebrate 100 years of Husqvarna motorcycles.

The TE510 engine is a single cylinder, 510cc, four-stroke unit.

Imme

1948 - 1951

In 1948, Norbert Riedel founded a production facility in Immenstadt, Germany which is where the abbreviated company name, Imme, comes from. (Imme is also German word for 'bee.')

The company produced a most unconventional lightweight motorcycle with very unorthodox front and rear suspension. The front suspension had a single leg, suspended by a spring and parallelogram links similar to a conventional girder fork. The rear wheel was carried on a swinging arm, suspended by a forward-facing spring. The tube that formed the swinging arm was also the exhaust pipe and extended rearwards past the rear wheel. A mix of tubular and pressed steel parts linked the steering head to the rear suspension pivot, plus supports for the seat and tank.

Production started in 1949. By 1950, up to 1000 machines per month were being built. Then financial and warranty problems caused the IMME AG to go out of business. Imme made a small numbers of 148cc, twin-cylinder versions shortly before production ceased.

A rare prototype, this 175cc machine was designed by Riedel, but never went into production. Imme had closed its doors by now.

The unorthodox engine and rear suspension design of the Imme.

Riedel designed this single cylinder, two-stroke machine in 1948. It was so different that people were rather suspicious of it.

Indian

1901- 1953

Of the 20 or more American motorcycle companies, there has only been one capable of competing with Harley-Davidson. This was the Indian Motorcycle Company, based in Springfield, Massachusetts, USA.

George Hendee was a bicycle builder in Massachusetts while his future partner, Oscar Hedstrom, teamed up with a man named Henshaw, building De Dion-powered tandems for motor-paced cycle racing. Hendee wanted to build a simple motorcycle for the average man and he felt that Hedstrom was the person to design it. The two got together and an agreement was made. In 1901, Hedstrom took his design to Hendee in Springfield. Both men were satisfied and the machine was advertised even before manufacturing facilities were established.

The machine used the Thor 1 _ hp engine unit as an integral part of the frame, which was basically a bicycle type. Drive was via a chain to a sprocket on the pedal shaft, and fuel was held in a crescent-shaped tank on the rear mudguard. Hedstrom designed and patented a spray type carburettor, which was also used on the new machine. Production of the machine increased over the next few years and minor changes were carried out. Both Hendee and Hedstrom, along with George Holden, demonstrated the machines. They produced a resounding 1, 2, 3 in the 280 mile New York to Boston endurance trial.

In 1905, some significant changes were made. The Thor Manufacturing Company still provided the engine, but now the original cast-iron cylinder head was replaced by a steel one. The front forks were sprung, but the real novelty was the first ever twist-grip throttle and ignition control.

In 1906, the Hendee Manufacturing Company announced it was intending to build its own engines and to use the Hedstrom carburettors. New premises were needed and were found on State Street, Springfield, Massachusetts. In 1907, the first V-twin-engined Indian was presented. Two years later, the

On display here is a 1908 Indian twin cylinder, board racing machine.

The 'F' head, V-twin, 994cc Indian of 1912. Designed by Hedstrom and one of the better designs to emerge from the United States.

first Indian leaf-spring front fork was fitted to the machine.

Between 1910 and 1911, Indians were present at the Isle of Man, obtaining resounding success in the 1911 Senior race, where they occupied the first three places. Ironically, they were all were ridden by British riders. At home, all seemed to be going well with sales of a staggering 35,000 sales in 1913. This figure nearly doubled in 1914.

Spearheading the line-up in 1914 was the amazing 7hp, two-speed Hendee Special, which came with electric lighting and electric starting – a worldwide first. On some models, swing arm rear suspension was adopted, along with a Corbin speedometer driven from the rear hub.

Unfortunately, a dispute now divided Hendee and Hedstrom. Hedstrom decided to leave the company in 1913, only to rejoin when Hendee retired in 1916. Hedstrom was replaced by Charlie Gustafson, who had worked at Reading Standard. He introduced the Powerplus twins, 990cc, 7hp models, in 1916. Alongside them was a 225cc, two-stroke machine with three speed gearbox and all chain drive. A flat twin was also introduced the same year, but never gained much popularity.

When America joined the First World War in 1917, the company concentrated on making machines for the military. After the war, not only

Compared to the bigger machines of the time, this 1928 Indian Prince with its 350cc, single cylinder engine probably seemed small, but it did cater to another area of the market.

This 1933 Indian 1340cc Four looks great in blue with gold pinstriping.

did Hedstrom rejoin the company, but Charles B. Franklin, the Dubliner who had taken second place in the 1911 TT, also came in. Later, he became company vice-president. He persuaded Indian to have another go at the TT. It was duly contested in 1922 and 1923.

The best-known Franklin design was the 500cc, V-twin Scout, probably one of the most loved Indians ever to leave the Springfield factory. An addition to the line-up was the smaller, 348cc, sv single, the Indian Prince, and at the top of the range was the huge, 1234cc Big Chief.

At the New York show of 1927, Indian announced the acquisition of Ace along with its chief designer, Arthur Lemon. Over the next

few years, the Ace Four was gradually assimilated into the Indian program with the Indian Four, although it remained distinctively Ace from its engine design and did not change until 1936.

In 1927, there was also a new design Four, which was not much appreciated by the buying public. It was less attractive, its new engine design requiring a nasty exhaust pipe arrangement. Indian responded quickly to the poor sales of this model and 1938 saw the introduction of an absolutely delightful, new machine. The Indian line-up consisted of the 500cc Junior Scout, the 750cc Sport Scout and the 1200cc Chief 74. The Four went through some general cosmetic changes, but by 1942, the last production model left the factory.

Since the Second World War was in full swing, the company once again turned to supplying the military with machines for the battlefield. Most went to the Canadian and American armies and some to the Great Britain. At this time, some Model 841 machines, transverse V-twins with capacities of 750cc, were employed in military work. They were very heavy, however, and therefore unsucessful.

The 1941 841 V-twin military model was heavy and not a great success.

In 1948, Indian brought out the 220cc Arrow and 440cc Scout, which were developed by the Torque Manufacturing Company. Torque wanted to get into motorcycle manufacture, but Indian bought the manufacturing rights and the machines were given the Indi-

an name. The following year, three versions appeared, each differing slightly in make-up. But they were not big sellers and the company decided to dabble in imports from Britain.

Vincent/Indian prototypes were seen, but never manufactured. A stream of 'so-called' Indians followed, which were, in fact, Matchless and Royal Enfield Bullets with Indian badges on them.

Before the final closing of the company gates, the Indian Sales Corporation became British-owned and an outlet for the Matchless-AJS-Norton group. Many have tried to resurrect the name. The latest, a Californian company, has also been forced to shut down due to lack of funds. It is better to let sleeping dogs lie!

This 1953 Indian 80 Chief is probably one of the last models left.

A beautifully restored 1937, upside down Four. Produced for only two years, it has a 1200cc motor with three-speed gearbox.

Innocenti

1931 - 1971

Innocenti got involved in the motoring world just after the Second World War, creating a scooter division within its steel works. The company assured its place in motorcycle history with its Lambretta products, which became a symbol of the classic Italian scooter and an icon of the 1960s.

The first model was produced in 1944 was a single cylinder, two-stroke, 125cc unit. The model C was presented in 1950 and used a central tube chassis in both the open and enclosed version. Both machines sold phenomenally, which is not surprising when you consider that for the average Italians after the war, car ownership was a wild fantasy. The machine became very popular abroad and was sold under license in many countries. The Lambretta was under continually developed, selling in 125cc, 150cc, 175cc and 200cc versions. In 1952, the D series appeared, followed the next year by the E (economy) version.

Lambrettas raced well. A machine with aerodynamic bodywork and 125cc engine broke many world records, including 63 miles at an average speed of 100 mph.

The silencing had been improved, the engine cooling was sorted and there were more body panels to hide the internal workings on the 1957 LD 150.

The base product of the Innocenti Company was the Lambrtetta in its various versions. There was an attempt to diversify with a series of mopeds and a three-wheeled van, the Lambro, constructed with 200cc, two-stroke engine. In the 1970s, the company merged with BMC England in order to construct their vehicles in Italy, therefore making the two-wheelers a secondary production item.

Although there were still micro-scooters and scooters on the books in the 1970s – one particular one was the Bertone-styled Lui, which did not help the company to get back into the motorcycle world.

The last Lambretta left the factory in 1972, although the Grand Prix 200 was still being made under license in India long after.

A truly naked machine, this 1948 model B, developed by Innocenti after the Second World War, was a cheap source of transportation.

The engine for the model B was a two-stroke, 25cc unit, which could reach about 40 mph. There is little protection for the rider.

James

1902 – 1964

The James Cycle Company started out as a bicycle firm in Birmingham, England, founded by Harry James in 1880. James took the brave decision to go-it-alone and make penny-farthing bicycles. Motorcycle manufacturing started in Constitution Hill. Trade was swift and new premises were acquired in Sparkbrook in 1890. A manager was employed – Charles Hyde – and the company went public in 1897. With this Harry James retired, leaving Hyde to run the company, who promptly employed Fred Kimberley.

The first machine, produced in 1902, used a 'clip-on' Minerva engine and later an alternative model with the engine placed within the frame diamond.

At the Stanley Show of 1908, a new James stole the show. Using a genuine James engine, it carried the fuel and oil tank at the front of the steering column and the saddle was mounted on two long, flat springs. The first internally expanding brake system was used here too. R.L. Renouf, the inventor, also contributed many other innovative ideas.

By 1911, a new machine was offered which used a two-speed countershaft gearbox, incorporating a muti-plate clutch with alternate steel and bronze plates. They acquired part of the Osbourne Company – the cycle makers - in the same year. 1914 saw the introduction of the 500cc model 7 twin.

Full production resumed with a 7hp twin after the First World War in 1922. During the 1920s, the company prospered and sold two-strokes, side valves, ohvs, singles and V-twins. James took over the Baker motorcycle company in

1931 and its founder built the first Villiers engines.

During the Second World War, about 300 Model ML – Military Lightweight, 125cc machines – were used on the beaches of Normandy on D-Day and about 6,000 motorcycles were produced for the Allies during the war. After the war, the ML continued in production, as did the Autocycle.

The company was acquired by AMC in 1951 and the Cadet, Cavalier and Commodiore were made with engines produced at the Woolwich factory. There were more machines and updates, but time was running out and the company ceased production in 1964, disappearing when AMC collapsed in 1966.

Seen here is a 1921, single cylinder James with outside flywheel.

The James 496cc, V-twin of 1924, which used a three-speed gearbox.

Connecting between the two cylinders is a Mills carburettor.

Kawasaki

1949 - to date

In 1878, Shozo Kawasaki started a dockyard in Tokyo before proceeding to manufacture locomotives, railway stock, bridge supports and steel components. 1937 saw the birth of the Kawasaki Aircraft Company and the start of its motorcycle manufacturing venture.

At the end of World War Two, the company had to search for an alternative to aircraft production and plumbed on motorcycle engine manufacture. By 1950, they were supplying various companies with 58cc and 148cc engines.

In 1960, the Meguro Works, Japan's oldest motorcycle manufacturer, entered into a business relationship with Kawasaki Aircraft Co Ltd., which led to a full merger in 1963.

The original W1 can be traced back to 1960 and the early K1, a motorcycle developed by Meguro, who modeled the K1 on the English BSA A7 to replace their single cylinder Meguro Z7.

The K1 was an advanced design for its day and showcased modern manufacturing techniques with its air-cooled, 4-stroke, twin, ohv, 496cc engine, mounted in a double-cradle frame. Although the K1 was developed and produced by Meguro, selling it was left to Kawasaki Motor Sales Co. the forerunner of Kawasaki Motorcycle Company Ltd. Since the K models were still in the transition stage from Meguro to Kawasaki, there were many problems associated with technology transfers and maintenance. However, work proceeded simultaneously on the development of a successor to the K1, the new W1. At the time, sales objectives concentrated on orders for police patrol motorcycles intended for the 1964 Tokyo Olympics. Since there was no time to develop a new engine, the only option

The W1 of 1966, a machine whose development was started by Meguro prior to their merger with Kawasaki.

was to use the K1 model as it was. However, because the company sales managers wanted to maintain the impressive appearance of the K1, it was sent only to United States for a test in response to the expanding American market for 4-stroke motorcycles. Unfortunately, it was rejected due to lack of power. The answer was the W1, developed as a large, high-performance, four-stroke based on the K2. Unfortunately, the W series was unsuccessful as well because it was too similar in basic structure to the K models and mimicked the BSA A7 too much.

Kawasaki rode the wave generated by what later came to be called the "Izanagi Boom" and the A1, more commonly known as the

Typical of the smaller Japanese capacity machines during this period is this 1967 120cc C2SS, equipped with TR (trail) kit.

"Samurai," took center stage in August 1967. It was a high performance machine quickly followed by a larger bore model, the A7. It was an era when Kawasaki laid the foundations for its current success.

Kawasaki now assembled a top secret plan known as the N100 Plan. Development got under way in July 1967. Kawasaki considered two different approaches to the construction of what would become the most powerful production motorcycle engine for its day. The first approach was to increase the bore of an existing engine and the second involved the development of a revolutionary, new engine layout.

In creating the fastest bike in the world, Kawasaki engineers had to rewrite all the technical manuals, building either parallel or

"L" design, air-cooled, two-stroke, three cylinder engines. Both twin cylinder and three cylinder engines were developed. The test results concluded that cooling efficiency would not be significantly impaired by arranging the cylinders parallel to one another and the company finally opted for the in-line layout. In this way, with the help of the latest technology, techniques and know-how of the day, the company developed famous models such as the A1, A7 and KR-3. Their efforts culminated in the successful launch of the H1 in June 1967.

Approximately 14 months after the N100Us initial planning phase began in July 1967, Kawasaki produced the first ever MACH III in September 1968. The new machine's popularity was nothing short of explosive and it became a best-seller almost overnight. June

The engine of the KH500, an in-line, triple cylinder, two-stroke, capable of over 112 mph. It had five gears and chain final drive.

Riding the KH500 was an experience. Acceleration was awesome, but taking corners at high speed was frightening to say the least.

1970 saw the launch of a candy-striped, red and white bike followed by the H1A in September 1971. In January 1972, the company brought out the H1B. A steering damper was also added and the machine debuted under the name "Rainbow Color." The H1D came out in 1973. The H1E evolved into the H1F with a different color and graphics. More than 110,000 units of this model left the factory for destinations all over the world.

In 1967, Kawasaki decided to develop a high-performance motorcycle to surpass the 650W1. As the United States was targeted as the main market for these high performance motorcycles, the development team was sent to the North America, where they secretly worked out a plan for the new model. The displacement was set at 750cc and a mock-up completed in October 1968. However, Honda announced a new, 750cc, single-over-head-cam (SOHC) motorcycle at the Tokyo Motor Show, so all development efforts were stopped.

In 1970, the Z1 (development code T103) project team was reunited. Management staff decided there was a strong market for a high-speed, eye-catching motorcycle with enough power to use as a reliable touring model. The specifications called for an air-cooled, four-cylinder, four-stroke engine with a double-over-head-cam (DOHC). The first prototype was completed in the spring of 1971. In the fall of 1971, the final prototype was complet-

The angular styling of the Z1R, launched in 1978, made it look like no other Kawasaki model. It was capable of 132 mph.

ed and the unit was approved for mass production after testing. The first production model was completed in February 1972, after reworking all weak points and the first mass-production model was built in May 1972. In September 1972, the Z1 was introduced to the American public and sales started in November of that year.

The "Z1" astonished the motorcycling world. At the time, its performance capabilities were world-class, earning the bike and Kawasaki great respect. The later Z1R and Z1000J were developed along the same lines as the Z1, but by September 1980, Kawasaki was aware that the appeal of the Z1's technology was beginning to pale. The decision was made to develop a brand-new, high-performance, next generation motorcycle. One year passed before a prototype was developed; the engineers had produced a DOHC air-cooled, 6-cylinder, 2-valve engine. For a first-time prototype, its engine layout was nearly perfect, but the Kawasaki engineers were not satisfied and they shelved the mild 6-cylinder and concentrated on a DOHC, air-cooled, 4-cylinder, 4-valve engine, thus initiating the development of the Gpz900R.

Towards the end of 1982, exactly ten years after the introduction of the Z1, the first DOHC, liquid-cooled, 4-cylinder, 4-valve prototype was produced and eleven years after the introduction of the Z1, Kawasaki's newest 900cc machine – GPZ900R – could again claim the title "World's Fastest." Its recorded top speed was over 150 mph and its 0-400 acceleration time was 10.976 seconds. After

Sleek, flowing lines and a four-cylinder, 908cc, powerful engine exemplify the world's fastest production machine back in 1983.

The beautifully designed front fairing allowed the rider to sit behind it and take full advantage of the high-speed aerodynamics.

tireless preparation, Kawasaki introduced the new GPZ900R to the public at the 1983 Paris Salon. In January 1984, sales of the GPZ900R began worldwide with the word "Ninja" added as a prefix to its name for the North American market. The Gpz900R yielded its flagship position to the ZZ-R1100 in 1990.

1972 saw a world-wide oil cisis, but Z1 continued to sell strongly. Realizing that demands for high-performance, supersport

machines existed, 1974 saw Kawasaki start work on a new flagship model to replace the famous Z1.

The decision was made to power the new machine with an in-line, six-cylinder unit, a first for Kawasaki. The original prototype was completed in August 1976 and its slim chassis seemed overwhelmed by the huge engine with its bank of six carburettors and a six-into-two exhaust system. As market tastes changed during its development period, so did the machine and it was given a larger fuel tank and restyled as a big tourer. When Harley-Davidson announced their 1,340cc engine in

Monster engine – six cylinders, 1286cc, double overhead camshafts, water-cooling and a capability to reach a top speed of 135 mph.

The shaft-driven Z1300 was a big machine, good for long distance cruising, but hard work without a fairing.

1977, the displacement of the new bike was increased from 1,200cc to 1,286cc. The final, restyled prototype was completed in March 1978 and the Z1300 made its world debut at the Koln show in September 1978. The liquid-cooled, 1,286cc, DOHC, two-valve engine had a maximum output of 120ps@8,000 rpm. It was truly a monster machine.

The Z1300, produced from 1978 to 1983, was given digital fuel injection ("D.F.I.") In March, the ZN1300A Voyager was added to the line-up, featuring fairing, saddlebags, top box, stepped seat, digital speedometer, AM/FM radio, cassette deck and trip computer with fuel gauge, stopwatch function and calculator for making fuel consumption/average speed calculations. After a twelve-year production run, Kawasaki's first, liquid-cooled, six-cylinder engine bowed out in 1989.

By the mid 1970s, Kawasaki were producing all types of machines from off-roaders – motocross and enduros to very fast two-strokers – H2C for example – and, of course, larger, multicylinder machines.

The racing scene saw Barry Sheen taking most of the honors, but the 'green meanie,' Kawasaki's 500cc racers, ridden by Mick Grant and Barry Ditchburn, were determined to give him a run for his money.

When the 1990s came round, the ZZR1100 was top dog, but the company also produced a range of machines of varying capacities. A new trend started with retro-style cruising machines and Kawasaki made the Drifter, with a choice of 800cc or 1500cc engine. The end of the 1990s saw the long, low ZL600

Good looks, comfort and speed make the ZZ-R 1200 ideal tourers.

The mighty ZZ-R 1100 has become a motorcycling icon for the designers of the ultimate tourer from the Kawasaki camp, the ZZ-R 1200.

The ZL 600 is a mid-range, laid-back, American-style machine with a smooth, responsive, four-cylinder motor.

Eliminator, which used the engine from the GPz series. The classic and retro trend hit hard and Kawasaki responded with the W650, a machine that paid tribute to the W series some 30 years earlier, but with all the modern equipment necessary.

The new millennium brought even more awesome machinery, including the ZX-12R, a pleasing sports tourer. The ZX10R was designed for any rider wanting ultimate super-sport performance. The ZX6R and RR are circuit ready machines and will hold their own anywhere. If you want adventure, try the latest KLE500. Go off-roading with a KX model, available in a variety of engine sizes, or if you prefer to cruise, then you cannot ignore the outrageous VN2000, the world's largest V-twin. In other words, Kawasaki provided many choices in their 2004 range.

Two versions of this machine are available: the road-going ZX6R or the tricked-up track version, the ZX6RR. Both extremely fast.

This is the multi-purpose KLE 500, a tall, fast machine which is as happy off-roading as running on tarmac.

The VN2000: the world's largest V-twin.

Ultimate supersport: the Ninja ZX-10, made for speed.

A little nostalgic, the W1 harks back to the days of Meguro.

For the younger enthusiast, the KX125 eats dirt for breakfast.

The totally awesome ZX 12 R. The 1198cc engine pumps more adrenaline than water from a tap.

Kreidler

1921 - 1940

Kreidler Fahrzeugbau was a company based in Kornwestheim, near Stuttgart, Germany. It was a sprawling factory supplying semi-finished metals to German industry. A small secondary production of Kreidler motorcycles was located here. The first bike to leave the factory was basically a moped – the K50 – a lightweight, 49cc, two-stroke machine. The success of this machine allowed the company to follow up with the K51, a more luxurious version of its predecessor which remained in production until 1953. Speed restrictions in Germany resulted in the engine being altered and late in 1955, alongside two other models, the R50 scooterette was introduced. The following year, however, the Florett, the machine that would determine the future for Kreidler, emerged.

The Florett was marketed as a motorocycle- which skirted speed restrictions on mopeds. It used an all-new, horizontal, 49cc engine and could reach a speed of 41 mph. The Florett was produced for many years and proved extremely reliable. At the time, the new 50cc racing category was starting to take hold, and many owners of the Florett found that its engine was ideal for tuning due to its exceptional reliability.

The first Kreidler racing machine appeared in 1959, basically a stripped-down, tuned version of the Florett. In 1960, Hans Georg Anscheidt joined Kreidler's research and development team and went on to bring many prizes home to

Wire wheels and slick styling made the Florett an attractive moped.

The Florett became the mainstay of the Kreidler production lines in the mid-1950s.

the company. The first was the 1960 Hockenheim Motor Cup. Kreidlers were present at the ISDT and took honors for several different countries.

In road racing, however, that Kriedler won its biggest prizes. In 1961, the FIM initiated the Coup d'Europe Endurance Championship. Anscheidt won and his team mate Gedlich came in second. In 1962, the 50cc class was promoted to World Championship status and Kreidler worked on the previous year's engine to prepare a 49cc, horizontal, single cylinder unit that produced 10hp and had straight finning and a four-speed foot gearchange. The new machine was the Renn Florett. Although the machines and riders performed beautifully, the title was not to be theirs and they were thwarted at the starting post by Ernt Degner's Suzuki.

Although 1961 was a good year for sales, 1962 was astounding. The company built more machines than all its German competitors put together. At the time, there were four models: the Florett 3.4hp motorcycle, the moped, the 4.2 model and the super models.

This is a Kreidker Van Veen 50cc racer from 1967.

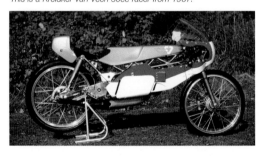

On the 1963 racing scene, although the machines did well again, Suzuki dominated. In 1964, the bike was completely redesigned, but even that was not good enough to beat the Suzukis. Although 1965 was a miserable year on the Grand Prix circuit, on 11 April 1964 at Hockenheim, Anscheidt broke the 50cc, 75cc and 100cc standing records with an average speed of 68.88 mph.

In 1966, following a boardroom disagreement, Anscheidt left the company and joined the

victorious Suzuki team, where he claimed the World Championship shortly after.

Kreidler had also lost out on the world speed record titles and therefore made the decision to produce a supercharged fifty to contest both the standing start and flying start records. The rider was Rudolf Kunz and he established the first world record for the standing quarter mile using a specially prepared streamlined machine. Kreidler went on to break several other records, while its road machines were also selling well. Kreidler also had some success on the race circuits, but was never able to topple the Suzuki domination. During the late 1960s, the company teamed up with the Dutch company, Van Veen, to break even more world records.

The 1971 line-up of road machines consisted of two automatic, two-speed, step-through commuter models and three Floretts – the standard TM, the R.S. Holland, was the principal market and the 100,000th came down the Kreidler line in 1971. It was also this year that a long-awaited World Championship was clinched by Jan de Vries on a newly designed, water-cooled machine with a 50cc engine and a new frame. In 1973, Kreidler dominated the scene and another World Championship was captured. The victories continued and Angel Nieto joined Kreidler to clinch the Championship in 1975. Although the trophy escaped the company for the next few years, Lazzarini brought it back in 1979. In 1977, there was a new record attempt with Kreidler's Black Arrow machine, ridden by Henk Van Kessel, running a mean average of 134.6 mph, followed up the next day with a new 50cc speed record at 141.7 mph and lastly, a speed of 137.38 mph.

In 1980, there was the upgraded Gelandesport enduro machine, now designated the GS50. By 1981, sales of Kreidler road machines dropped dramatically and the company introduced a new batch of machines for the 1981 season. Among these were the Sport-Mofa-Flott and a range of 80cc lightweight machines. Although other machines were designed, they never hit the market and Kreidler was liquidated in the summer of 1982.

KTM

1934 - date

In 1934, Hans Trunkenpolz opened a repair workshop in Mattighofen, Austria. By 1937, the company became the first distributors of DKW motorcycles as well as the largest motor car and motorcycle repair shop in upper Austria.

The first R100 machines left the factory in 1951. They used a Rotax 100cc, two-stroke engine, but were not a great success. By 1953, the company was producing three motorcycles a day and had entered five machines in the Gaisberg competition. They took the first three places. The company was now known as Kronreif Trunkenpolz Mattighofen.

In 1954, the thousandth KTM was delivered and the company took the Austrian 125cc championship. A year later, development of the 125cc Tourist model was started and in 1956, the company entered the ISDT in the 125cc category. Egon Dornaur won the gold medal. In 1957, a new 125 (the Trophy) was developed, along with a scooter, the Mirabell. Another new machine designed by Ludwig Apfelbeck helped Erwin Lechner to many racing victories in 1958 and 1959.

The crowd watch as David Tomasik navigates his KTM 420cc machine around a motocross circuit.

Like many other European motorcycle manufacturers, KTM cut back production in the 1960s. They consolidated by producing small mopeds, the first Ponny scooter, and bicycles. In 1963, the Comet range, powered by Sachs 50cc engines, was introduced. Cross-country competition resumed in 1964 and an official KTM works team participated in the ISDT.

65 SX - hydraulic clutch, 6 gears, Marzocchi forks, everything fully adjustable. Seat 2 @ ft high, ideal for 6 to 9 year-olds.

In 1968, the company produced the cross-country Penton Six Days for export to the United States. Four years later, it introduced its own 175cc, two-stroke, single cylinder engine. Russian-born Gennady Moisseev clinched the first of many World 250cc championships in it. There was success too in the ISDT, with which the company collected 51 gold, 34 silver and five bronze medals.

In 1975, KTM America Inc., the company's first American subsidiary, was established in Lorrain, Ohio. In 1980, the company officially changed its name to KTM Motor-Fahrzeugbau AG. The R&D department was constantly looking for new ideas. It produced a 125cc, water-cooled motocross machine, while development of a four-stroke, water-cooled engine began in 1982. In 1986, KTM won in all the categories at the ISDT in Italy and production of the four-stroke engine – a single cylinder, 560cc, ohc – started in 1986.

In 1988, a majority of KTM shares were sold to GIT Trust Holding Company. Scooter manufacture ceased and Trunkenpolz died. Sadly, 1991 saw the company file for bank-

The Duke series started in the early 1990s. This is the 2003 640.

championships saw two more victories at the Master Rally and the Tunisia Rally. The following year, production of the KTM LC4 engine began and championships were won in many categories. In 1997, the LC4 Supermoto road machine was produced along with the LC4 Adventure. New subsidiaries were opened up all over Europe and KTM presented their two-cylinder project at Intermot. Fabrizio Meoni won the 2002 Dakar rally riding a new 950cc rally twin, among numerous other titles. In 2003, KTM entered the 125cc class Road Racing World Championship. And the titles keep coming.

The V-twin cylinder, four-stroke, 999cc engine of the Super Duke.

ruptcy. A new company opened under new management and with a new name, KTM Sportsmotorcycle GmbH. Over the following years, 125cc, 350cc and 500cc championships were won. The company was renamed again in 1994 and production of the Duke series of machines began. In 1995, two more

The 990 Super Duke, latest creation from KTM, uses a chromium-molybdenum, powder-coated frame and aluminium sub-frame.

Laverda

1950 - date

Moto Laverda was founded by Francesco Laverda in the small town of Breganze in the province of Venezia, northern Italy in 1947. It was created to produce small-capacity motorcycles and mopeds.

In 1950, their first model was presented. Known as the Laverda 75, it was upgraded to sport status and raced in many long distance events on the National roads and in races such as the Motogiro d'Italia and the Milan-Taranto. Between 1952 and 1956, the little Venetian company gained great sporting success with the Laverda 75.

The 75cc bike was followed by a slightly larger, 100cc machine in 1955, which also proved a great success in the sporting world. With the credibility gained by these two machines, the company benefited and started to grow.

Through the middle of the 1960s, motorcycle production was restricted to the smaller cylinder size mopeds and scooters. In July 1958, the Laverdino 48 four-stroke moped was

presented and a year later, came a 49cc scooter. 1961 saw the launch of the 200cc, four-stroke twin – the engine was basically two 100cc cylinders put together – produced until 1969.

Massimo Laverda, son of owner Francesco, decided that the company should look at larger capacity machines, with a view towards increasing production. Thus the Laverda 650cc was presented by the company in 1968 and was well-received by the general public. It was not until the 1970s that the company gained real success with the launch of the Laverda 750cc, which was subsequently exported all around the world and gave birth to a grand series of sporting models from the small factory in Breganze. 1970 saw the stylish, 750cc, SF series, finished in a brilliant orange hue and produced until 1976. The 1978 SFC competition version won much respect on the race circuits. The machine was around until 1976 and raced in production racing all over Europe.

By the middle of the 1970s, the general public was looking at even bigger machines and Laverda stepped up production of their 1000cc and 1200cc machines. The production of the different 1000cc bikes, such as the 3CL and Jota, continued through the end of the 1980s. One of the most sought-after machines was the Laverda 1000 RGS (Real Gran Sport), presented at the 1981 Milan show. From the 750SF to the RGS, the super orange sporting machines from Breganze factory were loved by enthusiasts all over the globe.

The Laverda line-up was filled with smaller

The Laverdino, a 48cc, four-stroke moped introduced in 1958.

The 1981, awesome RGS1000cc machine.

size machines, the 350cc and 500cc, and provided the young aspiring riders of the day with 125cc and motocross machines.

One of the many innovative technical wonders to come from the Breganze factory was the development of a 1000cc, 90 degree, V6 machine, an amazing experiment which took some time to be refined and prepared for the race track.

In the 1990s, the company found itself in financial difficulties, a result of production diversification which did not go according to

Possibly the most expensive trail bike on the market at the time, the 2TR used a Laverda 247cc, single cylinder, two-stroke engine.

The three cylinder motor of the 3C, a 981cc, DOHC, four-stroke unit.

plan. The addition of the company to the Aprilia Group was initially a good sign. The company was going to return to current updated production, with a range of machines for many different markets. Unfortunately, there was a long period of difficulty and a lack of design concepts. The name Laverda was on every enthusiast's lips – what was going to happen?

Future production plans were unveiled with a strong view to producing medium to large capacity machines and to reviving a grand tradition, designed with the best technological advancement made in the motorcycling world to date. The machines distinguished themselves within the group by their eclectic styling and ability to experiment with new technical and

In 1978, Laverda produced this awesome V6 endurance racer, which made its debut at the Paul Ricard circuit in France, clocking 176 mph on the Mistral straight.

Brutally fast, the 3C was a sensational 130 mph superbike. Laverda planned a faster machine than the opposition and they got it.

The 1999 Laverda 750S Formula is a parallel twin, eight-valve, four-stroke machine, producing 92hp and with a top speed of 140 mph.

styling solutions. In the meantime, a new scooter was presented, the Phoenix 150, which was aimed at a now large scooter following. Thus the company started to rebuild the sales network and the after-sales back-up and was thus able to deal with future demands. At the same time, as the mark being relaunched, the Laverda Club Italia, a reference point for all the enthusiasts, collectors and workers around the world, was founded for those ambitious for Laverda's future.

The Laverda Strike is a classic 'naked' machine and has a 747cc, water-cooled, twin cylinder, four-stroke motor and six gears.

Levis

1950 - date

Daisy Butterfield and her two brothers, Arthur and Billy, lived in Stechford, a suburb of Birmingham, England. Bob Newey, a family friend, worked on a small motorcycle and tried to interest Mr Norton in it. After being rebuffed, he turned to Ms Butterfield, or rather to her brothers, who suggested it would be a good idea to produce the machine themselves. It was Ms Butterfield who came up with the name Levis – Latin for 'light.' The Butterfield brothers and Bob Newey went into business, building a lightweight machine. Ms Butterfield also became Mrs Newey and the company was launched.

In 1912, the company rolled out the 'Baby' Levis which used a 211cc engine. The machine was to remain in production until 1926. Like many motorcycle companies of the time, Levis was sure that races would provide publicity for the machines. In 1913, the company entered a team of 350cc machines in the TT (there was no 250cc race at the time). The riders were Arthur Butterfield, Albert Milner and, of course, Bob Newey. Unfortunately, the event was not a success for the small company, with only Arthur finishing, a lowly thirteenth.

During the First World War, the company continued to produce small numbers of machines – 211cc, single gear Populars. When hostilities ended and the TT resumed, a cup was offered for the best performance by a 250cc machine and Levis developed an engine of 247cc which used three gears. Levises finished the 250cc class race in first, second and third place. The following year, G.S. Davison, the most famous Levis rider, finished second in the 250cc class. It was the best period for the company as far as the TT races were concerned and it would never again achieve so much. It excelled in reliability trials, however, with the little, two-stroke engine winning many gold medals.

In 1925, a two-stroke machine known as the Model K was introduced. The engine was a

247cc unit and front and rear had expanding brakes . A three speed gearbox was fitted with chain drive and a kick start. A sports version, the Model O, was introduced the following year and the two machines remained in production until 1927.

In 1927, Newey produced his four-stroke, 350cc engine, a move away from normal, two-stroke production. The machine never sold well, but the company continued with the machine and entered it in the 1928 Junior TT. It was raced by Jack Amott, but without success because the cylinder castings were far too thin and broke on the first lap. The problem was rectified and the machine was entered in the Amateur TT, to be ridden by Tim Hunt. Once again, however, misfortune struck. On the last lap, a hare's breath from victory, one of the valves gave out.

Newey spent much time refining the two-stroke engine and introduced the 'Sixport' in 1929. The 'Sixport' used two exhaust ports and featured a detachable cylinder head for the first time. The machine had problems and was withdrawn in 1930, partly due to the success of the four-stroker. The 350cc was given another exhaust pipe – to keep up with the trends of the day – and renamed the A2. The success of the machine prompted Newey to develop a 250cc version, which also was very popular.

Soon a 500cc, ohv version was also available and a new, ohc, 250cc machine was designed by Newey for 1933. It was put on the market at an expensive price, despite the Depression and the global scarcity of money. In 1936, the Levis 600, designed by Newey and Ray Mason, who had joined the company the same year, was produced.

The Second World War put a stop to the development and manufacture of other machines. The company had to make air compressors for the war effort and continued to do so after the war. Thus no more motorcycles were made.

The single cylinder, two-stroke, 211cc unit of the Levis Popular.

The 1921 Levis: a popular, a simple, lightweight machine. The front downtube is split to let the exhaust pipe pass through.

Matchless

1904 - 1966

Unlike the majority of early 20th century manufacturers in Britain, the Matchless Motorcycle Company was not based in the Midlands, but in Plumstead, London. H.H. Collier was a maker of bicycles and he was joined by his two sons, Charlie and Harry. Between the three of them, they produced their first motorcycle, basically a bicycle with an engine attached to the downtube. By 1904, like many other manufacturers of the time, they had

The 1902/3 Matchless had its engine attached to the front downtube.

produced a tri-car. From then on, they concentrated on a V-twin, JAP-engined machine, introduced in 1905, which had swing arm rear suspension and leading front forks, a novelty at the time, but a later a trend.

In 1905, Harry Collier qualified for the International Cup Race in France, where he performed sucessfully. The following year, he was invited back along with his brother. Although they did get good results, they again failed to win. Legend has it that they returned to England with the Marquis de Mouzilly de St. Mars. Discussions on the journey concerned the possibility of having a similar race on the Isle of Man.

The Marquis followed up on the discussions and the first TT races on the Isle of Man were instigated. Charlie Collier went on to win the first victory in the first single cylinder race with his Matchless, fitted with a JAP engine.

The machine was exhibited at the 1907 Motor Cycle Show (replicas were available the following year), along with a sprung frame V-twin, a lightweight model with a two speed gearbox and a special racing model based on the V-twin Jap engine.

The company thrived and continued to race, with Harry winning the TT in 1909 and his brother the following year. Matchless also participated in races at Brooklands, where it was equally sucessful. By 1912, a step-through

This is the 5hp, 770cc, V-twin of 1912.

An essential piece of equipment, especially when racing or on speed trials, speedometers must be as accurate as possible.

Ladies' lightweight was produced and the company decided to manufacture its own engine. A single was produced, but dropped after a couple years.

The company concentrated on V-twins. The 8B model was produced with a three-speed, countershaft gearbox, kick start, fully enclosed chain drive and internally expanding hub brake in the rear wheel. The machine was powered by an 8hp, Swiss-made MAG engine.

By the outbreak of the First World War, the line-up consisted of the MAG-engined machine and the model 8B/2. The company was obliged to turn its skills to the war effort, making precision parts for munitions and aircraft. The company had a war motorcycle model ready, but no orders came. The machine was renamed the Victory after the war.

The company concentrated again on its V-twin machines and it was not until 1923 that a new single was seen on its books. The L2, as it was designated, used a 348cc Blackburn engine, an all-chain drive and expanding internal brakes. By 1924, a big, 591cc single was added to the range, along with other machines and sidecar models. The company also produced its own 347cc, ohc model, to be used in the 1923 TT. Unfortunately, it was not finished in time, but did remain in production for a few more years, even though it did not have great racing success. For 1925 came a Matchless-designed and manufactured V-twin of 990cc, loosely based on the 590cc machine. A year later, founder H.H. Collier died and the following year, the company went public as Matchless Motor Cycles (Colliers) Ltd. A 250cc light-weight, known as the Model R, was added to the line-up. It was the first to have an all-black tank with gold striping, and by the end of 1927, the range was given a complete makeover. The results were seen in the 1928 line-up, which consisted of the 246cc Model R, a Sports version known as the R/S, a new, 347cc, ohv Sports model, the standard 347cc, sv model, a new 495cc Super Sports model and the big, 591cc single. For the twins there were two versions, both using the 990cc engine. The single cylinder sports models came with twin exhaust pipes and silencers, a trend of the day. A year later, the R3 and a new V5 made their debut at the Motor Cycle Show.

In 1930, the Silver Arrow, a narrow angle V-twin with an engine capacity of 400cc and

The V-twin engine has cast iron cylinders.

The Model X had a V-twin, air cooled, side-valve, four-stroke engine and could reach 80 mph.

many new features, made its appearance. The frame had a triangulated rear section which pivoted behind the rear seat, its movement controlled by springing between the rear frame and the top tube. The engine valves were operated by a single camshaft driven from the crankshaft. Four valves, vertically positioned, were housed in a single casting which the two-cylinder heads and the inlet pipe formed between the two cylinders. The general public was wary of new ideas and the machine never achieved good sales. All the same, Matchless decided on another new machine, this time using a narrow, 593cc, V4 engine. The Silver Hawk was as innovative as the Arrow, but sales remained unimpressive. In 1930, the trends demanded sloping engines and new frames had to be designed. Sports models were introduced, their engines using upswept exhaust pipes and four-speed gearboxes. The now familiar Matchless chrome 'M' also came about, although initially without wings, which were added later.

In 1931, Matchless took over the ailing AJS concern, which had gone into liquidation. The AJS machines kept their own identity for a period, but then became identified as Matchless models.

A pretty unique machine for the period: the 1934 Silver Hawk. The front forks were the sprung girder type.

The taxation system at the time relied on a weight system and so all manufacturers were keen to keep down the weight of their bigger machines. Matchless produced a machine known as the Light Five Hundred, which used a 498cc engine and was designated D/5. The big, 990cc V-twin was redesigned also and renamed the Model X. This engine remained the backbone of the company right up to the beginning of the Second World War.

In 1935, the G models, mostly fitted with ohv engines (although the side-valve engine had not been left behind), were introduced. The G5 Tourist model had a 498cc engine of this type. Further expansion was seen in 1938, when Matchless took over the Sunbeam concern. At this point, the company went through a reorganization and was renamed Associated Motor Cycles Ltd. With this, the simple 'M' badge sprouted wings.

The Matchless badge acquired wings in the late 1930s.

The Silver Hawk had a V-four, ohc, four-stroke, 592cc engine, matched to a four-speed gearbox and chain final drive.

The Matchless G9 was introduced in the late 1940s. This is a 1955 model.

As the Second World War loomed, the company was asked to provide machines for the army. It presented the G3, a machine improved in 1941 with the 'Teledraulic' front fork system, designed at AMC. By the end of the conflict, the company had supplied some 80,000 G3 and G3L machines to the military. They were also manufactured after the war, but with a different color scheme. As people got back to normality, they also started racing again. Matchless bought out a new trials machine based on the G3L. It was higher, lighter and used competition tires. Many works sponsored riders and even privateers enjoyed great success on these machines.

The G9 had a 500cc, twin cylinder unit, which it shared with other machines from Associated Motor Cycles Ltd.

In 1948, a 500cc, vertical twin was added to the line-up. It had swing arm rear suspension controlled by oil dampers made by the company itself. Due to its shape, the bike gained the name 'jampot,' later the name of the AMC owners' club magazine.

The G9 twin model also became available and used almost the same units.

Developed from the G9, the G45 racing model was added to the catalogue in 1952. The G45 production model was based on the 1952 Senior Manx Grand Prix winner, ridden by Derek Farrant. In 1955, the G11 was added to the range and the company acquired the Norton, James and Francis-Barnett concerns in the

The G3 was supplied to the army during the war. This is a 1960 G3 LS, which used a 350cc engine.

The first G50 racers went on sale in 1959. Only 180 were built before production ended in 1962.

The G50 single cylinder, single ohc, two-valve, four-stroke engine produced a modest 52hp, but could reach 140 mph.

It is not difficult to notice the similarities between the AJS 7R and the Matchless G50, especially the gold-painted engine.

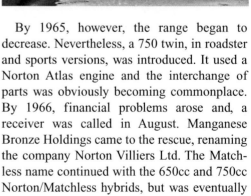

meantime, although these managed, for the moment, to keep their own identity. But consolidation followed inevitably.

By 1958, the Matchless range consisted of no less than 17 different models. To mention a few, there was now a medium-weight, 250cc single, along with the G2 and its odd circular gearbox. There was also the G12 CSR, a G12 scrambler and the single cylinder G50, which replaced the G45 racer.

By 1965, however, the range began to decrease. Nevertheless, a 750 twin, in roadster and sports versions, was introduced. It used a Norton Atlas engine and the interchange of parts was obviously becoming commonplace. By 1966, financial problems arose and, a receiver was called in August. Manganese Bronze Holdings came to the rescue, renaming the company Norton Villiers Ltd. The Matchless name continued with the 650cc and 750cc Norton/Matchless hybrids, but was eventually sacrificed to keep the Norton Commando on the market.

Megola

1921 - 1925

This short-lived German maker produced un-orthodox motorcycles. The company started production in 1921 and made motorcycles with five-cylinder, air-cooled, side-valve, radial engines designed by Fritz Cockerell and built into the front wheel. The unusual engine application meant that to change gears, the driver had to use different diameter wheels. For racing purposes, the radial engine had a very low center of gravity and handled well. It was possible to dismantle the engine cylinders without removing the spokes from the wheel. Sports Megola's featured saddles while the roadgoing models had bucket seats. Front suspension functioned by means of semi-elliptic springs in a substantial cradle and some models had semi-elliptic rear springs as well. The box section frame contained the main fuel tank, although fuel had to be decanted into a smaller, fork-mounted tank. The company made around 2000 motorcycles in total.

The radial, four-stroke, five-cylinder engine.

Featured here is a 1922, 637cc model Megola.

Merkel

1902 - 1917

Among the most innovative of pioneer motorcycle companies, Merkel, first appeared in Milwaukee, Wisconsin, USA in 1902 when Joseph Merkel set up shop producing single cylinder motorcycles. In 1905, they decided to compete and produced several racing machines.

With their racing experience, Merkel developed and patented spring front forks which became forerunners of the modern telescopic front fork. They were subsequently taken up by other manufacturers of racing and road-going machines. Merkel also developed a form of monoshock rear suspension, a system used in machines today. With all the springing and relative comfort, the new company slogan became "All roads are smooth to The Flying Merkel."

In 1909, the company was purchased by the Light Manufacturing Company and moved to Pottstown, Ohio where they started producing machines with 'Merkel Light' and 'The Flying Merkel' names.

A young test rider, Maldwyn Jones, raced the new Merkels and even beat the legendary Cannonball Baker on a 10 mile race. He achieved many good results for the company and finally turned professional, going on to win many more races on his 'Flying Merkel.'

In 1911, the company was sold once again, this time to the Miami Cycle Manufacturing Company and production was moved to Middletown, Ohio. The Miami Company built bicycles and Motorcycles under several names – Raycycle and Miami. Merkel would give them the high-end product necessary.

The factory racing team expanded and included such names as L.S. Taylor, F.E. French, C.F. Pinneau and W. Wikel. In 1914, The Flying Merkel won the National endurance run from

Chicago to St Louis and Maldwyn Jones broke a world record on the Vanderbilt Course, returning to Middletown a hero.

The First World War was looming and although the company had achieved success in racing and had come up with ingenious technical solutions in its time, its accomplishments were not enough to keep it afloat. Slow sales, a drop in demand and heavy competition finally caused production of the Flying Merkel to come to an end. The last machines left the premises in 1917.

Although unrestored, one of the last, very rare, 1916 Flying Merkels.

You wonder how good these tires really were, but having "non-skid" printed on them must have imparted a little confidence.

The big, V-twin engine of the 1916 Merkel. It had a kick-start and different intake system than the 1915 models.

Michaelson/ Minneapolis

1908 - 1928

The Michaelson and its sister bike, the Minneapolis, were first introduced to the marketplace in June 1908. The Michaelson motorcycle was conceived and realized in 1912 by four brothers in the great Twin Cities area of Minnesota, already the home of Wagner, Thiem and Cyclone motorcycles. The Michaelson brothers Jack, Walter, Joe and Anton developed a motorcycle whose design was considered one of the freshest and most advanced of its day.

The Michaelson Motor Company's manufacturing plant was located at 526-530 Fifth Street South in Minneapolis. Jack was president and treasurer, Walter was the vice president, superintendent and machinist. Joe had a considerable amount of mechanical experience. As company draftsman, he was instrumental in creating the advanced designs of both the Michaelson and Minneapolis models.

The Michaelson and Minneapolis were quite similar in their mechanical aspects and it must be admitted that most machines manufactured under the Minneapolis brand name was conceived strictly for public relations purposes. Both models were available in single and V-twin cylinder form. The Minneapolis used Thiem and Thor engines modified to fit its specifications.

Joe Michaelson also designed a single and twin engine for the Minneapolis motorcycle. Under his personal direction, the Michaelson engines were built entirely at the Michaelson manufacturing plant by expert workmen with years of experience. Every engine was tested to be sure it could produce maximum power and speed before being sent out. The cylinder and head were one piece. Mechanical overhead intake and exhaust valves with adjustable pushrods were used. The rocker arms on the intake and exhaust were covered with caps to keep out dust and grit. The rockers each had a large oil chamber packed with an oil-saturated wick, while the cylinders were nickel-plated and carefully polished. The all-aluminum engine case was highly finished for the sake of appearance. As for the mechanical details of the bike, there was a Schebler carburetor, a Bosch magneto, a chain drive and multiple disc clutches in oil. Overhead valves featured on both the single and the twin. The motorcycle also featured a leaf front fork suspension.

Several Michaelson Tri Cars were also made. The Michaelson was the first motorcycle to feature an integral engine transmission, and was thus truly advanced for its time. In 1908, the Twin Model A Michaelson cost $325.00, while the single Model B Michaelson cost $275.00. The successful production of these fine motorcycles continued until the late 1914 when the company began to run into financial trouble.

Lee W. Oldfield, a well-known racing driver from Indianapolis, Indiana, came to Minneapolis to take charge of the Michaelson Motorcycle Company. The company was reorganized with Oldfield as president and manager, while the new secretary and treasurer was I.A. Webb, a well-known mining promoter and capitalist who invested $50,000. Their plans were to increase production of the twin-engine motorcycles and delivery cars and suspend manufacturing of the single engine motorcycle. They would also build a larger manufacturing facility in the suburbs of Minneapolis. Walter Michaelson, head of the company at that time, felt compelled to resign.

Despite these changes and the many ambitious plans of the new owners, the company once again ran into financial difficulties. The stock, assets and parts supply of the company were bought out by the H.E. Wilcox Motor Car Company of Minneapolis. However, this company simply disappeared from the scene in 1928, along with all hope of reviving Michaelson Motorcycles.

Although disappointed by the fate of the family company, Walter Michaelson did not end his career with his resignation from the firm. As a pioneer designer of the original Michaelson Tri Car, he went on to manufacture a new tri car model, a radical departure from the previous machines. It had a foot starter and a two-speed, enclosed transmission with a multiple enclosed disc clutch. It also used an internally expanding 8 in drum brake, the largest featured on any American motorcycle at the time.

The Michaelson and Minneapolis were similar in mechanical aspects. Both were available in single and V-twin, cylinder form.

Walter Michaelson went on to manufacture the Michaelson Tri-car Motorcycle, a radical departure from previous models.

Minerva

1897 - 1909

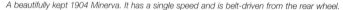

MINERVA. The Minerva Company only lasted about nine years, but it had a significant impact on the motorcycling industry. The Belgian engine-maker was supplier to many motorcycle companies – Triumph, Ariel, Matchless, and Royal Enfield, to name a few. Sylvain de Jong set the whole concern going. His bicycle company was established in Antwerp in 1897. The engine used on the first powered bicycle produced by the Minerva Company was designed by two engineers – H. Luthi and E. Zurcher. Their engine was intended to be positioned on the front of the downtube of the bicycle, while a leather strap was used for the drive to the rear wheel. This position was known as the 'Minerva position' and it was a jealously guarded secret.

By 1900, an improved and larger version of the engine was produced as a 239cc unit. It used a system where the exhaust and inlet valves were operated by cams. There was a Minerva-made spark plug and a Minerva spray-type carburettor along with an exhaust pipe with a small silencer. Minerva claimed that 75 cycle factories in Britain and Europe were using its engines. David Citroen was responsible for its brilliant salesmanship. Minerva was so sucessful that the two sales companies decided to merge under the name of Minerva Motors Ltd. The head office would be in Holborn, London, and both Citroen and de Jong would be directors.

It was not long before the introduction of new models such the 262cc, the 345cc and a 423cc engine aimed mainly at forecar or sidecar models. At the time, a new design was chosen. A second position for the engine would be between the 'V' of the frame of the bicycle, while the twisted drive belt would henceforth be a 'V' type.

In 1904, a new factory opened in Bechem, near Antwerp and the workforce now numbered about 1000 people. The demand from other companies, however, dwindled as they designed their own engines or turned to other manufacturers. So Minerva concentrated on making its own models.

Minervas were present in races around the world. They collected medals and prizes from many different events, even as far afield as Australia, where they finished in the top three

A beautifully kept 1904 Minerva. It has a single speed and is belt-driven from the rear wheel.

in the 1905 Sydney to Melbourne Reliability Ride.

Minerva, or rather de Jong, designed cars before producing motorcycles. He decided to pick up where he had left off. Motorcycles were of secondary importance and while some were listed for 1909, they had seen little development. Soon that side of the business ceased altogether, leaving Minerva free to concentrate on motor cars.

A Minerva engine used by the BSA Company.

The 1904, 345cc, 2 3/4hp engine.

MM (Italy)

1897 - 1909

Alfonso Morini, born in Bologna, Italy in 1898 started out in the motorcycle business in 1924. In 1922, together with businessmen Massi, Mattei and Mazzetti, he founded the "Fabricca di Motobiciclette Brevetti M.M. di A. Mattei & Co," or M.M. for short.

In 1924, they produced their first machine a 125cc two-stroke. Their first Grand Prix win came in 1927 when Alfonso rode the latest version of the 125cc machine to victory at the Gran Premio delle Nazioni at the Moinza track.

1930 saw their first four-stroke, a 175cc, ohc single. It was followed by 350cc and 500cc, four-stroke machines.

Morini left in 1937 to start Moto Morini, but the company continued to produce machines.

Mazzetti was a man who wanted perfection for his machines and this 1951 MM is a great example.

The beautifully finished, 250cc, ohc engine of the 1951 MM.

Montesa

1944 - 1982

Montesa was formed in 1944 by Pedro Permanyer and Francisco Bulto of Bultaco fame. The first machine was a small-capacity model of 93cc based largely on the Motobecane model of the period.

It was a difficult period in Spain's history. The Civil War had just ended and materials were hard to come by. Finding the right kind of machinery for the new company proved difficult, but fortunately, a local car company had gone into liquidation and the machinery needed was bought from the liquidated stock.

The demand for Montesa machines was staggering and round the clock production was needed. Of course, new premises had to be found to cope with the demand. The new buildings were in Pamplona Street, Barcelona, where there were three plants and plenty of space to operate. By now, a 125cc machine was sold along with the 93cc machine.

In the early 1950s, Montesa entered the world of competition, under the supervision of

This lightweight 1970s, 348cc, single cylinder, two-stroke Montesa is ready to confront the local terrain.

The Montesa Impala was awarded the ADI-FAD prize for the best industrial design in 1962. Seen here is a production racer.

Francesco Bulto. They entered a 125cc, two-stroke machine in the 125 class road race events. The machine was developed over the next few years, becoming very competitive and securing second, third and fourth places at the Ultra-Lightweight Isle of Man TT in 1956. The most successful machine that came out of the factory during the period was the Brio 80, a 93cc two-stroke.

Things were going so well for the company that they had to move once more in 1957, this

Geoff Connell, on his Montesa, comes to grips with the terrain during a 1970s International Six Day's Trial.

time to Espluges de Llobregat. All good things come to an end and certainly in the next few years, Montesa understood that first hand. The Spanish economy was once again in turmoil and sales suddenly slumped. The company found itself immeshed in deep financial problems. To cap it all off, the two owners, never eye-to-eye, decided to part company. Bulto left the company and started Bultaco, which would become Montesa's rival. Many of the Montesa staff went with Bulto and wages were cut. Everybody tightened their belts. So with most of his middle management gone, Permanyer had to appoint new faces. Leopold Mila became technical director, Pedro Pi went from chief test rider to development engineer while Permanyer's son Javier, at the age of eighteen, became sports assistant.

But once again, the economy started to revive and things started to look up. Pi began the development of new motocross machines and in 1960, Mila had come up with a new monoblock engine, a 175cc two-stroke used in the Montesa Impala models. These machines were tested by riders of the day on some of the worst African desert terrain to their durability. In 1965, a new model was presented, the Scorpion 250cc motocross machine and the first Montesa Trial machine was presented in 1967. In 1968, one of the machines, now called Cota, was raced by Pi who went on to win the Spanish Trials Championship. The original Cota had a 250cc engine, but was later enlarged to cover six machines of between 125cc through 348cc.

In 1975, the new Montessa motocross machines emerged. Known as Cappras and possessing engines varying from 125cc, 250cc and 360cc, they were presented, followed by a range of off-road enduro machines. Montesa, along with its rival Bultaco, dominated the international Trials scene and constituted a major threat in motocross as well.

The post-Franco period in Spain brought terrible industrial unrest, strikes and worker sit-ins, which risked destroying a healthy industry. Montesa was brought to its knees once again, this time by the workers themselves. Ironically, in 1980, the very year when it became virtually impossible to purchase a Spanish trial bike

because of strikes, Ulf Karlsson won the World Trials Championship. His victory should have been the icing on the cake for Montesa, but the many people hankering to buy Montesa were disappointed because of the strike. Things deteriorated so terribly that the government tried to resolve the situation, pointing out that Montesa should run all three companies (Montesa, Bul-

The ultra-lightweight 1999 Montesa Cota 315R.

The 315R uses a 249cc, two-stroke engine.

taco and Ossa). Montesa was also linked with the giant Honda concern and announced in 1982 that, with the Spanish Government's approval, they would buy Montesa. With its available cash, the company was able to to develop new models. Today, Montesa Honda S.A, as they are known, produces very competitive Cota trials from the Espulgas premises.

Morbidelli

1960 - 1990

Giancarlo Morbidelli was born in Pesaro, Italy in 1934. One of four children, he attended the local technical school and started work in a mechanical engineering factory.

With little money, but much ingenuity and great passion, he opened a factory selling woodworking machinery, eventually turning the factory into one of the best known in the world. His greatest passion was motorcycles, however, and he began to build racing machines to advertise his company. The machines were very successful in the 1970s, collecting four World titles. In the mid-1990s, he built a small run of 850cc, V8 machines, the design of which was far ahead of anything available at the time. Today, Morbidelli has assembled one of the finest motorcycle collections, a museum consisting of over 300 machines dating from the beginning of the 1900s to the 1980s.

The V8 machine was designed by Pininfarina.

Contemporary sports bike styling with integral seat, fairing and tank unit.

Morini

1945 - date

Alfonso Morini, born in Bologna, Italy, established himself as a great rider during the 1920s. He also gained respect as a technician and was a partner in the MM Company (Morini and Mattei). After the Second World War, he decided he wanted to start his own company. In 1945, the new Morini concern was born and the first machines were delivered to customers one year later.

The new machine was a single cylinder, two-stroke with 125cc, which was also produced in sports and racing versions. It was one of these racing models, ridden by Masetti in 1948, which captured the first Italian 125cc championship. Just one year later, the company turned to four-strokes for competition and produced a single, 125cc, ohc machine. The bike performed well, winning many races ridden by

Mendoni and going on to take the national title the following year, but it reached its peak in 1952.

In 1953, the company fitted their road machines with ohc engines, producing an interesting single cylinder, 175cc model followed by a sport version named Settebello. In 1955, the machines were raced, with excellent results, in long distance competition such as the Giro d'Italia and the Milan-Taranto races. The 175cc Touring version was joined by a new 125cc machine, a four-stroke called Corsaro. Morini

The Morini TreSette engine of 1960. This was a single cylinder, pushrod, four-stroke, 172cc unit, which could produce 10hp.

A sporty machine which could top 60 mph and weighed a mere 236 lbs.

continued to enter minor sporting events and produced sporting machines from their series production, although they were not able to enter international competitions. One of the models was the single cam, 175cc Rebello, from which a twin cam version also came.

In 1958, the company finally produced its first real Grand Prix machine: a new twin cam 250cc model which immediately took top spot on the winners' podium ahead of an MV at the Grand Prix of Nations at Monza. However, the machine saw its best results two years later when raced by Provini, conquering the world title. In 1967, it was still demonstrating its superior speed when Bergamonti captured the national title.

Morini remained faithful to four-stroke machines. Its off-road Corsaro even managed to be successful until the end of the 1960s, when off-road racing became increasingly dominated by German two-strokes. On the touring side, the 250cc GTI, derived from the famous 175cc machine, remained in production until 1973, when it was finally replaced by an all-new Stra-

Unrestored, but still a fine example of a Corsarino 50cc machine. An ideal, inexpensive ride for the time.

The little Corsarino was introduced in the 1960s and had an ohc engine, designed by Alphonso and used for road racing.

da 350cc V-Twin, with six gears. A sports version was produced for 1975 and a 500cc version of the V-Twin launched at the Milan show. In 1976, the 125cc and 250cc singles appeared, the engines of which basically consisted of the front half of the V-Twin modular design.

In 1980, a 250cc version of the V-Twin was introduced, alongside an off-road version of the 500cc, called the Camel or the Sahara in

The 1977 Morini 3½ Strada. A real treat to ride if you can get used to the stiff gearchange and slight lack of instrumentation.

The V-twin, air-cooled, 344cc engine was fed by two Dellorto carburettors, which gave the machine a top speed of 98 mph.

Britain. The following year, a six speed version of the 500cc machine was introduced, alongside a 350cc off-road bike, the Kanguro. Morini also showed a prototype turbo-charged, 500cc machine at the Milan show. In 1985, the end of production arrived for the 500cc roadster. The Camel was upgraded to 507cc, while the custom-styled Excaliburs made their first appearance in 350cc and 500cc forms.

In 1987, Gabriella Morini decided to sell the family firm to the Cagiva group. The first Cagiva Morini, the 350 Dart, was introduced. It was an updated Morini 350 engine in a Cagiva 125 Freccia frame with modified Freccia bodywork.

The engineer Lambertini developed the modular V-Twin engine into a 750cc 'Ducati beater.' Cagiva itself was far from happy and ceased further development. In 1989, a 400cc Dart was introduced to the Japanese market and Lambertini left for Piaggio-Gilera.

In 1993, Morini production finally ceased. The 501 Excalibur was the last production model. Three years later, Cagiva sold Morini and Ducati to the Texas Pacific Group, though there were no plans for further Morini production.

In 1999, TPG sold the Morini brand to Franco Morini Motori spa. Franco was the cousin of Alfonso. In 1954, he started his own business specializing in the manufacture of two and four-stroke engines. Lambertini decided to 'return' to Franco Morini. It was then announced at the Bologna Motor show of 2003 that Morini Franco Motori and the Berti family, owners of the Sinudyne brand, were to re-launch the Moto Morini name. A new factory was being built next to the Morini Franco Motori factory. In 2004, a new, 98 degree V-twin was seen on the dynamo and artists' impressions of new bikes came to fruition in late 2004.

The 3 1/2 legend, updated. The new 9 1/2 offers a powerful 998cc Bialbero CorsaCorta with 105hp at 9000 rpm.

The all new 9¹/₂ has a carefully designed tank, wheels with aluminium channel spokes and left side/under saddle silencer.

Naked, powerful and stylish, the Corsaro 1200 is the ultimate road bike and the Bialbero Corsacorta engine is its soul.

The tubular steel frame and the front cowl with its twin front headlight contribute to the Corsaro 1200's sporty aura.

Motobecane

1921 - date

 Charles Benoit and Abel Bardin were the two founders of the French Motobecane company in 1923. Based in St Quentin, the first machine was a 175cc, belt-driven motorcycle and it sold extremely well. The company was a conglom-

The 'Monsieur' version of the 1923 Motobecane. There was a lady's version, the 'Madam,' with a more feminine frame.

erate of three companies: Motobecane, Motocomfort and Polymecanique. Polymecanique made and supplied engines for the Motobecane machines, including the first clip-on type. In the 1920s, the company also assembled British Blackburn and French Zucher machines.

By the 1930s, the company was producing larger capacity machines as well – 500cc, 750cc, ohc and ohv, with four-cylinder and shaft-drive models. In 1937, Benoit produced the 100cc, four-stroke engine for the Type Z range. Machines of 125cc and 175cc followed. The range was in production until 1963.

In 1939, the Second World War began and the Pony 60 was introduced, but production was halted until hostilities ceased. Production was able to resume in 1946. The model, now known as the Pony 50, had a smaller, 49cc engine. It could be classed as the forerunner to the most successful bike produced – the Mobylette, which first rolled off the production line in 1949.

In 1953, the company moved into scooter production, but sales were not good and the machines were discontinued. The 1960s were more successful. The company produced the

The 1938 R55C used a single cylinder, four-stroke, 492cc engine. These machines were the French superbikes of the 1930s.

The S5C was possibly one of the best French ohv singles of the 1930s. It was styled by the legendary Geo Ham.

D52, a 5cc, lightweight, five-speed machine, which became the 75cc C52. The Moby XI fold-away also took its place among the many models manufactured at this time. When developed, it became the Moby X7, though this was not a fold-away.

Impressive twin exhausts of the R55C. The most powerful Culasse models, the 1938 Grand Sport and Super Cub, had single port heads.

Moto Guzzi

1921 - date

With the help of blacksmith Giorgio Ripamonti, the Italian technical genius and designer, Carlo Guzzi, constructed his first motorcycle: a horizontal, single cylinder, four-stroke, 500cc engine with four-valve cylinder head and overhead camshaft, a bore measurement of 88 mm and a stroke of 82 mm. The year was 1920 and the bike was presented to Emanuele Vittorio Parodi, a wealthy Genovese ship owner. After making an initial loan of two thousand lire, he agreed to finance the establishment of a motorcycle production company.

Carlo Guzzi and Giorgio Parodi met in the air force. Along with motorcycle rider Giovanni Ravelli, they nursed a burning passion for the motorcycle. On 15 March 1921, at Mandello del Lario on the eastern shore of Lake Como, Guzzi and Parodi, son of Emanuele, founded the 'Società Anonima Moto Guzzi' and one of the world's most famous motorcycle brands was born.

Unlike almost all other constructors during those years of constant striving for excellence, every component of the bike Guzzi had in mind was rational and essential. First and foremost, it had to guarantee functionality and reliability from the first prototype. It had to be radically different from other bikes in its engine configuration and low-slung frame.

The first motorcycles bore the lettering G.P. (Guzzi-Parodi), but to avoid confusion with Giorgio Parodi's initials, subsequent models were named Moto Guzzi. The eagle on the logo was added as a tribute to Giovanni Ravelli, who died suddenly in an aircraft accident. To promote the new make, Carlo Guzzi decided to make his racing debut immediately and entered the Milan-Naples race with the only two machines so far produced on 28 May 1921. They finished

Featured is the 1921 Normale, which used a four-stroke, 499cc, flat, single cylinder engine.

launched in 1923 with outstanding success – the Sport 15 model in particular – was followed by the launch of the GT in 1928, the first Moto Guzzi with elastic frame, an innovation criticized at first, but soon adopted by many constructors throughout the world.

The company's growth was dramatic. In 1934, just 13 years after it was founded, the original staff of 17 employees in the Guzzi factory had swollen to 700. The same year that the famous Guzzi 500 twin made its debut, it went on to dominate the World Championship circuits, unchallenged with its highly original 120° V engine. The definitive international racing glory came on the Isle of Man in 1935, where

in 20th and 21st place. Not a great result, perhaps, but a great experience. Only four months later, Gino Finzi's Guzzi was a sensational first at the finishing line of the famous and gruelling Targa Florio.

It was the start of an extraordinary series of successes (3,329), which included 11 Tourist Trophies and 14 World Championship Titles, just rewards for the Mandello Company's racing commitment between 1921 and 1957. Such racing experience was also reflected in the quality and technically avant-garde character of the standard production machines.

Thanks to its amazing success, the Guzzi name became well-known. The Sport series,

A 1928 500S model. It had a single cylinder, four-stroke engine, which produced 13hp and which gave the machine a 63 mph top speed.

The 1933 'Bici' was produced between 1933 and 1951. Part of its success was the low weight and compact dimensions.

Presented in 1946, the 65cc Guzzino was a cheap and easy mode of transport.

the Guzzi 250 and 500 twin, both with elastic frames, scored a famous victory with the Tourist Trophy. It was the first time that a non-English bike won the world's most important race. Moto Guzzi had truly established its place in biking history.

Official riders for the team also became legends in their own time: Tenni, Woods and later Ruffo, Lorenzetti and Anderson, to name but a few.

In the 1930s, two new models were presented to the public: the P 175 and the P 250 with its various versions the PE, PL, Egretta and Ardetta. Then the famous Airone 250, the most

For more than fifteen years the Airone 250 was the favorite mid-range machine for Italian riders. This is a 1956 Sport model.

popular medium-capacity motorcycle in Italy for almost 15 years, appeared in 1939. For private riders, racing models such as the Dondolino, Gambalunga and Condor were developed.

Second World War left Italy deeply scarred, with enormous damage to roads and buildings. The motor car was a plaything of the rich, accessible to a select few.

The motorcycle became a key factor in the mobility of the Italians, who looked for cheap and reliable transportation. Highly efficient, low-powered motorcycles were developed, thanks to technological progress. After the war, Italians got about on scooters and the so-called 'lightweight' motorcycles, which attracted a much larger public than their higher-powered relatives. Strong, relatively clean, easy to ride, capable of respectable speeds, the Guzzino 65 cc was launched by the company in 1946. The machine was designed by Antonio Micucci and was renamed the Cardellino in the 1950s. For more than a decade, the Guzzino was the best-selling lightweight motorcycle in Italy and Europe.

The unprecedented success of the Guzzino also opened the way for production of other low

This is the Galletto of 1952, with its 160cc engine.

Eight-cylinder, four-stroke, 499cc engine, four-speed gearbox: the awesome V8 engine of the 1955 Guzzi racer.

capacity motorcycles, including the Galletto, a highly original hybrid of scooter and motorcycle, the Zigolo, a 98 cc, lightweight motorcycle and the Lodola 175 cc, the last design to bear Carlo Guzzi's name. At the higher capacity end of the range in 1950, the then-outdated GTV 500 (later renamed the Astore) was replaced by the Falcone 500, becoming the dream machine of the majority of motorcyclists in the 1950s. In 1949, the first World Motorcycle Champi-

onships were held and in the years leading up to 1957, when Moto Guzzi participated for the last time, the company managed to accumulate a series of amazing wins and created a succession of innovative and consistently successful designs and machines.

Alongside Carlo Guzzi, the racing team included top mechanics such as Umberto Todero and Enrico Cantoni, together with a legendary designer, Giulio Cesare Carcano. After joining

Here is a 1953 first series Zigolo with partially enclosed 98cc engine. Not all Guzzi's were painted red.

Possibly the most extraordinary two-wheel machine never produced. Conceived in 1955 by Giulio Cesare Carcano.

Moto Guzzi in 1936, he was responsible for creating the sensational Guzzi 500 V8 cylinder engine, considered by many to be the most extraordinary two-wheeled machine of all time. As early as 1955, on its first official outing during the Belgium Grand Prix trials, the eight-cylinder bike gave just a hint of its extraordinary potential. The following year, with its 72hp and 171 mph top speed, it won its first victories. In 1957, the company withdrew from racing, preventing further development of the spectacular machine.

The 1960s brought major changes to the company. Giorgio Parodi died in 1955, Carlo Guzzi in 1964 and the motorcycle sector went into deep recession. Moto Guzzi found itself in financial difficulties. The company was acquired by SEIMM and focused on lightweight machines such as the Dingo and Trotter mopeds as well as on the development of a new 90°, V-twin engine designed by Carcano. It would become the symbol of Moto Guzzi up to the present day.

The Guzzi V7 was launched in 1967 and was the first to be fitted with Carcano's V twin, having a capacity of 703 cc. It was remarkably successful and after the V7 Special with 750 cc engine was presented, the legendary V7 Sport was launched in 1971. This machine, with its elegant lines and exceptional stability, was extraordinarily successful. For the American market, the Special, California and Ambassador versions were developed.

Change came again in 1973 when Guzzi became part of the De Tomaso Inc. group and began to produce a series of four-cylinder engines, culminating in the Guzzi 254. A Sport-type frame and engine were progressively adopted for all subsequent versions of the V7. In 1977, the frame was also fitted to lower capacity versions, such as the Guzzi V35 and V50, two models which provided the basis for the whole range of Guzzi machines in the 1980s.

The 1969 Guzzi V750 Ambassador was a machine for America. It was a long range tourer with a smooth, four-stroke, V-twin, 757cc engine that could do 115 mph.

A highly modified V7 of 1972. This machine has a 750cc engine and has been modified for endurance racing. Non-standard indicators are for road use. The original V7 was launched in 1967.

In the 1990s, there was a revival of the Guzzi spirit, with the introduction of the California series, the Nevada and the V11 Sport. In 2004, Moto Guzzi became part of the Aprilia group, in turn recently acquired by the Piaggio Group. The company boasts a variety of machines, varying from the stripped down MGS-01 racer to the latest cruising California EV Touring and the Nevada 750. Le Mans, a name that all Moto Guzzi enthusiasts know well from the past, has also come back in the form of the V11.

The 1999 V11 Sport, with V-twin 1064cc, air-cooled, four-stroke engine. The tried and tested V-twin has been technically undated.

The naked and muscular Griso is everything it looks. The engine is the four-valve, 992cc version of Guzzi's familiar 90°, V-twin.

The stunning MGS-01 Corsa, for which there is now a 'track only' version.

Munch

1966 - date

 Freidl Munch started off in the racing department of the Horex Company. He developed and sold his own racing brake and when the factory closed in 1959, he went on to develop a four-cylinder racing engine, completed in 1964.

In 1965, Munch was contacted by Jean Murit, the French ex-sidecar racer, who wanted Munch to build him the fastest, most powerful

The Mammoth was big, powerful and extravagant. It used an 1177cc, in-line, 4-cylinder engine and could reach 130 mph.

road bike possible. Munch decided the most suitable power unit was the 996 cc, air-cooled NSU car engine and he installed it in a special frame, calling it Mammoth. Munch was pushed to build more Mammoths and went into small-scale production. He soon gained a backer in American publisher, Floyd Clymer, who financed a move to larger premises. Mammoths were made in small numbers, with an increase to 1200cc in engine size. Munch also pursued numerous racing ventures and one aborted world record attempt with the 'Daytona Bomb' machine, but despite gaining a sidecar world championship in 1971, the cost of racing led to financial difficulties. The company changed hands in 1972 and became Hassia-Munch.

Bad management caused the company to go into liquidation and it was subsequently bought by Heinz Henke. The new company name was Heinz W. Henke and production resumed in 1974. Munch joined Henke and continued to develop the Mammoth, but he decided to leave the company in 1977. He went on to produce the Titan, another monster machine, in 1986. Today, the Munch brand is still active in Wurzburg, Germany, while the Munch 2000 (using a 1998 cc unit) is still available.

Looking nothing like its predecessor, this is the Mammut 2000. It has an in-line, transverse, four-cylinder, 1998cc engine.

MV Agusta

1948 - date

 The MV (Meccanica Verghera) company was officially born after the Second World War in Cascina Costa in the province of Varese, Italy. It was part of a larger aeronautical industrial complex, formed in 1907 and owned by Giovanni Agusta. When he died in 1927, the company fell into the hands of his widow, Giuseppini, and his son, Domenico, who soon found that aircraft were hard to sell. They looked at other areas to keep the company going. At that time, there was great demand in Italy for motorcycles, so it seemed like the right sector to choose.

The first machine they made was both inexpensive to produce and run, a two-stroke with 98cc capacity, with three port timing system, primary gear transmission, a clutch that ran in an oil bath and two gears.

Unfortunately, the Second World War interrupted any further work on the engine and the company was occupied by the Germans until the liberation of Italy. After the war, Domenico officially established Meccanic Voghera to execute his ideas and supply a market yearning for cheap and reliable transportation.

The first machine presented to the public in the fall of 1945 was going to be called the Vespa 98, but the name was already registered. So it was simply known as the 98 and was produced in sport and economy versions. The first machines were delivered in 1946, when the company officially started racing. It did not have to wait too long for a first victory, taken by Vincenzi Nencioni in La Spezia. Then at Monza on the 3 November, all three podium places were taken by MV riders Vincenzi Nencioni, Mario Cornalca and Mario Paleari. The sports version, featuring telescopic forks, a shorter frame and an altogether sportier feel, followed these successes.

A fine example of a 1956 MV Agusta racing machine. It had a transverse four-cylinder, 496cc engine.

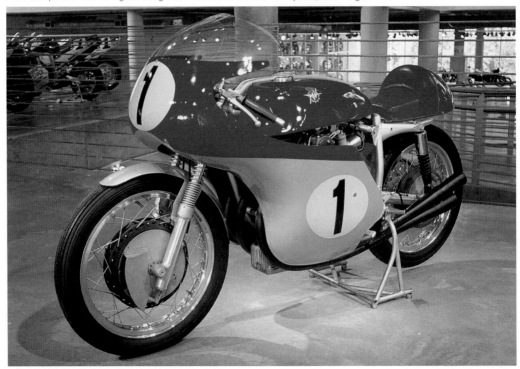

In 1947, a luxury version of the 98cc machine was presented. Alongside were the new two-cylinder, 125cc machines and the 250cc, single cylinder 4T models. The following year, a 125 category was introduced in the Italian Speed championships, allowing MV to enter its 125cc, three-speed machines. In 1949, the 98cc and 125cc models were replaced by the new 125 TEL models along with a 125cc type B scooter.

In 1950, the two new, four-stroke Grand Prix bikes, a single cylinder 125cc and a 500cc four-cylinder machine with shaft drive were introduced. The two machines would compete for years to come. In 1952, Cecil Sandford took the 125cc world title and Les Graham took the 500cc title. The 500cc machine was then fitted with a normal chain drive and five speed gearbox.

No ordinary MV: the 1953 125cc Pullman.

This is the MV Agusta 125cc Gran Turismo model of 1960.

The engine was a single cylinder, four-stroke, 123cc unit.

What could be any more beautiful than the stunning 1972 750S? A legend in its time.

In 1975, MV changed its line-up. The 750 America was one of the new models.

The awesome 790cc, four-stroke, four-cylinder unit of the America.

Les Graham was tragically killed at the 1953 TT and finding another rider who could handle the four-cylinder machines took some time. The problem was solved in 1956 when John Surtees joined the team and took the 500cc world championship in his first year. Following many years of Italian success by

companies such as Gilera, Moto Guzzi and Mondial, 1958 found MV the lone Italian company left to defend national honor. It was unfazed, going on to win world titles in the 125cc and 250cc categories, with Provini and Ubbiali as main riders. In the 350cc and 500cc classes, Surtees, Hocking and Hailwood took their four-cylinder machines to victory as well. The production machines were of an inferior cylinder size – 83cc, 100cc, 125cc, and 150cc.

Motorcyle production hit a slight low in the 1960s, but unlike many other companies, MV continued to develop and produce machines, including the 600cc four whose engine was derived from the Mike Hailwood 500cc Grand Prix machine and the 125cc Disco. The 600 cc four went on to become the 750S America, which could top 137 mph.

1965 was a significant year because Giacomo Agostini joined the racing team and a new 350cc Grand Prix machine was presented, followed by a similar 500cc machine. In both these classes, Agostini became world champion multiple times. The three-cylinder machine was replaced by a 500cc and given to Phil Reed, who won titles in 1973-1974. In total, between 1956 and 1975, MV captured 38 rider world titles and 37 for the factory. The last MV podium was cap-

The 1978 Ipotesi 350S was one of the last machines from the old factory.

tured by Agostini on 29 August 1976 at the Nurburgring in Germany.

Count Domenico died in the early 1970s and the company was faced with hard financial challenges and decisions. Some wanted to stop racing, others did not. A middle road was found and the production line-up was decreased to two sizes, the 350cc (which included a scrambler, the GTEL and the SEL), and the 500cc (which consisted of the Sport and Gran Turismo). The MV situation did not improve and the company looked for a new investment partner. It found one in the public financing giant EFIM (Ente Partecipazioni e Finanzimanto Industia Manifatturiera), which insisted, as a prerequisite, that MV move away from motorcycle production. As one can imagine, this was a difficult decision. The company left projects due for release at the up and coming Milan show of 1977 unfinished. The company continued to sell machines between 1980 and 1986. The racing machines were also sold off at rock bottom prices.

The name did not disappear from sight, however, and in the spring of 1992, the Cagiva Company announced that the ownership of the Cascina Costa trademark was to go to the Castiglione group. The trademark was questionable: as far

as any remaining stock was concerned, it had all been sold. If anybody could save MV it was the Castiglione family, who had created Cagiva from the ashes of the old Aermacchi concern and saved both Ducati and Husqvarna from extinction.

The challenge faced by the Cagiva engineers was huge: how could they revive such a legendary company? The new machine would have much to live up to. The engine would have to be an in-line, three or four-cylinder unit, which posed another question: should it be new or bought-in? Castiglione decided to start afresh on a project developed by Ferrari, referred to as F4.

The stunning rear end of the MV F4 Serie Oro.

An MV test rider puts the incredibly fast F4 through its paces.

Looking every bit as clean and mean as its predecessors, this is the 1999 F4 Serie Oro.

From this point, the engineers worked the project up to what it is today: a machine of quality and integrity with speed and handling to match. Massimo Tamburini, once of the Bimota Company, was left the awesome job of creating the aesthetic look and design of the new machine. On 16 September 1998, the prototype was presented to the astonished biking press. The initial production was for 300 Gold series machines and the first was shown in action at the Monza race track in April 1999. Today the machine comes with a much lower price tag and includes a special Senna series as well as the sporty SPR. There is also a new model in the stable, the outrageous Brutale. The company is not simply alive, it's kicking!

The now-familiar trellis frame used by MV.

Many versions of the F4 were produced after the initial launch.

A move away from the racey type of machine: the 749cc Brutale.

MZ/MuZ

1946 - date

MZ stands for Motorradwerk Zschopau and although the company only came into existence in 1953, it has a rich history.

As the Iron Curtain descended across Germany in the late 1940s, the MZ factory was created from the IFA works established in the DKW factory at Zschopau. Zschopau was in Saxony and found itself in East Germany under Russian rule.

Huge chunks of the German motor industry had escaped to the West, taking machinery and design plans with them. Factories were emptied and, fearing what was going to happen under the Russian regime, people moved to the West in the thousands.

Not much was heard from the East in those early days and still less about motorcycle manufacture. Parts of the old DKW factory survived the war and it produced DKW-like two-strokes under the name of IFA in 1946.

By 1949, road racing started to gather momentum in the East and one machine showed the way in the 125cc series. The RT 125cc was a single cylinder two-stroke designed by the DKW factory prior to the war. The design was given to the West as part of war reparations and out provided the inspiration for the BSA Bantam and Harley Davidson Hummer, to name just two.

The power output of this machine was increased over the next few years and in 1950, it claimed the 125cc championship of East Germany.

In 1952, Walter Kaaden joined the Zschopau team. He was a racer and engineer in his own right and he made the decision to fit a rotary disc valve to the 125cc engine, immediately increasing its power output. At this time, the company also started to use the MZ logo on their machines. A financial grant was granted by the state and the company was given comparative autonomy.

In 1954, the 125cc machine was upgraded and a new 250cc twin Grand Prix machine was introduced. The mid-1950s saw the arrival of Ernst Degner, who was not only an expert rider, but also capable of setting up a machine. The only way to become a successful team is to join

The 1956 RT 125 became very popular in East Germany. Cars were expensive and small-capacity machine were much sought-after.

The 1978 MZ TS 250 Sport 5. A bit boring to look at, but by no means boring to ride. This was the top of the range model.

the international stage. Thus the company began to travel outside its borders, a not uncomplicated feat during the restrictive Iron Curtain period.

The company also began to hire the better riders of the day. Alongside Degner came Gary Hocking who gave the company its first classic wins in the 1959 Swedish and Ulster 250cc Grands Prix. Luigi Taveri before securing a win on his 125cc at Locarno. Unfortunately, the company suffered due to currency exchange rates and restrictive travel passes. Hocking decided to leave the racing team.

The following year was the most promising for MZ and the company had one of the strongest teams. Degner was leading in points with only the Argentinian GP left to run. Then, as with so many East German athletes and sportsmen, Degner defected to the West and the championship was awarded to Tom Phillis on his Honda. Degner, with all his expertise and know-how, went to Japan where Suzuki and

The engine was a two-stroke, 243cc, single unit.

Yamaha racing machines benefited from his ideas.

The company first entered the ISDT program in 1956, but without much success, contrary to its racing fortune behind the Iron Curtain, where it seemed to win everything. By 1963, it was confident enough to move outside the eastern border again and this time, it was successful. The team consisted of Werner Salevsky and

The 1977MZ TS 150 had a single cylinder, two-stroke engine.

Hans Weber on their 250cc machines as well as Peter Uhlig and Horst Lohr on their 175cc models. It was the start of a string of victories and there was great admiration for the East German riders and their machines. MZ even had success in the ISDT competition during the 1980s. The everyday 125cc and 250cc road machines benefited from all the development even if, compared to machines in the West, they lacked style and finesse.

The fall of the Berlin Wall left the company devastated. It lost its currency stability and back-up from the state. Sales dropped off and the company went into liquidation. But there was hope. After Germany's re-unification, the company was forced to come to terms with the loss of its most important markets in the former Eastern Bloc and parts of East Asia. However, the company quickly shifted its emphasis to bring modern competitive machines into production. It renamed itself MuZ and looked at the western European and international markets. It was a tricky time, but with the participation of the

The Skorpion Tour and faired Sport models were based on plans made by the English design studio, Seymour Powell. A complete change for MuZ as they were now known. This is the 1977 Sport model.

The 1999 MuZ Mastif ceased to exist after 2000, but it was interesting because it used a Yamaha XTZ 660cc.

MuZ also have a huge commitment to racing, organizing competitions and events at amateur and professional levels as well as running a 500 GP team. There was also talk of producing bigger engines and creating more bikes for 2005 and beyond.

For 2004, MuZ presented the new Baghira, a single cylinder street bike.

Hong Leong Industries Berhad (Malaysia) in September 1996, MuZ felt it could face the future confidently.

In 1994, MuZ introduced the Skorpion range of motorcycles, which were designed by British engineers and featured a liquid-cooled, Japanese (Yamaha), single cylinder unit, Grimeca disc brakes, Paioli forks, and Metzler racing compound tires. In 1998, the company introduced two new, Enduro-style bikes, the Mastiff and Baghira, aptly named 'funbikes.' In addition to the full size machines came the 50cc scooter, the Moskito and the Charly electric scooter – a model compact enough to fold away and fit in a car trunk.

The new line-up of MuZ machines is supplemented by the 1000SF. An aggressive machine with street fighter looks.

Ner-A-Car

1919 - 1927

The Ner-a-Car company was based at 196 Geddes Street, Syracuse, New York, USA. Its first, highly unorthodox machine was designed by Carl Neracher in 1919.

The company's initial start-up capital was put up by none other than razor giant, Karl C. Gillette. The first machines were produced using a 221cc, two-stroke engine. The transmission worked by friction and the machine used hub-center steering. There was a foot-operated rear drum brake only. Once these machines were imported to Great Britain, they had to have an extra brake fitted to the rear hub, which was operated by a handlebar lever.

Sheffield Simplex, makers of luxury cars, obtained a licence to import these machines. The works were based at Canbury Park Road, Kingston-upon-Thames, England, the old premises of the ABC Company, which had just gone out of business.

Simplex decided to fit a larger capacity engine of its own – a 285cc replacing the 221cc – and a new, larger headlamp. The Ner-a-Car

won a reputation for comfort and handling. It was even entered in long distance trials events, taking home many a gold, silver and bronze medal. It took the team prize at the 1925 ACU 1000 mile Stock Machine Trial. It was soon realized, however, that a bigger engine was needed and Sheffield Simplex responded by fitting a 350cc, side-valve Balckburne unit.

By 1924, the Syracuse operation closed its doors. In contrast, the British-based company was doing well and by 1926, an even more powerful unit, a 350cc, ohv Blackburne, was fitted. In 1926, the top of the range model was fitted with a new chassis and swingarm rear springing, a large apron at the front to protect the rider, a windscreen and an instrument panel. It was practically a car! Unfortunately, due to other Sheffield Simplex concerns, money ran short and the Ner-a-Car venture had to be terminated.

This is the car-style, hub-center steering.

Tucked under here is the 348cc, single cylinder engine.

As the name suggests, it was almost a car. The machine was made both in Great Britain and the United States. This is a 1925 model.

New Hudson

1900 - 1941

New Hudson started out making bicycles. It was known as Hudson and Edmonds and was based in Birmingham, England. After a financial restructuring of Hudson and Armstrong (makers of the Armstrong rear-hub gear), the company was renamed New Hudson Cycle Company Ltd. The company grew, as did the popularity of the bicycles.

Initial steps towards motorcycle manufacture were made in early 1900, when it clipped a 211cc Minerva engine to a new Hudson bicycle. In 1910, however, the company anounced an Armstrong Triplex, three-speed hub gear with metal, multi-plate clutch for motorcycle use. It then presented two machines powered by a JAP engine of 292cc. By 1911, it produced an engine of its own, a 499cc, side-valve unit. These machines were raced and broke world records as far away as Australia.

The JAP 292cc engine was replaced by a long stroke, 350cc unit in 1913 and a new 770cc Big Six joined the team. In 1914, some new machines were introduced, but the war started and New Hudson was obliged to supply models for the war effort (in particular the 499cc Service Four). The company, however, was chiefly employed in making ammunition.

Featured here is the 1926 new Hudson Super Vitesse model, which used a single cylinder, 596cc, ohv engine.

After the war, there were detail changes and some older machines were upgraded. Then in 1924, new 350cc and 500cc ohv engines were prepared for the TT. Unfortunately, they lost.

In 1927, Bert Le Vack joined the company and its fortunes changed. Races were won at Brooklands, Jimmy Guthrie came second in the Senior TT and Le Vack broke the 'ton' for the first time on a 500cc machine. When Le

By the time this 1929 New Hudson machine went on sale, the company was already facing hard times.

This is the beautifully restored 1929 596cc, single cylinder engine. It still had a lever to change the gears.

Vack left there was a slump, but then came Vic Mole from Ariel. He refreshed all the machinery and the company won the Bronze Wing model. By now, however, the Depression had taken its toll. Too much money was invested in the new models and New Hudson was forced to cease production. One last attempt was made with an autocycle in 1941, but the company could not cope and was taken over by BSA.

New Imperial

1900 - 1939

 The story begins with Norman T. Downs buying the failing bicycle works of Hearl and Tonks of Birmingham, England. He reorganized the company and turned it into a profit-making concern under the name New Imperial Cycles. New premises were found in Hack Street, Birmingham.

New Imperial bicycles were displayed with strapped-on engines at the 1901 Stanley Show, but since not a single one was sold, they were

Clearly shown on the fuel tank, this New Imperial of 1912 used a 500cc, single cylinder, JAP engine.

returned to the factory and used as engines for chaff-cutting machinery.

In 1910, a JAP engine of 293cc was fitted to a conventional motorcycle frame and the light-weight machine sold successfully and remained on the books until the 1920s. It was joined a year later by a V-twin specially made for sidecar use.

It was important at the time to be seen at the TT, where you could truly advertise your product. Thus in 1913, New Imperial sent three 500cc, JAP models to the Isle of Man for the Senior TT. But the results were not good – all retired. It was not until 1921 that they were entered again and this time, Doug Prentice won the 250cc trophy with a company JAP-engined, 250cc machine.

Bert Le Vack, the renowned racer, joined the team the following year. With his JAP-engined special, he broke the 350cc one hour record at 74.17 mph and the flying kilometer record at 83.56 mph, good signs for the 1922 TT. Unfortunately, although Le Vack's machine was the fastest and he led most of the way, a gearbox seizure ended his race. In 1924, the loss was all but forgotten when the Twemlow brothers won both the Junior and the Lightweight races and the latter was taken again the following year.

By this time, the company had expanded and moved into more buildings nearby. Now it began

The 1930s was a good time for New Imperial as far as sporting events were concerned. This is the 1935 ex-works racer.

New Imperial finally closed its gates in the late 1930s, but not before producing nice machines like this one.

Nimbus

1919- 1959

The Nimbus history starts in 1919 when the original machine, often known as the 'stove-pipe,' was designed and produced by a Danish duo, Fisker and Nielsen, who had started his career by making vacuum cleaners.

to manufacture its own engines, mainly for road machines.

In 1931, a 150cc machine known as the Unit Minor was introduced and was soon followed by the 250cc Unit Super and the 350cc Unit Major models. During the early 1930s, world records continued to be broken with the 500cc V-twin, the 250cc and little, 123cc models. In 1936, a new works racer was produced for Bob Foster, who called it the 'Flying Pig Trough.' He went on to win the Lightweight TT on it and a few weeks later, came second to Ginger Wood, also on a New Imperial, in the 250cc Ulster Grand Prix.

The owner, Norman Downs, prompted New Imperial to pull out of competition. Besides, the company was running into debt. Located at Spring Road, the company finally closed its gates in 1938. In 1939, Jack Sangster bought the company and started production once more with a view to combining with Triumph and the other companies he had acquired. But then Britain went to war. The revival of New Imperial was doomed from the start.

The original machine used a four-cylinder unit with shaft drive in a pressed steel frame. The orders came rushing in (as did those for vacuum cleaners). Unable to cope with demand, the company decided to stop making bikes in 1928, after some 1200 examples had been produced.

The second part of the story starts in 1934, when a new factory was found for vacuum cleaner production and motorcycle production resumed. Looking very like a car unit of its day, the new machine also had a four-cylinder engine of 746cc and a shaft drive in a pressed steel frame. These machines also used telescopic front forks, supposedly invented by F&N for the Nimbus Model C, but the invention has been credited to BMW. The original bikes used hand gearchange, but had moved to a foot-change by 1935. There were four models: Nimbus Luxus, giving 22 horsepower and delivered in red with gold pinstripes; Nimbus Standard, giving 18 horsepower, with black paintwork; Nimbus Special, delivered in ivory yellow or

This is the single cylinder, 250cc engine of the ex-works racer.

The striking, four-cylinder engine of the pre-war Nimbus.

Despite upgrading, the Nimbus design changed little in 37 years.

The pressed steel frame and the shaft to the rear wheel are clearly seen in this photo.

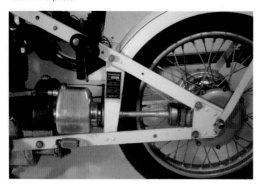

lavender gray; and finally, the Nimbus Sport, delivered in blue.

The machines changed very little up to 1954, when series production halted again to make way for vacuum cleaner production.

With their four-stroke, four-cylinder, 746cc engine, they had no problems towing a side-car, as shown here.

Norton

1902 - date

James Lansdowne Norton, from Birmingham, England, was not someone you would instantly associate with motorcycle manufacture. He was a religious man and a supporter of the Salvation Army. He apprenticed in the jewellery trade, where he learned his precision engineering skills.

In 1898, he founded the Norton Manufacturing Company, which supplied components for the bicycle trade. The first Norton motorcycle appeared in 1902 and consisted of a standard bicycle with a Belgian Clement engine fitted on to the front downtube. He took this idea from Charles Garrard, who was producing a machine himself called the Clemente Garrard which used a Clement engine in a similar way. Other machines followed, although bought-in, Peugeot, twin cylinder engines or Moto Reve singles were used, as fitted to the lightweight model Energette.

The break for Norton came when Rem Fowler purchased a Peugeot-engined machine to enter in the very first Isle of Man TT. Norton, acting as pit crew, accompanied Fowler and saw him take first place.

Buoyed by this success, Norton now decided it was time he designed his own engine. The result was the 633cc Big Four, a prototype exhibited at the 1907 Stanley show. Over the

The Norton 16H was often seen attached with a sidecar unit. The 490cc engine was more than capable of towing it.

next three years, Norton decided to enter the TT again. He rode the machines himself, but without luck. The machine he rode in the last event was a new, 490cc model, the forerunner to the 16H, a machine which lasted 40 years.

Norton, not a healthy man at the best of times, picked up an infection at the TT and was struck low for a considerable time. The company also suffered and finally had to go into liquidation. It was rescued by one of its supply companies – R.T. Shelley and Co – and a new firm was started under the name of Norton Motors Limited.

Having built up quite a record-breaking reputation for himself, D. R. Donovan was based at Brooklands and the Norton factory would send him engines for tuning. Each engine was tested and given a certificate, which would be passed to the owner once the engine had been returned to the factory and fitted to the appropriate frame. There were two grades of tuning – BRS, as in Brooklands Racing Special, and BS, as in Brooklands Special. The latter had to be 5 mph faster than the first. O'Donovan's own machine secured over 100 British and world records prior to the First World War. No wonder they called it 'Old Miracle!'

When the war came in 1914, Norton did not get a commission from the British armed forces.

In fact, the company ended up supplying the Russian Government. An increase in production meant a change of premises and the company moved to Bracebridge Street in 1916.

After the war, like many other companies, Norton bought up old army machines and refurbished them. Soon, however, the firm had to think about making a new model. Several designs were on the table. James Norton had been considering an ohv design and a desmodromic engine layout and eventually went with the ohv design. In 1922, a prototype was seen at Brooklands in the hands of Rex Judd. With this machine, he raised the 500cc record to 90 mph and the mile record to just over 88 mph.

The 31/2hp engine is a simple and reliable unit.

Not many machines are as perfectly named as 'Old Miracle.'

The Norton model 18 used a single cylinder, four-stroke engine of 490cc. It had a top speed of 78 mph.

The ohv Model 18, as it was designated, made little impact at the 1922 TT. But before the year was out, it had firmly established itself as one of the fastest bikes around.

A better year proved to be 1924, when Alec Bennett won the Senior TT with an ohv Norton, averaging over 60 mph the first time, and George Tucker wrapped up the sidecar race.

By 1926, four-speed gearboxes and internal expanding brakes were standard equipment on several Norton models, along with automatic primary drive chain lubrication. Stanley Woods won the Senior TT on a Norton.

Between 1926 and 1927, Walter Moore designed an overhead camshaft engine. The drive from the crankshaft was taken through a set of bevels, then by an enclosed vertical shaft to the cambox via another bevel set. The cambox was bolted to the cylinder head and the valves returned by coil springs. A new frame was also introduced, a cradle type with single top and front downtubes. The exhaust pipe was to the left of the machine, which was the standard Norton practice at the time.

Alec Bennett managed another win at the 1927 Senior TT and Norton riders were regularly on winners' podiums, though mostly in Europe.

In 1929, Arthur Carroll was asked to redesign the old ohc engine. He produced what became one of the most dominant racing engines of all time. Its racing pedigree would last for the next 25 years. Riders such as Jimmy Simpson, Tim Hunt, Stanley Woods, Jimmy Guthrie and Harold Daniel joined the Norton racing team. Then, in 1932, Bill Lacey raised the one hour record to 110 mph at Montlhery just as plunger rear suspension appeared on the works racers in 1936. There was one black moment however, when Jimmy Simpson at Chemnitz in Germany in 1937. A statue was erected to his memory in

Low-slung in the frame, this tall Norton CSI engine is a single cylinder, 490cc, sv, four-stroke unit, which produces 25hp.

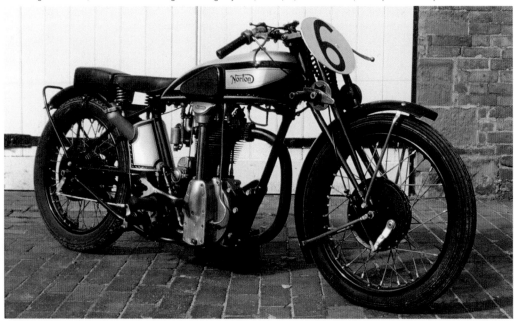

his home town of Hawick, and even in Nazi Germany, a memorial was placed at the crash site.

In 1938, the Manx Grand Prix racer was offered for sale, basically an Inter with all the latest, go-faster goodies, with the exception of the DOHC engine. In the late 1930s, the pace of the Europeans was starting to tell and Norton was having trouble keeping up. In 1939, the company withdrew from racing, the BMW victory at the TT was quietly forgotten as more

During the war, Norton manufactured over 100,000 machines for military use. They consisted of the two side-valve machines: the 16H produced to 1937 specification with open-valve gear and air cleaner for overseas use and the Big 4 for sidecar duty, with a disengageable drive to the sidecar wheel.

When the war was over, there was a glut of military machines, which helped with excessive civilian demand and allowed the company a

The Norton Dominator used a 'slimline' version of the Featherbed frame, contributing to its good handling.

important political events loomed. Britain declared war on Germany and civilian production of motorcycles had to stop.

The International of 1956 had a single ohc, 490cc engine.

breather so that it was able to resume production.

In 1948, Norton started taking an interest in the American export market. They entered a successful works team using American riders under Steve Lancefield, then Francis Beart, in the Daytona 200 race. The same year saw the launch of the Dominator, which had a 497cc, vertical twin engine and was designed by Bert Hopwood.

1949 was another excellent year for racing in the Norton camp, with legends such as Geoff Duke winning the Senior Manx Grand Prix.

The team of Duke, Oliver and Artie Bell went to the Montlhery track in France and together took 21 world records in the 350cc and 500cc classes. Then in 1950, the Featherbed frame, designed in Belfast by the McCandless brothers, was used on the works racers. Innovative and advanced, it became the benchmark for other frames for years to come. At the TT that year, the new frame helped Duke to a record-breaking Senior victory, while Bell took victory in the Junior. In both races, Norton bikes finished first, second and third.

Geoff Duke became world champion in both the 350cc and 500cc classes in 1952 and was awarded the OBE for his services to motorcycling.

In 1954, the last 16H model was produced and Norton celebrated its Diamond Jubilee, marked by the production of a new 250cc Jubilee twin, in 1958. The machine was followed in 1960 by a 350cc version, the Navigator.

On the racing scene, the leading riders on British short circuits were Mike Hailwood, Phil Read and Derek Minter, all on Nortons.

All was not well at home, however. It was announced in mid-1962 that the company would be amalgamated with the AMC Group, which meant a move from Bracebridge Street to the Woolwich factory in London. Worse news came when the AMC Group collapsed in 1966. The Manganese Bronze Holding Group came to the rescue and another move was made to Andover.

At this time, the development of the Commando began and the new anti-vibration system, patented as 'Isolastic,' was used. However, although the system insulates the rider from vibration, the mounting rubbers must be regularly fixed in order to maintain the machine's handling standard. Its fuel tank and matching tailpiece were made of fiberglass and a twin

The 1960 Manx Norton used a single cylinder, tuned-for-racing, 350cc engine.

The Manx Norton was a pure racer using the featherbed frame and a highly efficient, 499cc engine, developing over 50hp.

leading shoe front brake was standard. The 'S' Type version Commando made its debut in March 1969. It sported a high-level left side exhaust system, a small 2¹/₂ gallon fuel tank and naked front forks without gaiters or shrouds. Reverse cone silencers were also used for the

Conceived as a racer: the P11 from 1969.

first time, although the Fastback continued with the old Dominator cigar-shaped silencers.

In 1971, the Street Scrambler and Hi Rider made their debuts and the John Player-sponsored racing team started under the management of Frank Perris, once a racer for the Suzuki team. Peter Williams was the mainstay of the JPN racing effort and was partnered by various other well-known riders over the next few years.

The Commando and Roadster models became Norton classics and the manufacturing was moved back to Wolverhampton in 1968. In 1972, under the umbrella of NVT (Norton Villiers Triumph) and facing severe competition

The Commando, a parallel twin of 745cc. Although regularly upgraded, the engine's history went back to 1947.

Designed and built in the USA: the 2004 952.

A move away from tradition: the rotary Norton.

and a series of strikes at its factories, the company lost substantial sums of money. The British government refused to provide further financial assistance to NVT.

To avoid liquidation, the company changed its name to NVT Engineering Ltd and proceeded to go into liquidation in 1976, although it produced motorbikes until 1977. Heavy imports of Japanese motorcycles, increased production costs, strikes and shortage of funds temporarily defeated Norton.

In 1987, Philippe Le Roux and investors formed Norton Group PLC and the company started to produce again in Lichfield in 1988. In 1992, Norton won the Isle of Man TT races once again. Though F1 Norton had been heralded as the 'Porsche of the Motorcyle World' by Le Roux, he promptly departed from the company in 1991.

In 1993, ownership of the Norton name and brand ended up with a Canadian company. This concern merged with March Motors in 1998.

The new company is now called Norton Motorcycles and is committed to restoring luster to the name and carrying the Norton torch. The new 952 Commando has the soul and look of the original machine – it is a bike that feels as good as it looks.

NSU

1901 - 1966

In 1873, Christian Schmidt and Heinrich Stoll, two mechanics from Riedlingen, a town on the bank of the Danube River, set up a workshop to make knitting machines. In 1880, they moved to Neckarsulm and changed their company name to Neckarsulm Strickmaschinenfabrik AG four years later. It was another two years before they started making penny farthing bicycles, known as 'Germanias.' Production changed to standard bicycles soon after.

By 1892, the knitting machines had gone and the name changed to reflect the bicycle production to Neckarsulm Fahrradwerke AG. 1901 was the first year of motorcycle production and a test track was laid down at the factory in 1903. For the early machines a Zedel engine was used, but from 1904, NSU (accepted as an abbreviation for Neckarsulm) designed and used units of 2 to 3.5hp.

NSU were keen to get into competition and started immediately, gaining an impressive record – Martin Geiger won the 1904 Feldberg Trial on a Neckarsulm. Gertrud Eisemann, one of Germany's most famous lady riders, set up a number of records and recorded a string of successes in long distance events.

Another fine achievement went to Karl Gassert who won a gold medal at the 1911

British TT, followed by a win at the Sammering circuit in Austria.

Between 1913 and 1914, NSU riders won 375 first prizes in Germany alone and the company produced 12,000 bicycles and 2,500 motorcycles.

In 1906, a tricycle was produced, using a 3.5hp motorcycle engine located above the front wheel, which was driven by chain. It was known as the 'Sulmobil.'

NSU produced powerful twin cylinder bikes and lighter tourers in their motorcycle program;

A 1907 special racing machine with single cylinder, 243cc, four-stroke engine. The front forks have been strengthened.

By 1912, NSU were producing machines with their own engines. This is a V-twin, four-stroke, 350cc model.

rear suspension was available as early as 1911 along with chain or belt drive, two speed gearbox and sprung front forks.

The NSU Pony was the smallest in the range at 1.5hp and then there were larger capacity machines of 800cc producing 6.5hp.

As the First World War loomed in 1914, NSU was obliged to change its production to suit the needs of the military and the 3.5hp twin 'military' model was born in 1915.

When the hostilities ended, the first machine to come out of NSU in 1921 was a 350cc single

One of the earliest NSU machines: the 1902 model.

Clearly a machine from 1922, this is the 249cc, 4.8hp 'Pony' model, which has a two-speed gearbox and belt drive. A specification from the post-war years.

The 1924 twin-cylinder 502S sport model.

Another 'Pony' model, the 201 ZD of 1934.

which developed 3hp and had belt drive to the rear wheel. By 1928, chain drive had already been re-adopted and the NSU 201 R, a 200cc machine, and the 301 T, a 300cc machine, were introduced to the line-up. Two years later, they produced their first two-stroke machine, which used a 175cc engine.

By 1929, sales were picking up nicely and a new running-in track was laid down behind the factory. NSU employed the English designer Walter William Moore. He involved himself not only in the racing side but also with the OSL models – 200cc, 250cc, 350cc, 500cc and 600cc. These were the backbone of the NSU

line-up right through to the 1930s. At the lower end NSU also produced the 'Motosulm,' a motorized bicycle with a 1.2hp, two-stroke engine, followed by the ZDB models in the early 1930s.

At the 1936 International Automobile and Motorcycle Exhibition in Berlin, a machine of 100cc appeared, named the 'Quick,' an immediate success not just then, but for the future – they built and sold more than a quarter of a million examples.

On the racing scene, Moore engaged British rider Tom Bullus for the NSU team. Moore developed a new, 500cc supersport machine for

This is a magnificent poster depicting a triumphant Heiner Fleischmann on his NSU machine.

Bullus and the results spoke for themselves. In June 1930, he took the SS500 to victory at the Motorcycle Grand Prix at the Nurburg Ring and went on to win at the Solitude circuit, the Eifel event, the Klausen Pass Hill-climb, the German Hill-climb Grand Prix, the Gaisberg race near Salzburg and the International Grand Prix at Monza, Italy – thus becoming one of the most successful riders of all time. By 1937, the machine was revised slightly and a 350cc model was also available. Heiner Fleischmann, riding the 350cc version with an output of 36hp, walked off with the German championship of that class.

Moore left the following year and Albert Roder, who was asked to produce a supercharged version for sidecar racing, came in. Unfortunately, sidecar racing was banned before the machine was finished and so Roder turned his skills to a supercharged, 350cc twin with DOHC.

Misfortune raised its ugly head again, but this time it was due to the Second World War. All motorcycle development stopped. During the period, NSU were involved with producing materials for the war effort, including a half tracked motorcycle. By the end of the war, they had manufactured almost 8,000 multi-purpose vehicles.

The years after the war were no different for NSU than for any other German industry. It was time to clear away the dust and rubble and get back to low level production. Pre-war designs such as the Quick motorized bicycle, the 125cc ZDB and the 251 OSL models were dusted off and produced again.

1949 saw the company launch their first post-war design, the NSU Fox. It used a 100cc, ohv, four-stroke engine, which developed 5.2hp. At the Frankfurt Trade Fair in 1950, a Lambretta was shown with an NSU engine. Built under license in Italy, it used a 125cc, two-stroke engine and was enhanced over the years until it was replaced by the NSU Prima in 1956, by which time nearly 120,000 had been built.

It was 1947 when motorcycles finally got back to their race circuits. William Herz had built his own supercharged NSU and rode it to victory in the 1948 German 350cc championship. At the end of the year, NSU resolved to go racing once again with a factory team made up of William Herz in the 350cc class, Heiner Fleischmann in the 500cc class and Bohm/Fuchs with their sidecar outfit.

1950 was the last year of the supercharger. They were subsequently banned and the victories came with Bohm/Fuchs taking the German sidecar championship and Heiner Fleischmann taking the 350cc championship. 1951 was the first, post-war record breaking attempt by the NSU factory. In April, a streamlined, 500cc machine ridden by William Herz reached a speed of 180 mph, taking back the record set up by Henne some 14 years previously. Eight other new records were also set up.

On the 20 July 1952, Germany won the first World championship race since the war. The race took place at the Solitude circuit. Werner Haas was on the starting grid with his all-new, 125cc Rennfox, which he steered to a well-earned and notable first time victory.

In 1952, the Rennmax appeared a racing version of the production model. It used an inline,

The NSU Rennfox of 1953. Werner Haas won the World championship and German Mastercup in the 125cc class on this machine.

twin-cylinder, DOHC engine. It was so good that Haas started at the Grenzland Ring in the 350cc race with his 250cc Rennmax and beat everyone. The following year, NSU vowed to enter the world championships – Werner Haas excelled, capturing the 125cc class and the 250cc class as well as the German championship.

The following year, three newcomers joined Haas on the team: H.P. Muller, the 'Racing tiger,' as he was known, Hans Baltisberger and Rupert Hollaus. The Fox and Max machines were fitted with new fairings and were called 'The Dolphins.' 1954 saw the NSU team tie up the 125cc and 250cc championship classes, the machines now adopting the nickname of 'Blue Whales.' It was a glorious period for the NSU racing team and the riders.

A bombshell exploded the following year when NSU decided they were going to pull out of racing, but would support private entries. In 1955, H. P. Muller became the first private rider to capture the 250cc world championship and NSU now turned their attention to record-breaking. Gustav Adolf Baumm designed a highly aerodynamic vehicle with a 3.4 Quickly engine installed at the rear and another version with a 7hp Fox engine. He captured 11 World records in 1954. In July and August 1956, at Bonneville Salt Flats, USA, William Herz rode his fully

The engine of the 1953 racer: a 124cc unit producing 16hp at 11000 rpm.

This is the 1957 Rennmaxi, 175cc machine. The engine produced approximately 19hp at 9000 rpm.

NSU Fox from 1950 used a 98cc engine and could reach 62 mph.

streamlined, 500cc machine at 211 mph. H P Muller, in turn, took the Baumm 'Flying Deck-chair' up to 122 mph with a 50cc engine and to 150 mph with a 125cc engine installed. Thus NSU held all the three records that could be achieved by a two-wheeler set up.

In 1951, the new 200cc Lux appeared. It had a two-stroke engine and the type and model range was extended with two versions of a larger motorcycle, the Konsul 1 with 350cc engine and the Konsul ll with 500cc, four-stroke engine. The last pre-war design 251 OSL went out of production in 1952. In the same year, the Max, a four-stroke, ohv model designed by Albert Roder, was introduced. The machine used an unusual rod and crank system to oper-

Shown is a 1951 NSU Konsul, which used a 349cc engine and produced 18hp and was able to reach 68 mph. The Konsul ll had a 500cc engine.

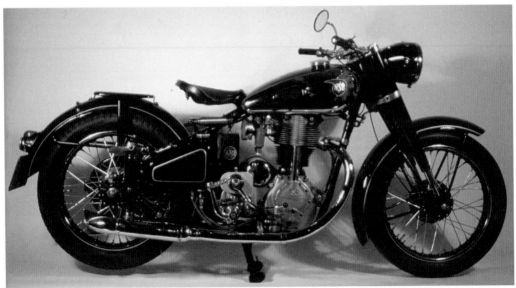

This single seater NSU is a 1951 251 OSL model and used a 241cc, single cylinder, four-stroke, ohv engine.

ate the valve gear, known as the 'Ultramax' valve gear system. The following year, the Quick

was replaced by the 50cc Quickly, which had pedals and only weighed 73 lbs. It was also possible to ride this without road tax or a driving license.

The mid-1950s saw machines with the word 'Super' placed in front of their model names, confirming their performance and comfort: Super Fox, Super Lux and Super Max. Even though the Quickly outsold everything in its class and a new design, the Quick 50cc, lightweight motorcycle, with two-stroke engine appeared in 1962, it was clear that motorcycle sales were on the decrease. Four years later, motorcycle production ended at Neckarsulm.

Part of the Quickly series of small-capacity machines: the single cylinder, 49cc Cavallino.

The Quickly T of 1960 had a 49cc, two-stroke motor.

In 1955, the company reached its absolute peak output with some 300,000 motorized two-wheelers, becoming the largest motorcycle manufacturer in the world. Since the company was formed, around 2,300,000 motorized two-wheelers were built.

NUT

1912 - 1933

The 4-port, V-twin engine of the 1933 NUT.

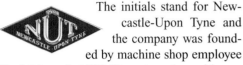

The initials stand for New-castle-Upon Tyne and the company was founded by machine shop employee Hugh Mason in 1906. He partnered up with cycle dealer Jock Hall and their first machines in 1912 had handle starting and the Mason 'HM' monogram.

They later built bikes under the names Jesmond and Bercley until NUT was used in 1912 – a JAP-powered, V-twin NUT machine won the 1913 Junior TT and other racing successes followed.

They moved to larger premises in 1914 and made military equipment during the war, but the company went bankrupt when their partners pulled out.

This 1933 NUT had a twin cylinder, 698cc engine.

The carburettor of the V-twin is tucked in between the two cylinders.

It was bought by Robert Ellis and restarted in 1921, under the name of Hugh Mason and Company, closing in 1922.

In 1923, they started once more under NUT, building their own 698cc engine. They continued with 698cc and 750cc V-twins, 172cc, single, Villiers, two-strokes and 350cc, Blackburne models. In 1933, the company closed because of financial problems.

This is a 1914 Sports V-Twin, 680cc machine. It has the early, distinctive, round, NUT-style fuel tank.

OEC

1901 - 1954

 The Osborn Engineering Company was founded by Frederick Osborn, who began by making bicycles before turning to motorcycles in 1901.

OEC made motorcycles under contract with Blackburne until 1914. But it did not make an impact until his son John Osborn took over around 1920, and decided to make motorcycles. The company took over the manufacture of Blackburne engines in 1921 and became known as OEC-Blackburne. However, it continued to use V-twin JAP engines in some machines.

In 1927, OEC introduced a patented duplex steering system and numerous other innovations followed. The company ran into financial troubles in 1930, but with fresh capital production was soon restarted.

In 1936, OEC produced the Atlanta Duo roadster which used a duplex steering system designed by Fred Wood. In 1926, Claude Temple rode an OEC-Temple to the world speed record of 121.3 mph and Joe Wright rode a JAP-engined OEC at 150.736 mph in 1930. Although the company resumed production after the Second World War, it finally stopped in 1954.

Single seater, 600cc, OEC from 1927.

Opel

1901- 1930

 Besides making cars, the Opel Company, based in Russelsheim, Germany, also produced motorcycles. The first models used 1.75 to 2hp and 2.25 to 2.75hp, single cylinder engines.

Although production stopped before the First World War, it resumed afterwards with a four-stroke, side-valve, 123cc bicycle attachment model. From 1922 to 1924, the company produced complete machines with 148cc engines using two-speed gearboxes. The following year, a 498cc single was produced.

In 1928, came a new model named the Motoclub. With its 499cc sv and ohv engine, it was produced in the old Elite-Diamant factory and was the last machine built by Opel.

The 496cc, single cylinder, four-stroke Opel engine.

Last of the line, the 1929 Motoclub model.

Ossa

1951- 1984

The full production of Ossa machines started in 1951, after Eduard, son of Manuel Giro, designed and built his own small two-stroke engine. Manuel was so impressed that he turned part of his factory in Badel, Spain, over to the production of his son's machines.

An early Ossa moped from 1955.

The first batch were two-stroke, ohv models up to 175cc, although the company concentrated on single cylinder, two-stroke machines throughout the 1950s and early 1960s. The firm grew and produced such machines such as the 250cc Wildfire, the 175cc and 230cc TS Sports.

At this time, Ossa was the smallest of Spain's three motorcycle anufacturers, and was not as well established. In the late 1960s, the company hired Englishman Mick Andrews as factory rider and technical adviser. The company had by now moved to the Poligona Industrial zone of Barcelona and Andrews and Eduardo worked together to produce the new line of machines.

The results came in 1970, when the MAR (Mick Andrews Replica) was introduced. Andrews won the first of three consecutive victories in the Scottish Six Days Trials. This was the beginning of many victories, which culminated in 1971 with the company's first European Trials Title – now the World Trials Championship. However, the ups and downs of corporate life saw Andrews depart in 1972.

In 1973, the Phantom motocrosser, a machine, which had been long on the drawing board, arrived, leading to a whole new range of Ossa

Ossa were competitive, capitalizing on the motorcycle boom in the 1970s. This is a 1975 250cc single.

The rather strange-looking 1982 Urbe.

P&M/Panther

1904 - 1963

machines such as the Pioneer, the Desert and the SDT models.

In the mid-1970s, there was a motorcycle boom in Spain and the company duly moved into road machines. The Tourist, for example, was a two-stroke single with a five-speed gearbox. Then came a parallel twin, the Yankee 500cc model. It was a well-equipped and good-looking roadster with alloy wheels and Brembo brakes. The Explorer 250cc, another two-stroke single, also made its appearance.

There was a lot of industrial unrest in Spain in the late 1970s and workers went on prolonged strikes. The company suffered badly until strike action finally forced production to cease.

The 250cc Copa, introduced in 1981.

A rider negotiates his Ossa trial over rough terrain.

Joah Pehlon was in business with Harry Rayner, producing their own machine, when Rayner was killed in an accident in 1903. Richard Moore offered to join Phelon and the two started Phelon and Moore in 1904. The first thing they did was patent a two-speed gear system, which became a standard fit on their machines up to 1923. They were based at first in Cleckheaton, South Yorkshire, England, but as orders increased, they moved to Valley Road.

At this time the main machine was a 500cc single, the engine of which made up the front downtube of the frame. A new 770cc V-twin, with the front cylinder making up the downtube, was next on the scene. The First World War was about to begin, which meant that production had to stop. The Royal Flying Corps, however, had been evaluating a 500cc, two-speed P&M in 1913, and they now chose it as their standard transport vehicle.

After the war, the 500cc single was offered for sale once more until 1923, when a new 555cc sports model joined it. Granville Bradshaw (once of ABC) was hired by P&M during 1923 and his creation that caused a sensation at the Olympia show. The machine had a single cylinder (still acting as front downtube), but was an ohv model with incased pushrods and a four-speed gearbox. This was the first Panther model.

Two of these machines were entered for the 1924 Senior TT. Unfortunately, they collided. The following year was better with a fourth

Pictured is a 1911 model with a single cylinder, 498cc engine.

The inclined engine replaced the downtube of the bike.

place obtained. This was enough to warrant a replica being offered.

In 1927, came the introduction of a 250cc, transverse V-twin, the Panthette, while two years later came the 'sloper' machines that were now using the Panther name designed by Frank Leach. A 500cc speedway machine was also on the books at this time, as were some Villiers-powered lightweights. In 1932, the Model 20, a 250cc, ohv single which used a conventional frame layout, made its debut.

By now, the company, like many others, was suffering financially. Only a deal with Pride and Clark Ltd. of London, to produce the machines at rock-bottom prices, allowed it to continue.

The outcome of this difficult period were the 250cc and 350cc Red Panthers, which were accompanied by the De Luxe 350cc Model 85 Redwing Panther.

Once the recession started to ease in the 1930s, Bradshaw was asked to look at new

The P&M was better known as the Panther: a 1934 model 70 with 248cc engine.

designs. He came up with a 600cc, in-line, vertical twin model. Unfortunately, war again intervened, and the introduction of this twin was terminated.

After 1945, the 598cc model was back, as were a new range of 250cc and 350cc singles. In 1949, the roadster models were joined by 250cc and 350cc competition specials, the Panther Stroud model. In 1950, the company produced a scooter called the Panther Princess and two-stroke Villiers-engined machines were present again. In 1964, the big single was enlarged to 645cc, while the 249cc, Sport Twin, two-stroke gained an electric start.

The Panther M120 of 1959 was handsome, reliable and solid.

The motorcycle industry in Britain was not healthy at this time and Panther struggled once again. Machines were being sold cheaply, but this time nothing could save the company, which ceased to exist in 1967.

The robust 645cc, single cylinder, four-stroke motor.

Peugeot

1899- date

PEUGEOT
Motocycles

The Peugeots have been known since the 15th century. The family resided at Vandoncourt in Montbéliard, a region which belonged to the Holy Roman Empire.

In the early 1700s, Jean-Jacques Peugeot, son of Jean (mayor of Vandoncourt), married Suzanne Mettetal. Their sixth child, Jean-Pierre, was born in 1734. He later founded the Peugeot industrial dynasty with a dyeworks, an oil-mill and a flour-mill. In 1793, in the aftermath of the French Revolution, the principality of Montbéliard was annexed by France and the Peugeots became French.

In 1999, it was exactly 100 years since the first Peugeot single cylinder, motorized bicycle was created in Montbéliard.

A beautifully restored 1932 model Peugeot.

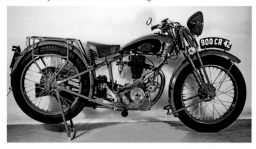

Single cylinder 242cc, producing 10.5hp at 5200rpm.

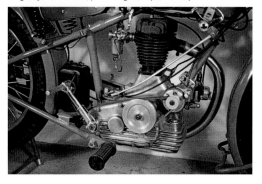

In 1905, their first V-twin was introduced. This was a four-stroke machine that could reach 87 mph. The first Peugeot scooter, the S55, 125cc two-seater, was launched in 1953.

Significant in 1970 was the 103 model range, while 1982 saw the company produce its first new generation plastic-bodied scooters, the SC and the SX. In 1996, came the introduction of an electric scooter, the scoot-elec, along with a sports scooter with single front arm fork, the speedflight. Then in 2002, the company launched the Elystar in 50cc, 125cc and 150cc engine sizes (there was also an exclusive combined braking system). It was followed in 2004 by the launch of the Ludix range of machines with their innovative styling and design.

The Ludix, 'twist and go' transport. Slim, light and zippy.

Small capacity fun: the 50cc XR6 Sport

Piaggio

1946 - date

PIAGGIO
L I M I T E D

The Piaggio concern was already well-established in the Italian shipbuilding, railways and aeronautics industry before it entered the world of motorcycles and scooters. In 1946, the two Piaggio brothers decided to take on different roles in the company. Armando dedicated himself to the aeronautics and railway activities while Enrico decided to busy himself with an ambitious plan to motorizing the Italian population by creating a simple, low-cost vehicle. He obtained the assistance of Corradino D'Ascanio, an ingenious aeronautic designer who designed the first modern helicopter. The first Vespa prototype was produced in Pontedera in April 1946. It was put straight on the market and, after a lukewarm welcome, 1947 saw production start to take off.

One of the first in Great Britain: a 1950 Vespa GS.

The spare wheel was tucked neatly away.

The 1978 Vespa P200E: Engine panels could be removed to reveal the two-stroke, 197cc engine on one side and the spare wheel on the other.

Around one million models were built and sold abroad in a 10 year period. A decision was taken to dedicate the Pontedera plant exclusively to Vespa, by now Piaggio's best-selling product. By 1965, more than three million models had been produced.

With the construction of the 'Leonardo da Vinci,' transatlantic ship-building came to an end. The aeronautic sector also showed signs of crisis. So in 1964, the company was split into I.A.M. Rinaldo Piaggio (the aeronautic and railway sectors) and Piaggio & C. (Scooters). In 1965, after the death of Enrico Piaggio, Umberto Agnelli succeeded to the presidency of Piaggio & C.

1967 saw the birth of Ciao, the first truly modern moped. In 1969, Gilera was taken over and a whole variety of bikes was produced.

In 1979, the new Società Piaggio Adriatica S.p.A. was created, while Bianchi was bought in 1981. At the end of the 1980s, there was a slow-down in sales of the Vespas, but this was counter-acted by the introduction of new vehicles, the Cosa, Superbravo, Grillo and ApeCar D. In 1988, Gustavo Denegri became the new Piaggio president, with Giovanni Alberto Agnelli on the board of directors.

In 1990, new vehicles were launched: an updated, three-speed Vespa 50cc, the four wheel Ape Poker commercial vehicle, and the Sfera in particular, the first plastic scooter to be made in Pontedera. Technological progress led to the launch of other new scooters such as the Quartz, Zip and Skipper. In 1994, the Hexagon, a landmark in the maxi scooter segment, was launched. In 1996, the 50th anniversary of Enrico Piaggio and Corradino D'Ascanio's revolutionary Vespa, was marked by the launch of a new Vespa, the ET4 125cc model, followed a few months later by the ET2 50cc.

After the premature death of Giovanni Agnelli in 1997, the Piaggio Group initiated a change in company ownership, with financial group Morgan Grenfell Private Equity acquiring the company in 1999.

The year 2000 marked Piaggio's entry into the prestigious maxi scooter segment with its revolutionary X9 250. On 23 October 2003, the Piaggio Group changed ownership once again to Immsi S.p.A, but continued to produce a wide range of safe, high-performance, environment-friendly, 50 to 500cc vehicles: the Piaggio X9 Evolution and X8, the Piaggio Beverly and the highly successful Vespa Granturismo.

A fully-equipped Piaggio B500, perfect for the city slicker.

The X9 instrument panel keeps the rider well-informed.

The 2005 Piaggio X9 500 Evolution, comfortable and aerodynamic.

Pierce

1909 - 1913

PIERCE In 1908, George Pierce already had a thriving motor car and bicycle business when he decided to hand the bicycle side over to his son, Percy. You can see the resemblance between the first Pierce machine and the FN machine of the day. Percy had returned from Europe with an FN and it spurred him to build the first, four-cylinder, American motorcycle. The Pierce used the 'T' head, side-valve system, the shaft drove the rear wheel and the engine was an integral part of a frame which carried the fuel and oil. Although the 1909 model was direct drive, a clutch and two-speed gearbox was fitted a year later.

The four was followed by a single cylinder, 5hp, 592cc model which used conventional belt drive to the rear wheel.

By 1913, the company was in financial trouble. It ceased to make motorcycles and instead concentrated on making Pierce Arrow trucks for the military.

Pierce based his 4-cylinder engine on the FN Four.

A 1910 Pierce with four-cylinder engine.

Pope

1911 - 1918

Lieutenant Colonel Albert Augustus Pope was one of America's transportation pioneers. He began by importing bicycle parts from England in the 1870s. He then built them up himself.

Pope bicycles were sold under various names and were also attached to motorcycles built by the American Cycle Manufacturing Company.

In 1914, the twin was offered with single or two-speed transmission, while the 8hp engine had roller bearings for the connecting rods, an eclipsed, multi-disc clutch and a Corbin-Duplex brake. The big Pope twin had a leafspring front fork and plunger rear suspension, which was very advanced for the period.

1916 saw the demise of the belt drive single, while the big twin was offered with a three-speed transmission. This engine was available in the 'short-coupled' frame for racing.

By 1918, Pope had reduced its line-up from seven models to two. Soon the company's financial difficulties became so great that production had to be abandoned.

A fine example of a 1914 V-twin, 998cc, four-stroke Pope. The machine is very large and sits high on the road.

Pope's own name was not applied to the motorcycles until 1911, two years after his death. The company had factories in Connecticut, Indiana, Illinois and Ohio.

By 1908, Pope's own financial situation had seriously deteriorated, and motorcycle production was moved to Westfield, Massachussetts. With the second generation of Pope machines came the single of 1911. This had a conventional F-head engine, a belt drive and was adapted for racing with overhead valves. The following year, the 1000cc, ohv V-twin was introduced.

In the center is the speedometer with mileage recorder and the gearchange lever is on the left.

Premier

1911 - 1918

Hillman, Herbert and Cooper, makers and inventors of bicycles and bicycle parts, changed their company name to the Premier Cycle Company Ltd. in 1891. The trademark was a kangaroo holding a crown since Kangaroo was the name of a bicycle they had produced years earlier.

In 1908, the first Premier machine made its debut at the Crystal Palace show. The following year, ridden by G E Stanley, it picked up first prize in the ACU Quarterly Trials. It used a White and Poppe, 427cc, side-valve engine, which was replaced the following year by the company's own engine. At the ACU event of 1909, two 548cc, V-twin prototypes were ridden by Henry Teague and Geoffrey Rotherham. The twin made its debut later this year at the London show and a Premier single of 499cc was also available by 1910.

In 1912, a new, 584cc V-twin joined the eight existing versions of the 499cc single models which ranged from a stripped racer to an open-frame ladies' heavyweight. In 1914, Premier was determined to have another crack at the TT. Equipped with a newly designed machine using

The V-twin engine of the 1909 model with exposed flywheel.

A fine example of a 1909 V-twin, 548cc Premier. The headlamp was a luxury.

The twin port engine of the 1912 Premier model.

The 1912 Premier 2 1/2hp, twin port, single cylinder model. It used belt drive.

A handy extra to warn people you're coming.

ed and for that reason, the 322cc Premier Pony, an in-line, two-stroke twin, never had time to become established. The company was now known as Coventry Premier Ltd. and it supplied a small selection of machines to the Russian military in 1914.

When hostilities were over, the firm decided to manufacture a three-wheeler car. But it went bankrupt rectifying all the development problems. Premier was bought by the Singer concern in 1921.

The 499cc, single cylinder engine of a 1914 Premier

This fine example of a 1914 Premier is exhibited at the Motorcycle Museum in Birmingham, England.

a 499cc, long-stroke engine, they set off to the Isle of Man. The riders were Harry Bashall, Jack Haslam and Len Cushman, but unfortunately, all were forced to retire.

The company had a new machine on the drawing board when the First World War start-

Puch

1903 - 1987

PUCH

Puch is Austria's oldest motorcycle manufacturer. The firm originally produced machines with it own single cylinder engines of 2.7hp, 3.5hp and 4hp, along with V-twin engines of 4hp and 6hp.

During the First World War it also produced a 6hp flat twin, but only in limited numbers.

After 1923 there were two-strokes with double piston configuration designed by Giovanni Marcellino which came in a variety of cylinder sizes: 122cc, 173cc, 198cc, 248cc, 348cc and 496cc.

Between the wars, Puch built a 490cc, JAP-engined, side-valve single and a four-stroke machine. Between 1936 and 1938 it added a 792cc, transverse-mounted, side-valve, flat four, four-stroke machine, but this was mainly for military use.

Built between 1936 and 1938, and very popular, was the S4, a single cylinder, 248cc two-stroke.

Puch had some success in competition. There were winning bikes such as the 1924 Monza works machine and the later 248cc, double piston singles which won the 1931 German Grand Prix among other well-known events.

When the war was over, the 1945 line-up included 123cc, single piston, two-strokes with pressed steel frames, while the older twin piston machines were also fitted with pressed steel frames. These machines stayed in production up to the early 1970s. After this, production was concentrated on 49cc mopeds and 123cc and 173cc motorcycles which used modern single cylinder, single piston units. These varied between normal road, motocross and trials machines. In 1977, came the M50 series, the Jet and Grand Prix models were road bikes while the M50 Cross was an off-road enduro machine. In 1980, the Maxi S, a step-through machine which came in a number of versions, was introduced. By 1987, the two-wheel department of Puch was acquired by Piaggio.

The two-stroke, single cylinder, 220cc engine of the 1926 Puch.

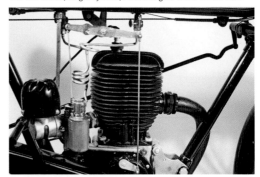

The 1926 Puch was a small-capacity machine with two gears, ideal for commuting.

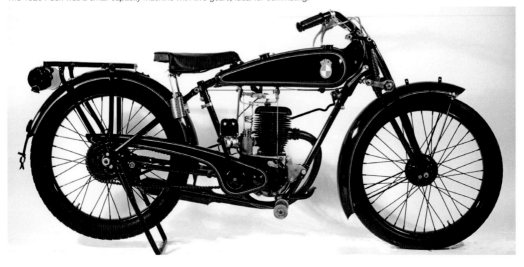

Raleigh

1899- 1960

 Raleigh started producing motorcycles in 1899. The first machine was a bicycle with a Schwann engine attached to the front steering head. In 1903, the company produced something a little more sophisticated: a 3hp unit with a twist-grip accelerator control and chain drive. There was a smaller 2hp version and a forecar, named the Raleighette, which used a water-cooled, 3hp, single cylinder engine. By 1905, the engine had grown to 3.5hp and in April 1905, the company started to reduce its prices dramatically. It was not long before motorcycle production was stopped.

There was some speculation before the First World War that Raleigh might start again and indeed in 1918, it produced a 654cc, side-valve model. This used a Sturmey-Archer gearbox bolted directly to the frame and a full swingarm rear suspension.

The range grew in the 1920s. At the lower end of the range was a two-speed, 174cc model, along with a variety of larger ohv and sv machines of 248 to 998cc. Raleigh did go racing, but achieved only mediocre results.

In 1929, there was a TT replica, even though it did not actually win. A better machine was the 495cc racer, which did achieve results: it came third in the Belgian Grand Prix and first in the Austrian and Argentinian Grand Prix. However, sales of Raleigh motorbikes tumbled in the 1930s.

Sturmey Archer gears are confirmed by the name on the gear lever.

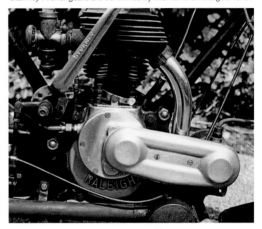

A single cylinder, 348cc model Raleigh of 1925. Gearchange functioned using the lever on the right of the tank.

A low seating position gives a sporty feel to this 1926, sv, 248cc, single-seater Raleigh.

Rex

1900 - 1933

The firm managed to hold out until 1933, but then shut down production.

The company returned to motorcycles in 1958 with a single gear Raleigh moped powered by a 49.9cc, Sturmey-Archer engine built under contract by BSA. It was not a great success and after a few years, another moped was built at the Nottingham factory. (In fact, these were Mobylettes made under licence.) Raleigh later bought the manufacturing rights for a 78cc Bianchi scooter, which went under the name of Raleigh Roma. But again profits were slight. The company finally decided it was better off building bicycles and ceased production for the last time in 1960.

Prior to going into motorcycle manufacture, the Rex Company was a car manufacturer from Birmingham, England. They moved to Earlsdon, Coventry in 1900 and exhibited a 1 3/4hp motorcycle at the Crystal Palace show the same

1907 V-twin engine with automatic inlet and side exhaust valves.

This 1921 Raleigh had a flat twin cylinder engine of 700cc, a move away from the everyday single or V-twin.

This 1907 Rex had a 5hp engine driving the rear wheel via a belt and single gear. There was no rear suspension.

year. The company was run by two brothers, Billy and Harold Williamson, who would enter their machines in as many events as possible to maximize publicity for the machines.

Over the next few years, a 465cc side-valve and a 726cc V-twin were also introduced. The company was looking at new ideas and experimenting with a rotary valve layout designed by G Pilkington. In 1909, it also started experimenting with a 470cc, two-stroke machine.

1910 saw a special version of the 5hp V-twin machine converted to 'step-through' style for a lady by the name of Muriel Hind, who went on trials and hill-climb events with the machine, which also acquired the nickname 'Blue Devil.'

A power struggle in the boardroom saw the two Williamson brothers leave the company in 1911. It was also now that the company was making the Rex-JAP on behalf of the Premier Company.

In 1912, the range had increased and was split into Tourist, Speed King and De Luxe models with engines of 499cc, 532cc and 896cc. A new, 952cc V-twin was added in 1914 and there was a 349cc two-stroke in 1915. Because of the war and work taken on for the military these machines did not reach the general public.

The first Rex manufactured after World War One was a 550cc, side-valve single. Rex bought out the Acme company next door, who offered a JAP-engined, 980cc V-twin, which was soon joined by a similar 980cc, Blackburne-powered Rex. In 1921, the first machine with the Rex-Acme name came on stream using a 350cc Blackburn engine and nicknamed the Impy. From here onwards, proprietary engines from Aza, Blackburne, JAP and Barr & Stroud were used.

In 1925, Wal Handley win two TTs in one week, also breaking the 250cc lap record. The following year, he rode in all three – Senior, Junior and Lightweight – races, results of which were second, third and failed to finish, respectively. Many more successes for the Rex-Acme company followed.

Like many motorcycle manufacturers during this period, the depression was starting to bite and they launched a 172cc Villiers utility model

Rex bought the Acme company next door and soon the two names were amalgamated. This machine is a Rex Acme of 1926 with single seat and chain final drive.

The company used many different engines for their machines. This 1926 Rex Acme has a Blackburn 350cc, single cylinder unit.

in desperation. This, unfortunately, did not help and in 1930, the company closed down. There was a glimmer of hope when Fulford-Mills bought them and produced a new range of 174cc and 250cc, ohv models, using Abingdon King Dick engines. By 1933, however, this closed down as well.

Rover

1903 - 1925

Like many companies, Rover made bicycles before moving to motorcycles and then cars. Rover, however, do have the distinction of producing a new type of safety bicycle during that period. In 1888, JK Starley unveiled a bicycle with wheels of uniform size and driven by pedals and a chain to the rear wheel (most bicycles of this period were of the 'penny farthing' type and quite dangerous to ride). This new bicycle was named the Rover.

After Starley died in 1901, steps were taken to produce a motorcycle and a 3 1/2hp Imperial Rover was shown to the public in 1903. It was a substantial machine with a proper diamond-style frame and the engine was positioned in the center.

After this, Rover did not produce any more machines until 1908, when a bicycle was made to take a clip-on type 1 1/4hp Motosacoch engine. By now, Starley's son had taken over the reins at Rover and he announced that a new machine would be available for 1911. The bike was designed by John E Greenwood and used a 3 1/2hp, 500cc engine. It stayed in production, with regular updates, right through the early 1920s.

Rover now became involved with sporting events, their two main riders being Dudley Noble and Chris 'Rover' Newsome. A sports model was presented in 1912 and a TT model was added for 1913, the riders bringing home the Team Award for the factory. 100 awards were won by riders in this year. The company was

The compact engine of the Rover Imperial.

Shown here is a 1915 Rover Imperial, with kick-start and gas lighting.

back at the TT the following year, but without success.

The First World War intervened and production slowed, although an order from the Russian military did keep the firm busy churning out the 499cc single. In 1915, there was a new, 654cc, V-twin, JAP-engined model and production of war machines continued, with 3103 machines being built between 1915 and 1918.

Rover were slow to make changes after the war, but in 1922, they announced a new 250cc lightweight, which had lighting and internal expanding brakes front and rear. Used in trials events, the machine picked up a gold medal when ridden by Noble in the 1923 ACU Six Days Trial. By 1924, the 250cc model was joined by a 350cc version, but the 654cc and 499cc machines were dropped from the line-up. The 350cc machine, discontinued in 1925, was the last to have a Rover badge.

A beautifully restored 1918 V-twin Rover is on display at the National Motorcycle Museum, Birmingham, England.

The Rover V-twin engine is a 700cc, JAP unit. Also seen here is the kick-start, which is on the left of the picture.

Royal Enfield

1898 - 1971

In 1893, the Enfield Manufacturing Company Ltd. was registered to market the bicycles produced by the Eadie Manufacturing Company. Then in 1896, the New Enfield Cycle Company was formed to take over the manufacture of cycles made by the Eadie Manufacturing Company and the Enfield Manufacturing Company. Soon the 'New' was gone and the company was known simply as Enfield Cycle Co. Ltd.

By 1899, Enfield was producing motor tricycles and quadricycles with De Dion engines. It experimented with a heavyweight bicycle frame and a Minerva engine clamped to the frame on the front downtube. The 1901 Royal Enfield had a 1 1/2hp engine clamped to the steering head and belt drive. In the following years, different versions were made, but by 1904, the firm lost interest in the motorcycle and concentrated on the motor car. A new company was started – The Enfield Autocar Company – but business did not go well and 1907 saw it go into liquidation. The assets were bought out by Alldays and Onions of Birmingham, who produced the Enfield-Alldays motor car.

It was not until 1910 that Enfield decided to get back to motorcycles. First, it produced a 2 1/4hp, lightweight, V-twin machine with a Motosacoche engine, quickly followed by a 2 1/2hp version. In 1912, the Model No 180 sidecar combination was introduced. It used a 770cc, V-twin, JAP engine which had two speeds and chain drive. In 1913, the company introduced its 3hp, 425cc, V-twin solo, which, in 350cc guise, was raced successfully in the TT and at Brooklands the following year.

During the First World War, the company supplied large numbers of machines to the military, including an 8hp sidecar model fitted with a Vickers machine gun. After the war, the firm continued to produce three pre-war machines – the 8hp model with sidecar, the 3hp twin, and

This is a 1914 model Royal Enfield. It could be bought both as a single or with sidecar outfit.

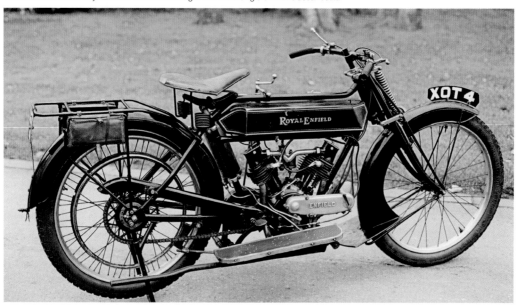

The 1914 Royal Enfield V-twin 450cc engine.

This is the two-stroke, 225cc Royal Enfield engine.

the 2 1/4hp two-stroke. However, the 3hp model was terminated in 1920.

In 1921, a new 976cc twin was introduced for sidecar use, the company's own design though it was built by Vickers. In 1924, they introduced a single cylinder, JAP-engined, 350cc, sporty model.

Between 1925 and 1930, the company decided to enter the TT and although it did not have great success, it did win the Manufacturers Team Award in 1927 and introduced its first 500cc, single machine, which had a four-speed gearbox. In 1928, there was a 225cc four-stroke with a new, bulbous gas tank which would soon be fitted to all models. By 1930, however, the Depression was starting to affect a lot of motor-

In the 1920s, this 225cc machine was designed to be cheap.

A single cylinder, 350cc Roal Enfield from 1926.

Cycar, a 148cc two-stroke with pressed steel forks and frame. In 1934, the 250cc, 350cc, and 500 sports models were given the Bullet designation and the company announced a new 150cc machine, the Model T. In 1936, the four-valve machine, model JF, was brought back while the three-valve model was dropped. Some of the bikes were also fitted with pressed steel forks. Then in 1936, it introduced a super competition model based on the two-valve Model J, which came in 350cc or 500cc capacity. It was highly

During the war, Royal Enfield supplied the armed forces. This is the WD/CO/B 350cc model, allocated to the 21st Army Corp.,

cycle companies. However, even though it made a loss, Enfield was able to fall back on cash reserves.

In 1931, a new, 570cc, sv machine was introduced and the model, J de luxe, was uprated to 499cc. At the motorcycle show in 1931, a 488cc ohv machine was presented, the model JF. Sadly, this was also the year that Albert Eddie, one of the company's founding members, died. The other founder, R.W. Smith, passed away in 1933.

In 1932, a 488cc Sport Special, the LF, was offered for sale. It had a foot-operated gear change and twin, upswept exhaust pipes. At the smaller end of the company line-up was the

tuned and had downswept exhaust pipes with upswept silencers. By 1938, the big twin models, K and KX, were on sale in Great Britain. These had 1140cc power units and had formerly been produced for export.

With the onset of the Second World War, Enfield began to supply the armed forces with machines, the 350cc, sv, WD/C model and the 350cc, ohv, WD/CO model were the main contenders. There was also a tiny, 125cc model that could be packed in a tubular crate and dropped with troops in gliders.

After the war, the 125cc 'Flying Flea' two-stroke, the 350cc model G and the 500cc Model

Designed in 1948, the Bullet is a survivor. This is a 1952 model with 346cc engine.

The rugged, ohv engine of the Bullet is simple and reliable.

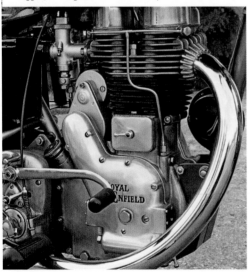

The 60 degree, parallel-twin, 692cc engine of the Constellation.

The beefy 1961 Constellation was the biggest British twin of its day.

J became available. There was a new 350cc Bullet at the 1948 motorcycle show, alongside a new 500cc, ohv, vertical twin. (The Bullet was available in both Trial and Scrambles versions.)

This was also a good year for competition, with the Bullet winning both the International Trophy and the Silver Vase in the ISDT. Then in 1950 and 1951, the company secured the Manufacturer's Team Awards in the Interna-tional Trophy. Johnny Brittain won the Scottish Six Day Trial and the Welsh Two Day Trial on a Model S51, and repeated this the following year.

At the motorcycle show of 1952, the new line-up was the 150cc Ensign two-stroke, the 500cc Bullet and the 692cc Meteor. In 1954, the 250cc Clipper was introduced. In 1957, the 250cc Crusader was presented and a year later, came a 350cc Works Replica and the Constellation. In 1962, the firm brought out a completely new machine, the Crusader Super-5, which had a 5-speed gearbox.

Major Frank Smith, son of R.W. Smith, who took over the company reins when his father died, died in 1962. He took over. In 1962, a larger twin, the 736cc Interceptor, was introduced. This could reach the 'ton' and cruise between 85 and 90 mph. Enfield merged with & H.P. Smith Ltd, a Mid-England engineering company.

In 1965, the 250cc Continental GT was presented, rated the fastest British 250 machine. Other models dribbled out of the Bradford-upon-Avon factory, but the long and glorious history of Royal Enfield came to an end when the machinery and stock were sold to a local development corporation in 1967.

The Royal Enfield name is by no means dead: a contract signed by Royal Enfield and the Indian Government in the 1950s has allowed Royal Enfield Bullets and other models to be made and marketed in India.

Based on a standard 350cc or 500cc Bullet, the Spartan kit transforms a road-going machine into a pre-1965 trial bike.

The 2005 Bullet Electra features the new, lean-burn, 500cc engine.

The 2005 Bullet 65 Sportsman is inspired by the Royal Enfield factory cafe racers of the 1960s.

Rudge

1911 - 1940

Dan Rudge had a workshop behind the Tiger's Head, a pub in Olverhampton, England, where he was innkeeper. In 1868, he was constructing velocipedes, the forerunner of the bicycle. When he died in 1880, his widow sold the thriving business to George Woodcock from Coventry.

Woodcock already had a hand in the bicycle business, with interests in Smith and Starley – who made Ariel cycles and Europa sewing machines – and Haynes and Jeffries. Woodcock now merged all the companies to make the 'D. Rudge and Company and Coventry Tricycle Company.' The new headquarters would be Crow Lane in Coventry and soon the name was shortened to D. Rudge and Company.

In the 1890s, Rudge suffered from financial problems because the bicycle market was flooded by the models of other companies. The lucrative American market established its own man-

ufacturers and the sudden death of Woodcock left nobody to guide the firm.

However, a short distance away in Birmingham, a company manufacturing screws and other hardware was about to get into bicycle production, having also produced bicycle parts for other manufacturers. With Charles Vernon Pugh as managing director and John Vernon Pugh as works manager, the Whitworth Cycle Company was started.

The company thrived and new premises were sought. Talks started between the ailing Rudge Cycle Company (another name change) and a final agreement was reached resulting in the formation of Rudge-Whitworth Ltd. in October 1894. The headquarters were at Crow Lane and

Rudge adopted an overhead inlet valve, over a side exhaust valve layout.

The Rudge Multi of 1913 used a single cylinder, 750cc engine. The front forks were girder type with an enclosed central spring.

The drop handlebars give this away as a racer, it is a magnificent 1920 Rudge Multi TT with a single cylinder, 500cc engine.

the Rea Street works in Birmingham acted as a parts supplier to Rudge-Whitworth.

Initial dabblings in the motorcycle world came with an agreement to sell Werner motorcycles through the Rudge-Whitworth distribution network in South Africa. But it was not until 1910 that Rudge produced a prototype, a 499cc-engined machine which was put on sale in 1911.

It did not take Rudge long to show its potential. That year Victor Surridge set a new Brooklands lap record at 66.47 mph and his machine became the first 500cc model to complete 60 miles in one hour. Unfortunately, Surridge crashed in the TT in 1911, going down in history as the first person to be killed in the TT series. Even so, the company machines continued their winning ways, Stanhope Spencer establishing a new world motorcycle record by covering the flying mile at 72.5 mph in August 1911.

John Pugh had been trying to enhance the gearing of the Rudge machines, coming up with a new system in which the outer face of the engine pulley could be closed inwards while, through a linkage, the flanges of the rear wheel pulley would open out. There would, therefore, be variation in the driving belt ratio, but the tension of the belt would remain constant. All this would be operated by a long lever that could select up to twenty different ratios: the well-known Rudge Multi gear system. In 1912, the Multi machines were offered at a slightly higher price than the single gear machines.

By 1913, Rudge was producing some 80 machines a week and all was going well. There were no fewer than twelve Rudge entries for the TT, but Rudge machines only achieved second place. An accident also took the life of Frank Bateman while he was leading on his Rudge. The following year, Cyril Pullin – the well-known designer and rider – took the Senior event at a speed of 49.5 mph.

The First World War saw Rudge involved with military contracts, supplying British, French, Belgian and Russian troops with machines. After the war, Rudge finally presented the 998cc twin engine that John Pugh had been working on before hostilities and alongside it were the 499cc and 750cc singles.

By now, the belt drive and the Multi gearchange system were starting to show their age and John Pugh started work on a three-speed gearbox. In 1920, a twin cylinder machine with the new box was fitted and a year later came chain drive on the 499cc single. In 1924, the cylinder machine which came in a 350cc format and later in a 500cc version with four overhead valves and a four-speed gearbox.

Three machines were entered for the 1927 TT amongst great fanfare, but all of them were forced to retire. Not all was lost, however. The machines were very capable and still did well in other races, including a second in the Belgian and Ulster Grand Prix and a third at the German Nurburgring.

The following year, the rider Graham Walker joined Rudge and although success did not come right away, he did win the Ulster Grand Prix at the same time, setting a new average speed of 80.078 mph. It was the first time any

A decision had to be made and after much discussion it was calculated that the bikes would last eight laps, the actual race being seven laps long.

In any event, the machines prevailed and Tyrell Smith won, followed by Graham Walker second and Ernie Knott third. The engines were stripped after the race and it was quite clear they would never have been capable of one more mile.

Booming sales should have resulted from the victory, but at this point the Depression intervened. This, along with the huge amount of money spent on the development of new engines and machines, left Rudge in a shaky financial

Kept at the Moray Motor Museum in Scotland, this is a 1928 Rudge Special with 500cc motor.

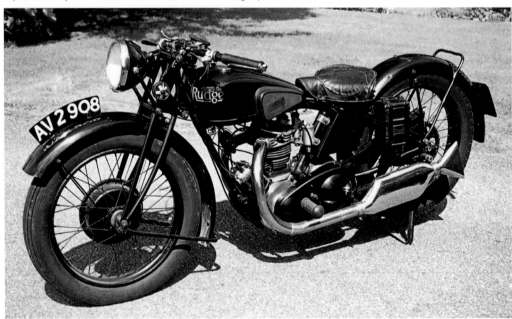

road race had been won with an average over the 80 mph mark and not only did the Ulster circuit become the World's Fastest Road Race, but it also gave a new name for next year's race replicas – Rudge Ulster, thus marking the beginning of a great racing period for Rudge, with many more wins in 1929. In 1930, first one, then three machines were sent to the Isle of Man with great drama. In practices, it was noted that the pistons were starting to break up and would probably never see the race through.

position. All the same, a new, 250cc, radial valve machine was presented in 1931 and Graham Walker won the Lightweight TT, his only TT trophy.

To help with the finances, Rudge took on engine manufacture under the Python name. These engines were taken up by Cotton, AJW, Grindley-Peerless and others. Nevertheless, in 1933, an official receiver was brought in and the racing department was closed. John Vernon Pugh died in 1936 and soon after the company

The 1931 Rudge Ulster, here in full racing trim, is small and sporty, more so than the later machine.

The Ulster engine is a mass of tubes, pipes and wires.

The clean lines and engine of the 1939 Ulster derived from racers.

The 1939 Rudge Ulster had a 499cc, single cylinder engine.

Pugh died in 1936 and soon after the company passed to the Gramaphone Company Ltd., part of the HMV group.

Sales did begin to pick up and development continued, though not on a great scale. In 1938, HMV, now known as EMI, moved the company south to be next to the EMI plant at Hayes. Rudge did get involved in producing an autocycle with a 98cc, Villiers, two-stroke engine, but production went to Norman, based in Kent. There were plans for new machines in 1939 and a 250cc machine was on trial with the army, but all this came to a grinding halt when the Second World War started. The company was obliged to gear up for radio and later radar production. Not long after, the manufacturing rights for Rudge machines were sold to Raleigh, which also bought Norman later.

Rumi

1949 - 1958

A 1954 Rumi Sciaotolo scooter is a very rare sight.

Donnino Rumi of Brescia, Italy, began his adventures in motorcycle production soon after the Second World War. In 1949, the Rumi firm produced its first bike, a horizontal, twin cylinder, two-stroke, 125cc machine designed by Pietro Vassena. Variations followed including a 'competizione' model used for racing. One of these machines won the Italian National Championship and henceforth the logo had the Italian flag and the words 'Campionate d'Italia.'

In 1954, a four-stroke, 125cc, the Bizbero Competizione, was produced. In 1955, the Junior Gentleman replaced the Competizione and a racing machine, the Junior Corsa, was also listed. A scooter called the Squirrel appeared in 1953. It used the 125cc, two-stroke Rumi engine, and was followed the next year by the Formicino, of which several versions were made, the most popular being the Bol d'Or. The company was given a large arms contract in the late 1950s and production of two-wheeled machines was halted.

The 125cc, two-stroke, twin cylinder engine of the Rumi racer.

The 1954 Rumi racer was capable of 93 mph and the engine was an integral part of the frame.

Sachs

1899 - 1960

 The precursor of the current Sachs Fahrzeug und Motorentechnik was founded by Carl Marschütz on 5 April 1886 as the Nürnberger Hercules-Werke in Neumarkt, Germany. He initially manufactured bicycles with eight employees, eight years later the company had already grown to a total of 170 employees.

In 1895, the company moved from Neumarkt to the Fürther Strasse in Nuremberg and the company used not only Sachs engines in their machines, but also other proprietary units over the following years.

Karl Fichtel and Ernst Sachs founded the Schweinfurter Präcisions-Kugellagerwerke Fichtel & Sachs (Schweinfurter precision ball bearing works) in 1895. Both company founders immediately recognized that the future lay with motor vehicles. Driven by the success of the legendary Torpedo hub, the young corporation had already registered over 100 patents by 1905. The company supplied engines for many different motorcycle manufacturers around the world.

In 1963, that Sachs took over the Nürnberger Hercules-Werke GmbH. Machines with the Hercules and the Sachs names were now available. 1987 saw the introduction of the Saxonette, a bicycle with a 30cc, wheel-hub engine. In 1995, a restructuring of the company saw the bicycle department sold to the Dutch ATAG-group and the motoring department renamed Sachs Fahrzeug-und Motorentechnik GmbH.

In 1998, SACHS Fahrzeug-und Motorentechnik GmbH was sold to the Dutch Winning Wheels Group and in 2000, the Roadster range of machines was presented with 650cc and 800cc engines. This same year saw the Sachs Beast 1000 presented at Intermot in Munich.

In February 2001, there was a management buy-out and 2004 saw some interesting machines produced from motorized bicycles to off-road machines such as the Dirty Devil.

One of the 2005 machines: the 50cc Dirt Devil.

Sanglas

1942 - 1981

 Talleres Sanglas SA was a motorcycle business started by the Spaniards Martin and Javier Sanglas Camps in 1942. Their original works were at Pueblo Nuovo, but in 1960, they moved to Hospitalet in the suburbs of Barcelona.

The original machines were four-stroke, 350cc singles made from the 1950s to the early 1960s, with regular developments. Even the Spanish police were impressed, placing an order with the company in 1956. The following year, a 500cc model appeared, although both the 350cc and the 500cc looked the same. A tourer version was used in Spanish production bike racing and a sportier 350cc machine was also produced.

With the move to new premises, the company decided to enter the two-stroke market and bought both Villiers and Zundapp engines for their machines. Initially, the Villiers 250cc and 325cc engines were fitted to the new line of bikes, which was called named Rovena.

The four-stroke machines were kept on as an alternative to the two-strokes and the machine line-up was increased with 50cc and 100cc Zundap engines in 1964. In 1968, Sanglas decided that two-strokes were no longer viable and the last model rolled off the production line. The four-strokes were still selling well and were even exported to the police forces in South America.

In 1972 and 1973, new machines were presented. The 400E, followed shortly by the 400T and F. Sales increased and at the motorcycle show of 1976, the company introduced the new 500S, a sports roadster which followed the design of the 400cc models and used a fully enclosed front disc brake. By 1978, there was a sportier version.

By 1981, the company was involved with Yamaha and even produced a machine with a 392cc Yamaha engine. Yamaha then took over the company and no more was heard of the Sanglas name.

The 1973 Sanglas 400cc was the first with electric starting and was widely used by the Spanish police.

Scott

1908 - 1969

The Scott motorcycle was the product of an engineering genius called Alfred Angus Scott. He began to take a great interest in two-stroke engines after helping his brother build a single cylinder gas engine. He built his own twin cylinder engine soon after, attaching it to the front steering head of a Premier bicycle. The machine was modified over time and he took out a patent for the vertical twin cylinder, two-stroke engine in 1904.

By 1908, Scott designed and patented his new frame as well as a new 333cc engine. This engine had water-cooled cylinder heads and two-speed gears and the time seemed right to manufacture this machine.

Scott, however, had no capital. He came to an arrangement with Ben and William Jowett to use their premises for the construction of his machines, a situation which proceeded smoothly until the Jowetts decided to concentrate on building their own motor car and the extra factory space was needed. Scott, therefore, had to raise money to set up his own company.

The new company was named the Scott Engineering Company and was based at rented accommodation in Grosvenor Street, Bradford, England from 1910.

The machines were already starting to gain a reputation and Scott himself claimed many a gold medal from hill-climbs. With the move to new premises, the machines began to include new features, such as a Scott-designed radiator and kick start along with an enlargement of the engine to 450cc. Legend has it that the use of purple paint, of which there was good deal, was inspired by the color of Scott's sister-in-law's

Shown here is the 1914 31/2hp model Scott.

Unconventional in most respects, the 1914 machine used a parallel twin cylinder, water cooled unit, with a capacity of 532cc.

The strangest racing machine: Scott has a 1925 vintage and a two-speed gearbox.

favorite dress, while the two stripes used on the tank represented 'two-stroke.'

By 1911, the engine size was increased to 486cc and a new radiator and better water cooling was included. The machine was raced in many different events, including the TT, where results up this point had not been impressive.

In 1912, however, the company luck changed and of its two riders – Frank Philipp and Frank Applebee – it was Applebee who came in first at an average speed of 48.60 mph. It was the

More conventional in appearance than its predecessors, this is a 1928 Scott Squirrel. It was reputed to be a fuel thirsty machine.

first time a two-stroke won the TT. With this victory, more orders came in, followed by an increase in production, leading to a need for more space. The company went public to raise funds for a new factory at Shipley. In 1913, the Senior TT win was repeated by new rider Tim Wood.

The outbreak of the 1914-1918 war halted the production of civilian Scott motorcycles.

During the period, the company supplied the military with a sidecar outfit with machine gun attached. Scoot himself was very taken by the idea of sidecars. Just after the war, he left the company he founded so that he could pursue the

This is the lever that selects the three-speed gear change.

development of the Scott Sociable, a three-wheeled vehicle, half sidecar, half car.

In the meantime, the Scott Motorcycle Company continued under new management, and the production of a new model, the Squirrel, was introduced in 1922, followed by the 1925 Super Squirrel, which had both 498cc and 596cc engines, and the Flying Squirrel in 1926, which was basically a 1926 TT model with a choice of either 498cc or 596cc units. The Depression years were as hard for Scott as for other motorcycle manufacturers, but somehow the firm managed to scrape by. A TT replica was produced in 1929 and a cheap 298cc single between 1929 and 1930. The company appointed an official receiver in 1931, but a Liverpudlian by the name of Albert Reynolds bought some of the Scott production, which he customized and sold as the Aero Scott and Reynolds Special.

At the Olympia show of 1934, the Scott Three cylinder bike made its debut as a water-cooled, 750cc, in-line machine, shortly superseded by the 1000cc version. The firm also tinkered with a small-capacity, 98cc machine called the Cyk Auto in 1938. Unfortunately, these motorcycles were never produced in large numbers because of the start of the Second World War.

The Squirel's engine is a 596cc, parallel twin-cylinder, water-cooled, two-stroke unit, which could propel the machine to 70 mph.

The beautiful TT Replica of 1930 used the same mechanical design as the Squirrel.

Racing features, such as a foot-change gearbox, are evident.

Shortly after the end of the Second World War, the company re-launched the Flying Squirrel model. Available in 500cc or 600cc form, the machine was even heavier than its pre-war predecessor. The machine was relatively expensive for the performance it offered, which did nothing to enhance sales. The company limped on for a few more years until going into voluntary liquidation in 1950.

In 1956, Matt Holder, who was to restart Scott motorcycle manufacture in Birmingham, announced a 596cc model with a duplex frame, telescopic fork front and swinging arm rear suspension. In 1958, the Scott Swift, which had a 500cc engine fitted with flat top pistons, was announced, but never went into production. These Birmingham Scotts remained in production right up to the end of the 1960s and they featured some of the key characteristics of the original models built 60 years earlier.

Shaw

1903 - 1917

Stanley Shaw offered strap-on motorcycle engines. They advertised that 'Everything is complete and we send it to you all ready to attach to your bicycle in just a few minutes without the aid of an expert mechanic.' The engine was a single cylinder, 240cc unit, could be attached to the front downpipe and drive was operated through a belt to the rear wheel.

The company produced a complete machine later while still selling the strap-on engine. They stopped selling in 1914 and later sold tractors.

This is the 1910 version of a Shaw machine with strap-on engine.

Once attached, the leather belt was fitted to drive the back wheel.

Silk

1976 - 1979

The Silk Company was started by the British men, George Silk and Maurice Patey. In fact, George Silk was involved with two-strokes in the 1950s when he worked for a company that renovated them.

George Silk had an interest in vintage motorcycle racing and one of his early ventures was fitting a Scott engine into a Spondon frame. Meanwhile, he was also talking to Matt Holder – now owner of the Scott name – to see if he could buy the production rights for Scott. This did not happen and Silk decided to build his own engine loosely based on the Scott two-stroke. Design assistance was given by David Minglow and the two looked at eliminating the bad aspects of the current two-stroke engines and maximizing the good aspects. When the design was complete, the pair sent the finished engine to Dr Gordon Blair at Queen's University, Belfast, Ireland, where the porting could be optimized and the performance checked by computer. The engine was a water-cooled, 656cc twin and had a top speed of around 115 mph.

The first Silk machine, the 700S, was produced in 1976 and was accompanied by the SPR production racer. There was no doubt that these machines were innovative, reliable, eco-

nomical and fast. There were other prototypes in hand, such as a trial 350cc and ideas for a larger capacity two-stroke. The British motorcycle business, however, was in trouble. A lot of companies had gone under and larger component suppliers were uneasy about selling the odd part here and there to a fledgling enterprise. Components were being bought by Silk in small quantities, which proved expensive. Silk had been taken over by Furmanite International in 1976. Furmanite soon called a halt to Silk production, and the last machine came off the line in December 1979.

Certainly the Silk instrumentation was more than adequate.

The Silk liquid-cooled unit derived from a Scott design from 1908.

One of the best handling machines of its day, the Silk 700.

Simplex

1899 - 1968

 There were several Simplex companies, but probably the Dutch Simplex company is the best-known. The story starts back in 1887 in Utrecht, Holland, when it was part of the Simplex Weighing Machine Company set up to build bicycles. The business did very well and as it expanded, the firm decided to move to Amsterdam in 1892.

Reorganization brought about the NV Rijwielfabriek Simplex – Simplex Bicycle Factory Ltd – which was founded in 1896. The name was changed again in 1899 to NV Machine Rijwiel-en Automobielfabriek Simplex when the company started producing motor cars. Three years later, a motorcycle appeared, taking the traditional lines of machines of the day: a Minerva engine was attached to the downtube of a bicycle frame, followed in 1903 by a machine that had the Minerva engine fitted between the front and rear downtubes in the now traditional 'Werner' fashion. By 1905, the company was building water-cooled, three-wheelers and a forecar.

Holland experienced a recession in 1907, but the company struggled on, making motorcycles, bicycles, motorcars and even special vehicles for the railways. During this period the company also changed its engine supplier, using the Fafnir Company in Aachen, Germany.

By 1911, Simplex was able to introduce three new models, a 5-6hp V-twin, a 2hp and a 4 1/4hp single. In 1913, it changed supplier again, this time to the Motosacoche MAG, buying company units for both singles and V-twin models.

As the First World War deepened, the company ceased making motorcars and concentrated on bicycle and motorcycle production. After the war, not only did sales increase, but four machines and their riders gained gold medals at the Anglo-Dutch Trials of 1921, and took of advantage of the publicity by exhibiting five models at the RAI exhibition in 1922.

These were 1100cc, 750cc, 600c and 500cc twin cylinder models, along with a 300cc single cylinder machine. All were powered by MAG engines.

In 1925, the company introduced a 350cc, Blackburn-engined machine, which could be bought in ohv or sv design. There was also a Bradshaw 350cc version, of which only three were made.

At the beginning of the 1930s, Simplex moved into the lightweight sector and started constructing a small-capacity machine using a German Sachs 72cc engine, which was subsequently replaced by a 98cc unit. During the mid-1930s, Simplex tied up with Villiers and produced several machines with its engines, ranging from a 98cc to a water-cooled, 248cc unit.

Following the Second World War, the company returned to making bicycles and mopeds. It finally merged with the Locomotif Company, which also made mopeds. All went well for a while, but then another merger was took place with the Dutch Juncker organization. Finally, the whole consortium was taken over by Gazelle in 1968 and the Simplex name disappeared.

A beautiful poster depicting a Simplex rider.

Singer

1900 - 1915

The Englishmen Perks and Birch made power wheels which could be fitted to either the rear wheel of a bicycle or the front wheel of a tricycle. At the beginning of the 1900s, this was quite unique and allowed bicycles and tricycles to be instantly motorized. In October 1900, Perks and Birch sold the manufacturing rights of the wheel to the Singer Cycle Company of Coventry, England.

Singer modified the wheel so that it drove forward to the pedal shaft and then back again to the rear wheel, using a chain. Accessibility was also improved by making the spokes large only on one side of the wheel. These wheels continued to be sold right up to 1904, but more conventional machines were produced with their engines between the two downtubes.

Singer ceased motorcycle production for a while, but came back again in 1909 with their Moto-Velo, followed in 1911 by a larger machine using a 299cc engine and a 535cc, sv single and intended mainly for side-car use. George E.Stanley took one of the 499cc singles with direct belt drive to Brooklands in 1912. There he managed to break the one-hour record,

increasing it again at a later date from 67 mph to 75 mph. The company also entered the TT, but without great fortune. In 1913, there was an open frame lady's variant of the 299cc machine, while the big single had been upgraded to 560cc.

The company also aided Stanley's bold attempt at the Brooklands Six Hour Race of 1913. Once again, the 'Wizard,' as he was known, came away with great success. Even though he retired prematurely, Singer was the first rider of a 350cc model to cover over sixty miles in an hour.

Just before the war, a new, 350cc two-stroke of the company's own design and make was introduced, but was short-lived. The war stopped further record and racing attempts. After hostilities, however, Singer went to the TT again, although without great success. Then the com-

The Singer used a 299cc, single-cylinder, four-stroke unit.

A light and sturdy 1911 model. It was beautifully engineered and all components were made in-house.

pany decided to concentrate on the manufacture of motorcars and no more motorcycles were made.

A complicated gear change mechanism.

High handlebars and hand gearchange: a 1912 Singer.

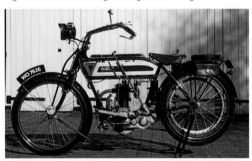

The 500cc, single cylinder engine unit of the 1912 Singer.

Standard

1825 - 1951

Wilhelm Gutbrod had been with the Klotz factory when it floundered in 1925. He then went on to start his own company, calling it Standard. Initially, he fitted 248cc and 348cc JAP engines to the machines, but changed to Swiss MAG engines in the late 1920s. These ranged from small singles to large V-twins.

In 1929, the factory produced 347cc and 497cc racing models with MAG ohc engines, along with a few 998cc racing V-twins. In the 1920s, the company bought the Swiss Zehnder factory and continued making well-respected lightweights in Switzerland. Another Swiss company Standard owned was also building larger capacity machines, including a 846cc V-twin using a MAG sv engine.

In 1930, Standard began making its own

The Standard BS 500 model introduced in 1932.

The BS500 used a MAG, 497cc, four-stroke, single cylinder engine.

This is a single seater Standard Rex Sport of 1935 vintage.

The 491cc engine pushed out 22hp and the machine could reach 81 mph.

The hand gear-lever, seen here, worked the Hurtl gearbox.

198cc and 248cc, single cylinder engines for the machines. During the late 1930s, it started building cars and 198cc and 248cc two-strokes. Swiss-built versions of the popular German Standard models also appeared in the 1930s, but unfortunately, Gutbrod died soon after the Second World War. His son took over the reins of the company, but chose to concentrate on making light cars and agricultural machinery such as lawnmowers.

Sunbeam

1912 - 1957

John Marston was born in 1836 in Ludlow, England, to a minor landowning family. He was sent to Wolverhampton at the age of 15 to be apprenticed to Edward Perry as a japanware manufacturer. When he was 23 years old, he left and set up his own japanning business, making any and every sort of domestic article. He did so well that when Perry died in 1871, Marston took over his company and incorporated it in his own.

He moved into making bicycles with great success, and on the suggestion of his wife Ellen, adopted the brand name Sunbeam. (The Paul Street works were called Sunbeamland.) He then started to make cars, but his business suffered from the slump affecting car manufacturers and eventually pushed Marston into making motorcycles.

Marston personally disapproved of motorcycles, which he considered dangerous, but the demand was high and he made thousands. He never rode one and he never drove a car. He was a dedicated cyclist nearly all his life, most often using a tricycle. A good businessman, and a harsh employer (workers who made a mistake were bluntly told 'Get your jacket!') he lived most of his adult life in The Oaks, on Merridale Road, Wolverhampton.

In 1903 and 1904, John Marston Ltd. carried out some experiments fitting engines to bicycles, but most were unsuccessful. John Marston's aversion to motorcycles did not encourage further development, and the company started to produce cars well before it produced motorcycles. The first motorcycle appeared in 1912 when Marston was 76.

John Greenwood, formerly of Rover and JAP, was engaged to develop a suitable machine and Harry Stevens (later of AJS) was engaged as a consultant. Harry did the mechanical design work and developed a single side-

This beautiful 1915 Sunbeam Solo is on show at the Black Country Museum, Dudley England.

The engine of the Light Solo is a 493cc, sv. 3.5hp unit.

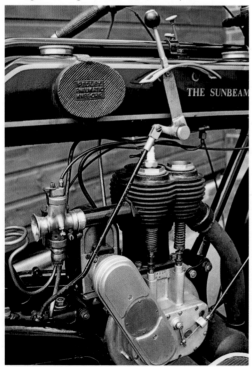

design was to place the magneto at the rear and use a Renold chain, running in a little oil bath chain case, connected to a Sharp divided rear axle. The exhaust pipe led to a 'pepperpot' type silencer and was finished in the usual Sunbeam black. The early gas tanks were finished in green with a silver panel bearing the Sunbeam name.

The first machines appeared in 1912 and were hand-built. Almost immediately, the machines featured in competitions and were very successful. Two Sunbeam machines won gold medals in the London-Exeter-London trial in December 1912. The Sunbeam name soon became well-known to enthusiasts throughout the country.

Minor changes were made to the 1913 model and the familiar black and gold-lined finish made its appearance. June saw the launch of a 6hp machine powered by a JAP twin engine. It had a three-speed gearbox and was similar in design to the 2.75hp machine, but with a larger and stronger frame. Then in September, a 3.5hp machine was launched. A Sharp divided axle was fitted to the rear wheel, which allowed the easy removal of the inner tube and the rear mudguard hinged upwards for easy removal of the rear wheel.

valve, 349cc, 2.75hp engine with a two-speed transmission and forward-mounted magneto. The only changes John Greenwood made to the

Sunbeam machines were entered in many sporting competitions while employees John Greenwood, Tommy De La Hay and Howard Davies became familiar figures at the events and won many medals. Over the summer of 1913, Sunbeam machines were ridden up three mountains for a publicity exercise. Snowdon was climbed on 6 June, Ben Nevis on 13 July and Mount Tosari, in Java, was climbed a little later. It was altogether a successful year and sales were good.

For the rider, visibility was at a premium.

The 1918 Sunbeam was used by the French troops during the First World War. It had a 550cc engine.

The first two Sunbeam sidecars made their appearance in 1914. The 3.5hp machine was named Gloria Number 1 and the 6hp machine Gloria Number 2.

Sunbeam's success in sporting events continued. Tommy De La Hay and John Greenwood, riding 6hp machines, won gold medals in the Midland Reliability Trial, while Vernon Dudley, Charlie Nokes and Joe Dudley won awards on the 3.5hp machines. The best result of the year was achieved by Howard Davies, who came in second in the senior TT. Sunbeam also won the team prize the same year.

At the outbreak of the First World War, Sunbeam started to develop machines for use in the armed services. The 3.5hp machine was modified and given an improved magneto drive. A new gearbox was fitted with constant-mesh gears and the fuel tank had three separate compartments, one contained gas, another contained oil and the third contained paraffin. The machines were finished in matte khaki with black lining and gold lettering.

In 1915, it was becoming difficult to obtain JAP engines due to sales to the War Department and so the 6hp machine was modified to accept a Sunbeam 6hp twin engine and then also sold to the War Department for service in Russia and Italy. Sunbeam also launched two new sidecars, Number 1 and Number 2. They were built by Charles Hayward, who later joined AJS. Nine gold medals were won by Sunbeam in the 1915 Style Cop hill climb, thanks to the efforts of George Dance on a newly developed 4hp single.

In 1916, large numbers of Sunbeam motorcycles were supplied to the Russian army for use on the Eastern front. A new 8hp twin with a three compartment fuel tank was developed fitted with a machine gun and armored sidecar. The machines were powered by a Swiss 996cc MAG engine and had Brampton 'Biflex' forks. The sidecar was also produced as an ambulance (stretcher carrier) and there was even a double-decker version. At the same time, a 4hp and later a 3.5hp belt drive version was sold to the French army. On 3 November 1916, the Ministry of Munitions suspended civilian production for the duration of the war and so Sunbeam had to rely on War Department contracts. The company stepped up production of vehicle and aircraft radiators, which were needed in large quantities.

1918 was a sad year for the Marston family. John Marston's third son, Roland, died at the early age of 45. He had been groomed as his father's successor and his untimely death came as a great shock to his parents. At the time, John and Ellen were staying at their house at Colwyn Bay. The loss was too much for John, who died on the 8 March, the day after Roland's funeral. Ellen died just six weeks later.

The armistice was signed on 11 November 1918 and all fighting ceased. The government immediately cancelled the surviving wartime contracts and ex-Sunbeam men returning from the war found themselves on a waiting list for their former jobs, which had been filled in their absence.

By 1918, JAP engines were available again and so the 8hp MAG engine was replaced with a JAP equivalent which gave the machine an extra 4 in ground clearance. John Marston's eldest son, Charles, was in charge at Villiers and rapidly expanding the highly profitable Villiers works. When faced with a claim for death duties

after has father's death, he sold John Marston Limited to a consortium of wartime munitions manufacturers who had done well in the war and were looking to invest their money. In 1919, the consortium was taken over and became part of Nobel Industries Limited. Civilian production was again authorized by the government.

Sunbeam quickly produced a new catalogue, which included the new 3.5hp Sporting Model, which was nearly identical to the WD 3.5hp model. There was also a 3.5hp Standard model. There was a new 8hp machine, which was basically the 8hp, JAP-powered, WD machine.

The new models were well-received by the public, while the press considered them the handsomest machines on the road. The 3.5hp single was even described as the Rolls Royce of singles. Motorcycle sporting events restarted in 1919, with competitions being dominated by Sunbeam riders such as George Dance, Tommy De La Hay and John Greenwood.

Celebrating the 1921 TT: the Sunbeam Sporting TT replica.

The engine of the TT race replica was a 499cc, 3.5hp unit.

A new Sunbeam range was developed for 1920. The new machines included the famous laminated leaf spring front fork, an important feature of future Sunbeam machines. Larger cylinder cooling fins were introduced along with drum brakes on the 3.5hp model. Detachable and interchangeable wheels were also introduced.

1920 was important for the Sunbeam competition team. The company achieved its first TT victory when Tommy De La Hay came first in the Senior Race at an average speed of 51.79 mph. W.R. Brown came third on a similar machine and George Dance had the fastest lap at nearly 56 mph.

The 1921 catalogue included three versions of the 3.5hp model, the Standard, the Semi-Sporting and the Sporting Solo Sunbeam TT Model. Prices reached an all-time high, but soon began to fall as ex-WD machines became available to the general public, which caused a lot of problems in the industry. Many manufacturers suffered from over-production when the motorcycle-buying public snapped up these ex-WD bargains in preference to new machines. In 1921, George Dance made a series of superb runs at Brooklands. In the 350cc class, he set a new record at 82.25 mph in the Flying Kilometer and achieved 82.19 mph in the Flying Mile. In the 500cc class, he achieved 93.99 mph in the Flying Kilometer, 87.35 mph in the Flying Five Miles and 82.69 mph in the Standing Ten Miles.

Two new models were introduced in 1922: the Longstroke TT 3.5hp machine and the 4.25hp Sunbeam, which was mainly sold as a combi-

This 1923, 350cc, Sport model is still seen on race circuits today.

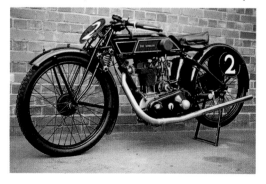

nation. Sunbeam gained its second TT win in the Senior Race with Alec Bennett in the saddle. In 1924, the 8hp twin was discontinued and a new model numbering system introduced.

In the 1920s, sprint meetings were a very popular form of motorcycle sport. They were often held on a public road which was closed for the event. George Dance made quite a name for himself in the post-1918 years, with sprint and hill climb machines based on standard 350cc and 500cc Sunbeams with cut-down frames. The Sprint models were discontinued.

In 1927, Nobel Industries amalgamated with Brunner Mond Ltd. to form ICI, a vast con-

Low-slung and with short rear mudguard: a 1926 Sprint model.

The Sprint model has a single cylinder, 500cc, ohv engine.

glomerate of which John Marston Ltd. was but a small part. However, the Depression hit hard and motorbike sales slumped. The Elms works on the Penn Road opened in 1928. The buildings contained the Service and Spares Department

TT races are often celebrated with replicas like the 1928 machine.

The 1928 replica used this 493cc, TT90, ohv engine unit.

run by Joe Dudley, the stores run by Freddie Simpson, the Competition Department, the canteen and the Social Club and offices. This was another good year for the Sunbeam racing team as the company gained its third TT win when Charlie Dodson came first in the Senior Race at an average speed of 62.98 mph.

In 1929, Sunbeam finally adopted the saddle tank invented by Howard Davies in 1924 and Charlie Dodson won the Senior TT for the second year running, making the fastest lap in 30 minutes and 47 seconds at a record speed of 73.55 mph. Teammate Alec Bennett came second and Arthur Simcock finished in seventh. To cap it all, Sunbeam also won the team prize for the third year in succession. Sadly, this was the

company's last successful TT and 1930 started badly. Sales were decreasing because of the Depression and a new range of models was announced in preparation for the Motorcycle Show.

The Model 6 Longstroke was restyled and called the Lion after one of the ICI trademarks.

Reputed to be Charlie Dobson's machine, this is a model 90 TT machine from 1930.

As the Depression hit, engines became smaller. This is a 1931 model 10.

The design of the fuel tank was a departure from usual Sunbeam practice and the soldered gas tank was replaced by a welded, crome-plated tank. The new 344cc Model 10 had an overhead valve single engine and was designed by Stephenson and Greenwood.

The 1931 catalogue listed just four models: the Model 19, Model 9, Model 90 and the Lion. Prices were reduced due to the continuing economic depression. Sunbeam continued to take part in trials events, but racing was discontinued. In 1932, only minor changes were made to the models. New, detachable and interchangeable wheels were fitted to all models along with a four-speed, constant mesh gearbox. Sales continued to decrease and more economies were introduced at the works. The Model 10 was dropped in 1933 and the old 350cc Model 8 reappeared. Sales were still decreasing and a re-assessment of the cycle and motorcycle production was started at the works. The writing was on the wall.

At the 1934 Motor Cycle Show, Sunbeam introduced the 'High Camshaft' Model 16 designed by George Stephenson with a duplex cradle frame and a Burman gearbox. It was powered by a 249cc engine. In 1935, ICI looked to sell their two-wheeled subsidiaries and Associ-

The engine of this model 10 was a 344cc, ohv unit.

ated Motor Cycles Ltd. bought the bicycle and motorcycle business in 1936. That is, they bought the goodwill, the brand name and the dealer network. They formed two new companies, Sunbeam Bicycles Ltd. and Sunbeam

Seen here is a 1934 Sunbeam, model 9, with 598cc, ohv engine.

Motor Cycles Ltd., and moved production to London. ICI absorbed the whole of the cycle and motorcycle workforce into large-scale radiator production.

After the Second World War, Sunbeam did not reappear until 1947 when it introduced a completely new machine, the S7, which used a longitudinally fitted, twin cylinder engine with shaft drive. There was a lot of interest, but not too many sales. The follow-up S8 never caught the public's attention and the Sunbeam name had disappeared by 1957.

The ignition key hole and amp guage were just below the seat.

The first post-war machine was the S7. This is a 1954 version.

The handsome and conventional 1952, 487cc, S8, ironed out many of the S7's problems.

Suzuki

1952 - date

Suzuki was originally a textile engineering company. It was founded in 1909 as the Suzuki Loom Works by Michio Suzuki in Hamamatsu, Shizuoka Pref., Japan. In 1920, it was reorganized, incorporated and capitalized at 500,000 yen as the Suzuki Loom Manufacturing Co. Michio Suzuki was voted president. The company goal was to produce the best, most user-friendly weaving looms in the world.

The production of motorcycles started in 1952, when the company built the 36cc, two-stroke, Power Free, motorized bicycle. It was not long before it was fitted with a two-speed transmission joined by a slightly more power-

The first cyclemotor made was a 36cc engine named "Power Free."

In 1953, a new model, the 58cc "Diamond Free" was introduced.

ful, 60cc version called the Diamond Free. This machine was simple and easy to maintain and the engine was mounted on the front wheel of a bicycle. But in 1954, Suzuki made its first real motorcycle, the Colleda. At this time, it was producing 6000 motorcycles a month, and developing bigger, more powerful machines. The Colleda was a lightweight, 90cc, single cylinder four-stroke and it won a national Japanese race in its first year of production, which made it an instant success and ensured its future.

Suzuki Loom Manufacturing Company presented the single cylinder, side-valve Colleda in 1954. The first real Suzuki motorcycle.

In 1954, the company changed its name once more to Suzuki Motor Company Limited, promptly entering a period of phenomenal growth. The Colleda series of machines was upgraded and newer and bigger specification engines produced. In addition to two-stroke engines, the company produced outboard motors, light 4x4s, cars, bicycles, motorboats and even prefabricated housing units.

Suzuki started racing in Europe in 1960 in the smaller classes. In 1962, it won the first ever, 50cc Grand Prix World Championship. A year later, the company won the title again, as well as the 50cc class at the Isle of Man TT.

In October 1967, the 500cc Titan road bike was introduced. During its 11 year production period, it was known as the Cobra, the Titan and the Charger and it finally finished in production as the GT500. It used a 500cc twin cylinder, two-stroke engine. Suzuki started competing in off-road events. In the World Motocross Championships, long dominated by European makes, it won the 1971 500cc title with rider Roger

This 1968 SuzukiTC 305 was also known as the Laredo.

DeCoster. The Belgian and his bright yellow Suzukis won the World Championship four more times: 1972, 1973, 1975 and 1976. Suzuki extended its Motocross success with an incredible string of victories in the 125cc World Championship, winning the eight quart title

The Stinger engine was a 125cc, twin cylinder unit.

Twin carburettors fed the 305cc engine of the Laredo.

The 1969 T125 Stinger had a 124 cc, air-cooled, dual carburettor, two-stroke, parallel twin engine.

The ideal environment for a 250cc Trail machine from 1978.

from 1975 to 1984. Brad Lackey became America's first 500cc World Motocross Champion on his works Suzuki in 1982.

By 1970, Suzuki was racing teams and riders such as Barry Sheene, soon to become a riding legend. He won two straight World Championships aboard the exotic RG500 Square Four and, with Italians Marco Lucchinelli and Franco Uncini at the helm, the machine went on to two more title wins in 1981 and 1982.

Suzuki initially concentrated on two-stroke production, but was forced to add four-strokes to its range because of the increasingly stringent emissions regulations in the United States, one of Suzuki's largest export markets. By now the company had plants in Malaysia, Taiwan, Indonesia, the Philippines, Mozambique and Nigeria.

In 1971, the GT750 was marketed. This was a liquid-cooled, two-stroke, in-line triple that could reach 60 mph in around five seconds. It was typical of the time, with disc front brakes and a drum rear spoked wheel. Its water-cooling system earned the GT750 the nickname 'Kettle' in Britain and 'Water Buffalo' in the United States. (However, it was outlawed in the United States after 1977 because of emission regulations.)

In 1976, the RG500 appeared. It was a two-stroke race bike which took Barry Sheene to World Championships two years in a row. It earned John Williams numerous Isle of Man TT wins as well victories for Mick Grant, Mike Hailwood and Phil Read. Suzuki gained considerable knowledge of two-strokes when Erst Degner, MZ's leading rider, defected from East Germany taking many of Walter Kaaden's secrets with him.

The water-cooled GT750 acquired many nicknames, including 'the kettle,' because of its problems with cooling.

1977 was the last year of production for RE5. The model was introduced in 1974. It was powered by a Wankel Rotary engine and was innovative for its time. Unusual features included a cylindrical instrument binnacle which rotated open when the ignition was switched on. In many other ways, however, it was conventional, based on a tubular steel swinging arm frame and telescopic forks. The 1977 four-stroke range introduced by Suzuki to ensure success in its export markets can be identified by the GS designation. Models such as the GS1000cc, the 850cc, the 750cc, the 500cc and the 400cc appeared over a number of years.

Graeme Crosby on his Heron Suzuki at the 1980 transatlantic races.

Another 1980 designation was GSX. This identified a double overhead camshaft and a four-stroke, 16-valve engine. However, it was produced in various engine sizes. The GSX 1100

The 1978 GS1000 was a beautiful and very fast machine for its time.

was the largest of the models introduced. It had cast alloy wheels, disc brakes back and front and boasted a very high performance.

In 1982, Suzuki produced the Katana range of machines. The GSX1100S, as it was designated, was available in various sizes including 997cc and 1074cc. It was to prove a high performance sports bike.

Designation GSX meant double overhead cams. This is a 1981 1100 model.

In 1986, Suzuki originated the mass-production repli-racer Superbike with the revolutionary GSX-R750. Such a 'racy' bike had never been offered to such a wide range of riders. The first GSX-R was distinguished by its full fairing, a then-unusual, square-tube, aluminum frame and design features that made it the lightest bike by far in its class. Many riders of the period honed their skills on the GSX-R and some rode to championships and even Daytona glory. For example, Kevin Schwantz won the Daytona 200-miler in 1988 and numerous other Superbike races on his GSX-R. Jamie James added to the Superbike championship tally with a title win in 1989 and Suzuki started its long-time ownership of the near-stock AMA 750cc Supersport Series.

In the 1990s, Japanese motorcycle factories started building custom-designed, American motorcycles, a move prompted by the renaissance of the Harley-Davidson mark.

Suzuki joined in and built the Intruder series. Like its other bikes, the Intruder was built in a variety of engine displacements including 750cc, the larger 1360cc variant and the VS1400GL. The engine was a V-twin with shaft

The Bandit started out as a 600cc machine. This is the 1200.

The Bandit has an 1157cc, DOHC, 16-valve, four-stroke, inline-4 engine.

drive and a typical upright riding position. Off-road, under the guidance of Roger DeCoster, now motocross team manager, Suzuki claimed many podium spots and World Championships both in Europe and the United States.

The Suzuki DR350, introduced in 1993, was a dual purpose trail bike designed for both on and off-road use. Powered by a single cylinder, four-valve engine, it features long travel suspension and disc brakes front and rear. The year also saw the introduction of the RM250, supplied race-ready. It used a water-cooled, 250cc, engine and was extremely light. In 1995, the Bandit 600cc was offered for sale. It had a very upright riding position and little in the way of bodywork. It was soon joined by a semi-faired version and larger engines. In 1998, Suzuki, although already producing scooters, came up

with the Bergman model, which used a 250cc engine and was not only comfortable, but had some kick to it. As if this was not powerful enough, the following year saw the introduction of the 400cc version. Then, in 1999, came the outrageous Hayabusa GSX1300R, which could reach a staggering top speed of 200 mph. In late

The Hayabusa could reach a stunning top speed of over 200 mph.

The AY50, has a liquid-cooled, direct-injection, two-stroke, 50cc unit.

1999, the SV600cc model was introduced, followed by a larger, 1000cc brother unlike the semi-faired 600.

Suzuki has produced an array of new machines for the new century. The company now caters for all kinds of riders and makes all-purpose bikes. From the powerful GSXR1000 to the VZ1600cc Intruder cruiser, from the latest Bergman 650 Executive scooter to the Van Van 125cc and the smallest AY50A Katana scooter…. Take your pick!

The Burgman AN650 Super scooter has a 2-cylinder, 4-stroke, 638cc unit.

The Suzuki GSX-R1000 has gone through years of development and is one of the best-looking, fastest machines on the road today.

Motovision Suzuki team member, Tanel Leok, in action on his RM250.

Terrot

1901- 1961

Terrot motocycles were founded in 1901 in Dijon, France, by Charles Terrot. At one point, the company was the largest motorcycle producer in France. In the 1920s, Terrot also acquired Magnat Debon, another French motorcycle manufacturer. The company produced 98cc, 174cc and 246cc two-stroke, side-valve machines and 246cc to 746cc, ohv models. Proprietary engines were fitted over the years from Bruneaux, Dufaux, JAP, MAG, Zedel and even Blackburne. In 1937, a 498cc machine was produced with a transverse mounted V-twin engine, and was used by the works race team.

After the Second World War, Terrot continued to produce ohv models up to 498cc and two-strokes including scooters. In the 1950s, the firm was brought into Automoto, which was part of the Peugeot group. Production under the Terrot name ceased in 1961.

A beautiful period advertisement for the four-stroke Terrot.

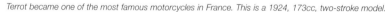
Terrot became one of the most famous motorcycles in France. This is a 1924, 173cc, two-stroke model.

Tornax

1926 - 1955

Ernst Wever, from Wuppertal in Germany, started the Tornax motorcycle company in 1926. Inspired by the British machines of the period, he decided to use a 600cc, 18hp, JAP engine for his first machine designed with Petrol Karpe.

When the Nazis came to power, it became increasingly difficult to obtain parts from other countries and therefore, local engines were used. One machine that became very popular was the Tornado model with its 800cc Columbus parallel twin engine. Other larger capacity machines up to 1000cc were produced before the Second World War.

Between 1950 and 1955, Tornax concentrated on everyday machines with two-stroke engines supplied by Sachs and Ilo. Possibly the best-known was the Tornax S250cc. The rounded rear fender of this machine earned it the nickname 'Black Josephine,' a reference to the shapely behind of the black dancer, Josephine Baker.

Tornax also built racing machines, the last of which was a 1952 124cc single which used a Kuchen engine. Most of the JAP-engined racing machines were V-twin, 746cc and 998cc units. They were ridden successfully by a number of riders including Kurten, Gosse, Theisen, Hobelmann and Ehrlenbruch. The company closed in 1955.

The speedometer was inlaid in the fuel tank.

This 1934 Tornax used a JAP, 592cc engine coupled to a Hermes gearbox. It was capable of a top speed of 111 mph.

Triumph

1902 - date

The seed of what was to become one of the most famous names m motorcycling was planted in the late nineteenth century when German business-man Siegfried Bettmann made his way to England from Nuremberg. At first involved in the sale of sewing machines, Bettmann was impressed with the craze for bicycles that was sweeping Victorian Britain and decided to set up his own firm, selling bikes made in Birmingham by William Andrews.

Rather than call them 'Bettmanns,' the shrewd industrialist chose 'Triumph,' as a name that would be understood in all European languages. In 1887, two years after he started his enterprise, Bettmann was joined by engineer Mauritz Schulte, also from Nuremburg. Both decided that the brightest future lay in manufacturing their own machines and Schulte found suitable

The 1905 triumph 3 1/3 was little more than a heavyweight bicycle with a 363cc engine fitted to it.

The single cylinder, four-stroke machine could do about 50 mph.

premises in Coventry, where production started in 1889.

As the turn of the century approached and the internal combustion engine began to make an impact, Schulte considered the next step for the Triumph Cycle Co.

In 1902, the first motorcycle emerged from Triumph's Coventry works. Known as 'No 1,' it was essentially a strengthened bicycle with a 2.25bhp Minerva engine hung from the front downtube. Drive functioned through a belt from the engine's crankshaft to the rear wheel while the bicycle's pedals, chain and crank were retained. Schulte chose the Belgian-made Minerva engine.

By 1905, Schulte, in collaboration with Triumph Works' Manager, Charles Hathaway, himself a gifted designer and motorcyclist, produced an entirely in-house machine, the Model 3HP. Featuring a 363cc, single cylinder, side-valve engine, it was claimed the Model 3HP produced a heady 3hp at 1,500 rpm and had a top speed of around 45 mph. In 1906, Triumph equipped their bike with a controversial 'rocking' front fork, which pivoted

The reliable 3 1/3hp, sv, four-stroke engine of the 1913 model.

around the bottom crown against the springs at the top.

By 1908, the Triumph engine was displacing 476cc, putting out 3.5HP and equipped with a 'variable pulley' to deal with difficult inclines. An Isle of Man TT victory in 1908, with Jack Marshal in the saddle, helped underline Triumph's reliability and road worthiness. As was said at the time, 'Eight Triumph's started, and eight finished…'

In 1910, a new advance was made to make riding a Triumph even easier: the 'free engine' device. Essentially a small, foot-operated, wet drum clutch which meant that the engine could be started with the bike on its main stand, via the pedals. Once the engine was fired, the clutch could be disengaged, the bike placed on its wheels and the rear hub clutch selected for forward motion.

In 1911, the TT races moved to its present home on the 37.5 mile Mountain Circuit and although Triumph's performed well, they struggled against the mighty Indians. However, many other records were set by Triumph motorcycles in 1911, including the 900 mile Land's End to John O'Groats run, which Ivan Hart-Davies rode in 29 hours 12 minutes at an average speed

The 3 1/2HP model acquired a good reputation and within a year of its 1907 launch, it was selling 3000 per year.

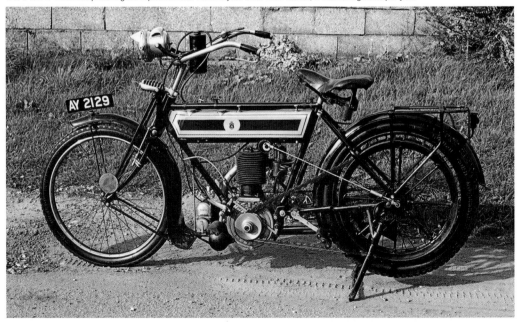

of 30 mph. Hart-Davies used a specially prepared bike with a huge fuel tank, but considering the almost medieval roads and lack of suspension, it was quite a feat.

By the outbreak of the First World War, the Type A had a 550cc engine slugging out 4bhp. The British Government placed orders with Triumph and the now legendary Triumph Type H

The single cylinder, 494cc engine of the 1926 'P' type machine.

was pressed into service from late 1914 onwards. It was the first Triumph without pedals. The Type H proved wholly reliable in the face of the mud and misery that existed for its riders in the Great War and earned itself the nickname 'the Trusty.' Schulte parted company with Triumph in 1919 after disagreeing with Bettmann's desire to diversify.

Deciding to diversify Triumph's manufacturing base, Triumph purchased the deserted Hillman car factory in Coventry early in the 1920s and started producing a 1.4 liter saloon car. On the motorcycle front, two years after the end of hostilities in Europe, Triumph unveiled another evolutionary motorcycle. The Type SD, which stood for 'Spring Drive,' its clutch now featured a shock absorber in the transmission. More importantly, it dispensed with the belt final drive of all previous models – the rear wheel was now chain driven.

With a capacity of 550cc, the Type SD was too big to enter the Senior TT and Triumph fielded six bikes, with all-new single cylinder engines of 500cc capacity, in 1921. Harry Ricardo, of Ricardo & Co Ltd, designed the cylinder head and barrel which featured four overhead valves set 90° degrees apart, pushrod

The 1926 'P' type had a hand gear selector and chain drive. It cost about £43 new.

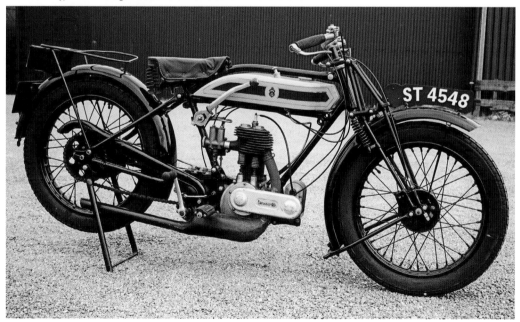

operated. The race was a disaster for Triumph. The 'Riccy,' as it became known, went on to collect many world speed records, including the flying mile at 83.91 mph.

But in spite of the high profile endeavors, the 1920s were not a great time for Triumph. In the face of global depression, the firm needed to generate income, so a cheap basic bike was developed. 20,000 of the side-valve, 494cc Model P were produced.

Towards the middle of the decade the Riccy was discontinued and another new engine, developed by Victor Horsman, was introduced in a new model. The TT or Two Valve, as it was called, displaced 498cc, with twin over head valves and a three-speed gearbox. The Two Valve became the mainstay of Triumph's range and proved a very worthy design.

In 1927, Tommy Simister finished third in the Senior TT on one, in spite of crashing twice.

Until his death in 1934, Charles Sangster headed a large engineering company, Components Ltd., which owned Ariel, a firm with a reputation for building top quality motorcycles. Like Triumph, the Great Depression was drain-

ing Components Ltd of cash and in 1932, the company folded, but Jack, Charles' son, turned the Ariel business around. Triumph, meantime, was struggling, with cars proving extremely difficult to sell. Bicycles and motorcycles, still produced under the Triumph Cycle Co. guise, were held up for sacrifice. The pedal bike plant went first in 1932 and then four years later, Jack Sangster purchased the motorcycle division. Ironically, Val Page, an ex-Ariel man and extremely talented engine designer joined Triumph in 1932 and set about designing a brand-new range of bikes, including a whole host of varying capacity ohv and side-valve singles and a 650cc, ohv, vertical twin. Sangster immediately installed two of Page's Ariel ex-colleagues at the new Triumph Engineering Co Ltd - Edward Turner became Works' Manager and Bert Hopwood was appointed designer. 1937 proved a landmark year for Triumph with the launch of a range of revamped singles, known as Tigers, together with the 498cc Speed Twin Tl00. It had a reported top speed of over 90 mph, defining everything a modern motorcycle should be and the essence of the motor-

A beautifully restored Triumph model N of 1928.

Shown here is the handsome 1938 Speed Twin 5T.

The model N used a 494cc, single cylinder engine.

The Speed Twin engine, a 498cc parallel twin, four-stroke.

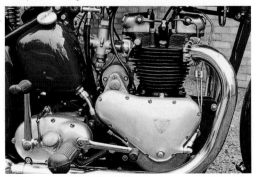

cycle Triumph would build for the next thirty years.

The outbreak of World War Two affected Triumph's commercial aspirations because all production was geared towards military production. The 343cc Model 3H became Triumph's warhorse and was renamed the 3HW for service application. A prototype 350cc twin, the 3TW, was on the blocks and approved as the standard service bike when, on the night of the 14 November 1940, the Triumph factory was completely demolished in the Coventry blitz.

Undaunted, motorcycle production resumed in temporary facilities in Warwick while a brand-new factory was built in Meriden. The new plant opened its doors in 1942.

The Tl00 impressed the American flat track racing community, proving itself repeatedly in competition in the late 1930s. Turner, sensing a business opportunity once hostilities finished, looked hard at the possibilities for Triumph motorcycles on the American market. The post-war range on sale consisted of three models: the Tiger 100, Speed Twin and the smaller, 'tour-

This 1948 GP model has an all alloy engine, racing megaphone silencers and sprung hub rear suspension.

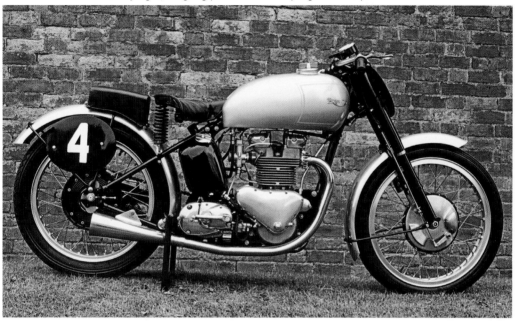

The Parallel twin engine of the 1948 Triumph GP 500.

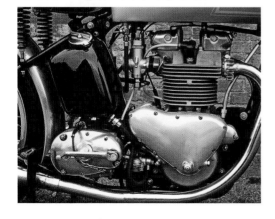

ing,' 349cc 3T. In 1946, Irishman Ernie Lyons won the Manx Grand Prix on a Tiger 100, beating a host of Norton's. 1949 saw in the same three bike line-up, but with the addition of the headlight and clocks enclosed and mounted in a nacelle, a feature unique at the time. Two additions as the decade drew to a close were the off-road 500cc Trophy, and the big bore 649cc Thunderbird, built in response to the constant American love for power.

The 1950s proved a golden decade for Triumph, even though they started with the sale of the firm to rivals BSA in 1951, to avoid crippling death duties. Sangster eventually took over

The 1959 Tiger Cub helped put many people on the road.

The Cub's single cylinder, four-stroke, 199cc engine could top 60 mph.

In 1954, the Tiger 110 was introduced. In essence a 'sports' makeover of the 649cc Thunderbird twin, it had swinging arm rear suspension and a bigger front brake. Two years later, Johnny Allen set a new world motorcycle speed record of 214.5 mph on the Bonneville Salt Flats, USA, using a 649cc Triumph engine in a streamlined vehicle. His record was rejected, due to alleged timing gear problems, but provided something that, for Triumph, would become invaluable.

Adding a pair of carburettors to the T110 and tuning the engine in 1959, created Triumph's most famous bike. The T120, or as it was called to commemorate Allen's speed run – the Bonneville – was the very essence of cafe-racer cool. The Bonneville had the right spartan look and, just as importantly, the performance to go with it.

The 1960s proved a fabulous decade for motorcycling in general and Triumph had a winning formula. The Bonneville was a fantastic success and was, without question, the definitive sports twin of the 1960s, both in Britain and in the United States. Competitive success at the TT and Daytona spawned a myriad of models.

Bert Hopwood returned to Triumph as Director in 1961, thanks to Turner's efforts. Turner was to retire eventually as chief executive of the BSA Group in 1964, but not before he got a glimpse of things to come after a trip to Japan. He was stunned by the ability of the Japanese to manufacture vast quantities and the speed with which they could research, design and produce a bike to very high standards. However, it was felt that the Japanese would always build small bikes. So if a motorcyclist wanted more power, they'd have to buy British.

the chairmanship of the BSA Group in 1956. Friendly competition continued between the two factories and a new breed of Triumph bike arrived in 1953 with the advent of the 149cc, ohv Terrier, which had a four-speed unit gearbox and the look of its larger siblings. The 199cc Tiger Cub followed a year later - essentially the same bike with a larger capacity. It proved massively popular and eventually (after two years), replaced the Terrier.

Shown here is a 1968 T120 Bonneville.

The 1969 Daytona: the fastest road-going 500 of its time.

The 1969 Daytona engine was a 490cc, twin-cylinder, four-stroke unit.

Although the seeds of disaster were being sown, sales of Triumph motorcycles at this time were very healthy. Harry Sturgeon, an ex-MD of a BSA group subsidiary, took over from Turner in 1967.

Eventually rumors of a Japanese 750cc machine could not be ignored and Sturgeon needed to know how his group was going to counter this new threat. As it happened, Hopwood and Doug Hele had been working quietly, without official sanction, on a three-cylinder, 750cc machine. The design was rushed through the prototype stage and became the Triumph Trident Tl50 and BSA Rocket Three.

The 1970s proved disastrous for Triumph. Sturgeon died three years after taking the helm and Lionel Jofeh, a man who, like Sturgeon, was on the 'outside' of the business, replaced him. He did not last long and was replaced by Brian Eustace. Management of the BSA group as a whole was in a state of flux, constantly changing and lacking a consistent strategy. Some of the emerging products were of dubious quality. Ironically, the three-cylinder motor was proving almost unbeatable on the race track and in its 'Slippery Sam' guise won many Formula 750 races as well as the Isle of Man Production TT five years in a row, from 1971-1975.

Throughout the 1960s, a healthy profit was generated, but times had changed. Thanks to the internal confusion and the rapid progress of the Japanese factories, Triumph was in deep trouble, with the BSA group recording a loss by 1971 of £8.5m. A year later, a £3.3m loss was posted and things were looking bleak. In July 1973, in a government sponsored move, a new company was formed Norton-Villiers-Triumph. Against the wishes of the Triumph workforce, Norton-Villiers-Triumph planned to move Triumph production to the BSA factory at Small Heath, Birmingham. As a result, the Meriden workers staged a sit-in that lasted almost two years. It finally ended in March 1975 when a workers'

The 1973 X75 Hurricane used a four-stroke, triple, 740cc engine.

co-operative was set up to manufacture the Bonneville in 750cc form, primarily for the American market.

Although there were some noteworthy bikes built during the period, the 1977 Bonneville

Time was running out for Triumph. This is the 1978 T140 'Bonnie.'

A beautiful machine, but the 1978 Tiger TR7RV was on borrowed time.

Jubilee Special and T140D Special with cast wheels, the writing was on the factory wall.

The Meriden factory closed its doors in early 1983. It seemed like the end of Triumph and the British motorcycle industry. Fortunately, it was not. Property developer and self-made millionaire John Bloor bought the Triumph name and a new, privately owned company – Triumph Motorcycles Limited – was born. Initially, the Devon-based firm, Racing Spares, which had previously been making parts for Triumph, were licensed to build the final incarnation of the Bonneville, principally to keep the Triumph mark alive while the new company laid plans for Triumph's return to the world stage.

A new factory was built in Hinckley, Leicestershire and by 1989, rumors were circulating. The new Triumphs would be totally different to

those before – three and four-cylinder, water-cooling engines with four-valves per cylinder and double overhead camshafts. In other words, they would be competitive with Japanese technology. Six brand-new Triumph motorcycles were unveiled to the bike industry and press at the Cologne Show in September 1990. Based on two different engine formats, these models – the unfaired Trident 750 and 900 Triples, the touring-oriented Trophy 900 triple and 1200 four

The 1995 Speed Triple: a modern machine for a new company.

and the sports-slanted Daytona 750 triple and 1000 four – employed a modular concept, meaning that many parts were common to all. Thoroughly modern in performance and technology, they were well-received in all quarters. The line up evolved in 1993 when Daytona grew in capacity, becoming a 900 triple and 1200 four. Soon after, a Triumph once again wore the name 'Tiger' on its tank, with the introduction of an off-road style, 900cc triple that won legions of fans. But it was the advent of the Speed Triple

The 1995 Thunderbird, with three-cylinder, 885cc engine.

The Daytona T595 rapidly established itself as a bike with the ability to compete with the best.

in 1994 that really caught the press and the public's imagination. Just as the hopped-up Thunderbird had metamorphosized into the Bonneville in the 1960s, the new Speed Triple captured a piece of cafe racer chic. It had a ton of character, plenty of performance and a raw look that was just right for the time. It also had its own one-make race series, which ensured that the public saw the potential of the Speed Triple on a racetrack.

Ever growing volumes meant the opportunity to evolve away from the modular concept and the T595 Daytona was launched to an expectant world in 1997. Dispensing with carburetors, its brand-new, three-cylinder engine used state-of-the-art fuel injection, a rarity at the time. It also had a chassis to match almost any production sports bike available, marking Triumph's ability not only to exist as a manufacturing entity, but to lead the way once again. Subsequently, the fuel-injected engine was adopted to power new versions of the Tiger and Speed Triple, together with the unveiling of a brand-new sports-touring machine, the Sprint ST.

The dawn of the twenty-first century saw Triumph build its 100,000th bike at the Hinckley plant and release two brand-new motorcycles.

The first, the sports middleweight TT600, met the Japanese manufacturers squarely on their turf. With a 599cc, fuel-injected, in-line, four cylinder engine and a chassis that won universal praise, the TT600 was and still is, the only non-Japanese contender in the class. Perhaps even bigger news for Triumph was the unveiling of the second new model, the Bonneville. An evocative, 790cc, air-cooled, parallel twin, the new Bonnie combined the look and feel of the

The all-new, naked-style 1999 Speed Triple.

legendary late 1960s T120. It was an immediate success, not only in Europe, but also in America. The cruiser-style Bonneville America followed hard on its heels, specifically designed for the American rider.

Then fate intervened again. Just as Triumph geared up for the busy coming season, the factory was devastated by fire. The blaze of 15 March 2002 saw the complete destruction of the chassis and final assembly lines and the injection molding area. The machine shops, engine assembly area and paint shop were affected by water, heat and corrosive soot. Almost six months to the day, the rebuilt factory was fully operational. Soon after, at the 2002 International Motorcycle Show in Birmingham, England, the four-cylinder Daytona 600 supersports bike was shown publicly for the very first time. Visually stunning and packed with state of the art technology, the Daytona 600 is the fruit of hard-earned knowledge and experience, gained from the TT60O.

The all-new 2002 Triumph Daytona being put through its paces.

A new Tiger was launched in 1999: a real all-terrain machine.

In 2004, Triumph continues to be a force in the motorcycling world, producing new models, coming up with new ideas and possessing an enviable array of machines. Take, for example, the Rocket Ill, the first production motorcycle to break the 2-liter barrier, or the Bonneville Thruxton, just to mention two. No doubt Triumph has many more surprises in store for us.

The name lives on: the 2002 Bonneville.

From the front and from the rear, the amazing Rocket III is the ultimate, classy cruiser.

Ural

1941- date

The Ural story begins in 1939. The Soviet Union knew it would soon be going to war and mobility would be of paramount importance. Discussions were held on what type of motorcycle the Red Army would need. One story goes that, after lengthy discussion, the BMW R71 motorcycle was chosen. Five units were covertly purchased through a third party, stripped and copied. A more likely story is that the BMW factory supplied the construction drawings and casting molds as a result of the Molotov-von Ribbentrop Pact which agreed on the transfer of German technology to the Soviet Union.

A factory was set up in Moscow to produce hundreds of Russian M-72 sidecar motorcycles. In 1941, the Nazis invaded Russia. Soviet strategists decided to move the motorcycle plant further east. The small trading town of Irbit, located on the fringe of the vast Siberian steppes in the Ural Mountains, was nicely removed from the bombing range. On 25 October 1942, the first batch of motorcycles was built. Throughout the war, a total of 9,799 M-72 motorcycles were delivered to the front.

After the war, the factory was further developed and the 30,000th motorcycle was produced in 1950. Over three million motorcycles, mainly sidecar outfits, have been produced.

The Ural machine was built for the military until the late 1950s, when another plant in the Ukraine took over that job and the Irbit Motorcycle Works (IMZ) began to make bikes for domestic market. The popularity of the outfits grew steadily and the plant was turned over to non-military production in the 1960s. The main products of the plant today are heavy-duty URAL sidecar motorcycles, designed for rough Russian roads and the custom Wolf.

Ural motorcycles use a four-stroke, air-cooled, flat-twin engine and a four-speed gear box with reverse gear and shaft drive. There are new solo models for the western markets, and water-cooled engines also available.

The future looks bright for IMZ. The bike is growing in reputation as an economic form of transport which is both fun to ride and easy to maintain.

1970s Ural with complete sidecar attachment.

The 2004 Ural with sidecar attachment and modern additions.

The 746cc, ohv, air-cooled, 45hp engine with electric and kick-start.

Velocette

1904- 1971

Johannes Gutgemann was the son of a merchant from Oberwinter, a German town on the banks of the Rhine. He moved to England after his father died and changed his name to Jack Taylor. He started a pill company named Isaac Taylor and Company, and expanded into bicycle manufacture, opening a small shop on Great Hampton Street in Birmingham. The meeting between him and another cycle maker, William Gue, led to Taylor, Gue and Company, manufacturing cycles under the Hampton name. The company grew and made other products, such as rickshaws and a prototype forecar.

A London company by the name of Kelecom Motors Ltd., had fallen on hard times and was taken over by Taylor Gue towards the end of 1904. Taylor Gue was already supplying Kelecom with frames for its single cylinder, 3hp Ormonde models. Only a year later, these machines were marketed under the Veloce name and a new 2hp engine was introduced. Unfortunately, this failed and the company went into liquidation in 1905.

John Taylor, however, did not lose faith in bicycles. He started a new company under the name of Veloce Ltd., and moved to premises near Spring Hill in Birmingham. Taylor's two sons, Percy and Eugene, decided to branch off on their own: one went to India and the other started to work as an apprentice at New Hudson. But a little later, the two brothers reunited to start New Veloce Motors and they produced a motor car in 1908. (The venture failed and in 1916, Veloce Ltd. absorbed New Veloce Motors as well.)

In 1908, John Taylor became interested in motorcycles again. With his two sons, he set to work on a new machine. Engines were to be the responsibility of the two brothers at the Spring Hill works and the frames and cycle parts would be made by John at the Fleet Street works. By 1909, the design of a 276cc, 2 1/2hp, four-stroke motorcycle was complete. It comprised many innovative features such as the overhung crankshaft, a hallmark of the later Velocettes. The public seemed reluctant to buy this innovative machine, and so the company decided to make a more conventional model, a 499cc machine with direct belt drive to the rear wheel. The new model would also carry the VMC – Veloce Motor Company – logo. Sales began to pick up and the company catalogue was able to advertise several options for the two machines.

In 1911, John Taylor took British citizenship, and changed his name to Goodman. Soon after, the company introduced a 206cc, two-stroke ladies model. It was also the first machine to carry the Velocette name and three models were available.

The First World War broke out soon after and the company started producing munitions for the war effort.

After the war, the company continued to supply the two-strokes, but only two of the three original models were available, the D1 and DL1. Their capacity was increased to 206cc and 220cc. They were followed up by two new models, the D2 and DL2. Three D2s were entered in the ACU Six Days' Trial, where they duly won three gold medals. Over the next few years, these machines were upgraded to include front

The little 1922, two-stroke, 220cc model. It had a top speed of 40 mph.

internal expanding brakes, a clutch and a kick-starter. Two sports models were introduced in 1922. Intended for racing, they had engines of 249cc. The following year, a Colonial model, with designation GC, was added for export. A side-car model was also introduced.

In 1924, the Model A, a two-speed, belt drive machine and the Model B, a three-speed, chain drive machine, were launched as economy models. Then, in 1925, the G-model range became the H model range, although the Ladies' models continued to be called Es.

In 1925, the company produced a 348cc, ohc prototype. Initially, it had the Veloce logo on the tank, but that was later changed to Velocette. Three model K machines, as they were known, were entered for the Junior TT that year, but results were poor. But the following year, Alec Bennet came in first on his 348cc machine, some 10 minutes ahead of the field. There were two more wins in 1928 and 1929. The K had been followed up by the KSS in 1925.

By now the company had move to Six Ways in Aston. However, as orders piled up because of the success achieved in the TT, it looked at

moving once again, this time to York Road, Hall Green. The late 1920s saw several new models introduced: an upgraded two-stroke model U, its supersport brother the USS, the KS, KE, and KES. There was the basic Model 32, with its blue gas tank and the KTT, a replica of the KSS. In 1930, the 249cc GTP model appeared, and the KTP was around for a year or so. The M series came three years later, the first of which was the MOV, a 248cc, high cam, four-stroke model. It was soon followed by a 349cc version, the MAC, which, in turn, was followed in 1935 by the 495cc MSS.

The single cylinder, ohc, four-stroke engine used in the 1929 KTT.

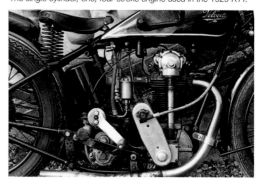

Modified for racing, this KTT left the factory in 1929 and took fourth place in the Manx GP the same year.

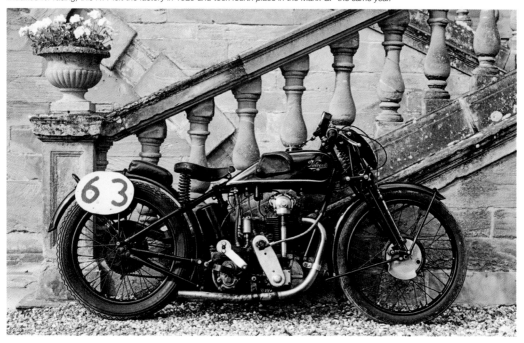

Shown here is a 1939 350 'cammy' KTS Mk II model

The instrumentation was minimal, but adequate.

On the sporting scene, 1939 saw the Mk VIII KTT model Velocette, ridden by Stanley Woods, win the Junior TT, where the supercharged 490cc Roarer racer also made a guest appearance. The Roarer never raced because work was disrupted by the Second World War and the FIM governing body banned superchargers after 1945, along with another development, known simply as the Model O, a 580cc parallel twin. During the war, the company supplied the French troops with the MAF model, a special version of the MAC. Later, these also

Instrumentation on the LE was at either side of the tank.

One of the best-known Velocette models is the LE. This one has a 192cc engine.

found their way to British troops in the Western Desert.

In 1946, the GTP was again produced and the MOV, MAC, MSS and KSS were also on the line-up. The following year saw Velocettes take the first four places in the Junior TT and in 1948, one of the most famous Velocettes of all time, the LE, was announced. It was unlike anything the company had produced previously, using a 149cc, water-cooled, flat-twin unit with shaft drive. Gearchange was achieved by hand and the machine had to be cranked to start. It was almost completely enclosed and had foot-boards and leg-shields. Unfortunately, the public never really took to it. It is widely remembered today as the main mode of transport for the local policeman.

The Velocette KTT series was a great success: the Mk VIII of 1949.

The single cylinder, ohc, 348cc engine of the 1949 KTT model.

In 1949 and 1950, Freddie Frith and Bob Foster took the 350cc World Championship on the ageing KTT. But Velocette were a spent force, and the race shop closed after the death of Percy Goodman in 1951. A scrambler and an endurance machine were announced in 1955 for the US market, and in 1956 there were two super sports machines, the Venom 500cc and Viper 350cc. This year saw the introduction of an up-rated LE called the Valiant, which was phased out in 1963, but not before the Vogue version was introduced.

A great feat was achieved when a Venom set the 24 hour world record for a 500 cc motorcycle, reaching 100.05 mph at the Monthlery banked circuit south of Paris in France on 18-19 March 1961.

One of the last great machines to come out of the factory at Hall Green was the Thruxton in 1964. One of the machines went on to win the Production TT in 1967. But, the company finances were not doing well. In February 1971, the company went into voluntary liquidation.

The Thruxton engine was a high-cam, ohv, four-stroke unit.

The very simple and compact 1967 Thruxton.

Victoria

1899- 1966

The Victoria bicycle factory was founded by Max Frankenburger and Max Ottenstein in Nuremberg, Germany. The company's first motorcycles appeared in 1912 and used proprietary engines from Fafnir and Zedel.

In the years between the two world wars, the company utilized BMW flat twins. But when BMW went into production of complete motorcycles in 1923, Victoria employed a former BMW designer, Martin Stolle. He went on to design several engines for the company.

By 1924, Victoria engines designed by Gustav Steinlein were good enough to break the German speed record and the company had added single cylinder models to its range. Many of these had advanced, pressed-steel frames and unit-construction engines.

After the Second World War, production began with small two-strokes, but Victoria launched the sophisticated V35 Bergmeister in 1951. This was a clean, shaft-drive, transverse V-twin of 347cc engine capacity.

The bike eventually performed well, but so much work had to be carried out on it that it almost bankrupted the company. The first bikes finally went on sale in 1953, together with a wide range of lightweight singles and a new scooter.

Victoria launched an extraordinary machine called the Swing in 1955. This 197cc single had short, leading-link forks and an engine which pivoted with the rear suspension. It was a design produced by Norbert Riedel of Imme fame. You could change gears with a set of buttons positioned on the handlebars.

By the 1960s, production consisted of a small range of lightweights and mopeds. Victoria went

Beautifully designed instruments positioned neatly on the tank.

The 1931 KR 50 S model had a 495cc engine and produced some 18hp. It weighed 331 lbs.

into partnership with the Italian company Parilla and fitted its engines. When the Zweirad Union was organized, the Victoria Company was absorbed into it. Motorcycle production stopped, although mopeds and scooters continued to feature the Victoria badge.

This is the 1951 world record machine which used a 39cc engine.

Handlebars were positioned down so the rider could lean on the machine.

The strange-looking Victoria Swing had a single cylinder, 197cc engine.

Vincent

1928- 1956

Philip Conrad Vincent was born in London, although his parents lived in Argentina. His father, also born in England, sent him back for preparatory and public school education.

By the time Vincent graduated from Cambridge University, where he studied mechanical science, he had already decided that he wanted to be a motorcycle manufacturer. He persuaded his father to put up the money for his first machine.

The bike was finished in 1927. It used a 350cc MAG engine and was capable of 80 mph. He decided to continue in motorcycle manufacture and extracted more money from his father. Now an engineer, Frank Walker, joined Vincent in his enterprise and the two found suitable premises in Stevanage. At the same time, they heard that HRD Motors Ltd. was for sale. Vincent was particularly keen to use the HRD brand name because he wanted to emulate the achievements of Howard R. Davies, founder of the HRD mark. Like Davies, he intended to build limited numbers of high quality sporting motorcycles.

By 1930, Vincent-HRD was well-established. The new company used proprietary engines from Rudge and JAP, but unhappy with their reliability and performance, began to manufacture their own engines later. Vincent also obtained help from Australian engineer Phil Irving, who joined Vincent-HRD in 1931.

What emerged from all this development was a single cylinder, 500cc engine which incorporated, for the first time, valves operated by splayed pushrods running parallel to the valve stems, while the camshaft was positioned high in the engine to accommodate them.

The new engine was presented at the Olympia Show in October 1935 and was fitted to three machines – the standard Meteor, the

A rare, early Vincent: HRD with a JAP engine unit.

on the pre-war machine, major work had been done on the design. The angle of the cylinders was increased to 50 degrees and the wheelbase was shortened using the engine and gearbox as a structural member suspended below a box-section top tube that doubled as an oil tank. The

Shown here is a 1938 Vincent-HRD series A Comet.

sporty Comet and the TT Replica. They sold well and became very popular. Now there was a new machine on Irving's drawing board. Basically two singles matched to make one 1000cc, 47 degree, V-twin. There were problems with the clutch and gearbox, which had

The Vincent Rapide was a phenomenally fast machine. This is a 1937 version which had a V-twin, 998cc engine.

trouble coping with the awesome power. But by 1939, the Rapide was on the road and over 70 had been sold before the onset of the Second World War.

After the war, Vincent started planning the next step – the Rapide series B. Although based

machine made the headlines as 'the world's fastest standard motorcycle' and with a top speed of around 110 mph, there was little doubt about it. Production started in 1946. Just two years later, a monster arrived, the Black Shadow – named for its entirely black look. Not only were

Series B Rapide - headlined as 'world's fastest standard motorcycle.'

the frame and tank black, but so were all the exterior engine parts and the brakes. The machines could be easily distinguished by the large 150 mph speedometer attached to the top of the forks and although the standard model could only do 120 mph, the racing version, the Black Lightning, could reach the maximum speed marked on the speedometer. This machine was supplied without lights, kickstart or stand and used TT style carburettors and unbaffled exhaust pipes.

The following year, the C series Rapide made its debut. It was not so different from the B,

though it did have new style Girdraulic front forks and rear damping.

These powerful machines were breaking records all over the world. On the Bonneville Salt Flats in America, for example, Rollie Free, dressed in only swimming trunks and without a front brake, took his Lightning to a new American record of over 150 mph. George Brown, who left the company in 1951, was establishing records and winning sprints and hill-climbs with his three machines: Gunga Din, Nero and the supercharged Super Nero.

This is the awesome, V-twin, 998cc engine of the Black Shadow.

There was little around, on two or four wheels, which could catch the Black Shadow. It had a top speed of 125 mph.

The all-enclosed Black Prince of 1955. Strip off the bodywork and you find a Black Shadow.

A new single was added to the range for 1950, the Gray Flash, which was built for racing. As with the Black Lightning, it had no lights or other road equipment. There were three models of Gray Flash listed.

The Series B models were dropped and only Series C models were built from 1951 on. Production continued until 1955, when the Series D models were announced. These were fully faired machines with a hinged rear mudguard enabling access to the wheel. There was a windscreen and the fairing extended outwards to protect the handlebars. Under all this bodywork was a slightly modified Vincent. Thus the Rapide became the Black Knight and the Shadow became the Black Prince. Unfortunately, although the machines created great interest, there were problems with the manufacture of the bodywork. The D series, therefore, suddenly lost their bodywork and reverted to the open style while incorporating all the modified details.

Unfortunately, however, financial worries were beginning to take their toll on the compa-

Instrumentation tucked behind the large winscreen.

ny. After a period of co-operation with the German NSU Company and fulfilment of all outstanding orders, production of Vincent motorcycles came to halt in 1956.

Wanderer

1902- 1929

The German Wanderer-Werke AG, Schonau/Chemnitz was founded in 1902 and became well-known as a manufacturer of up-market machines. The company produced 327cc and 387cc singles and side-valve V-twins of 408 and 616cc displacement with engines of their own design and manufacture.

The company supplied a number of its motorcycles to the German Army during the First World War and produced a novel 184cc machine in which the single overhead valve cylinder was horizontally positioned. It also manufactured larger displacement V-twins of 708cc and 749cc, some of which had eight valves.

Wanderer too excelled in competitions and employed such riders as Schister, Urban, Kohlrausch and Ebert in the 1920s.

Towards the end of the 1920s, a new machine designed by Alexander Novikoff went into production. It used a 498cc, single cylinder engine of unit-construction, had shaft-drive to the rear wheel and the frame was of the pressed steel type. The production run of this machine was short and the whole design and all the production equipment was sold to the Janacek Com-

This is the 500cc V-twin engine of the 1915 Wanderer.

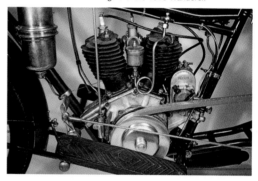

The 1915 4hp Wanderer. Drive was via a belt to the rear wheel and the top speed was around 53 mph.

The beautifully kept 327cc, single cylinder engine of the 1921 model.

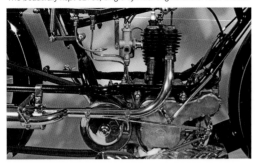

This is a 1921 Wanderer: 2.5hp model, with three gears.

pany, now known as Jawa, of Czecho-slovakia in 1929. The Janacek-Wanderer tie-up produced the name for the Czech company, using the first two letters of each word to make 'Jawa.' This sale signified the end of Wanderer motorcycle production, although it later manu-factured motorized bicycles with NSU for a short period.

The 1924 Wanderer was fitted with chain drive to the rear wheel.

The 184cc single, lay flat in the frame of the 1924 model.

Wanderer produced this single cylinder, 498cc machine in 1928. It was shaft driven to the rear wheel.

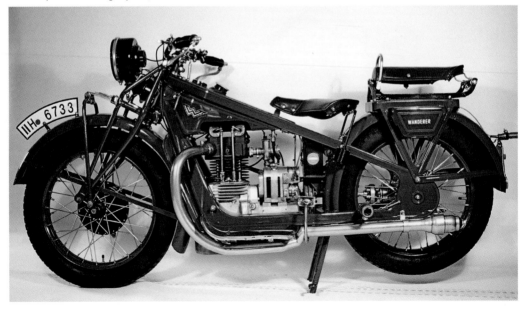

Wilkinson

1909- 1916

The Wilkinson Sword Company of Pall Mall, London made swords for the armed forces for many years. But wars come and go, and during peace the company had to diversify. One such 'diversification' was into motorcycle manufacture.

Bike manufacture started around 1903 with the introduction of two single cylinder machines using 21/2 and 23/4 capacity Antoine engines. These were marketed, though not very successfully, for the company by a garage in Chelsea. A few years later, the company decided to venture into motorcycles once again, this time with a completely different machine. The approach was military: a designer called PG Tacchi had created a rather unorthodox scouting machine equipped with a Maxim machine gun (also made by Wilkinson) positioned on the handlebars. It was demonstrated to the British Army in 1908, but was turned down. Wilkinson therefore decided to produce it as a touring machine

and the next time it was seen, the V-twin engine had been replaced by an air-cooled, four-cylinder unit of 676cc with shaft drive to the rear wheel. This became the Wilkinson TAC (Touring Auto Cycle) and was unveiled at the Stanley Show in London in 1909.

Production got under way at the Oakley Works, Southfield Road, Chiswick, with the odd modification being carried out. By 1911, it had a new title – Wilkinson TAC (Touring Auto Cycle). The engine was now water-cooled and its capacity increased to 848cc. Development

The four-cylinder engine of the Wilkinson was an 848cc unit.

Luxuriously equipped with a sophisticated design, the Wilkinson was dubbed the 'two-wheeled Mercedes.'

The large 'Jones' speedometer is well-positioned for the rider.

Wooler

1911 - 1955

The Wooler Company presented a novel, 230cc, two-stroke machine John Wooler's 'anti-vibratory' frame at the 1911 Olympia Show in London. To produce the machine, Wooler joined forces with the Wilkinson Sword Company, building it alongside Wilkinson's four-cylinder machine. Engine size grew and several modifications were also made. The First World War halted production, but the machine re-appeared in 1919. It now had an engine with a capacity of 348cc facing fore and aft.

In 1923 came a complete redesign which resulted in 350cc and 500cc models and which also used a new style fuel tank. By 1926, there was a completely new, single cylinder, upright-engined machine of 511cc with semi-conventional frame and forks. It seems that this machine may never have gone beyond prototype stage, as Wooler had recently bought the P & P Company and was concentrating on producing its machines. In 1943, however, a new Wooler design appeared. This was a 500cc transverse four. Assembly of the prototype started in 1945, shaft drive was used while the old style, protruding fuel tank was brought back. It made its debut at the 1948 Earl's Court Show, but not much more was heard of it. Wooler and his son, Ron, produced a transverse four. Only a few hand-built examples were ever produced.

was carried out on the machine over the years and an alternative 996cc model was available for side-car use by 1913.

By now, however, war was looming and Wilkinson was gearing up for their traditional supply of swords and bayonets: all motorcycle manufacture came to a standstill. Manufacture of the TMC was taken over by Ogston Motor Company of Victoria Road, Acton, but the firm closed down in 1916.

There was shaft drive to the rear wheel.

A Wooler from 1920 with a 348cc, horizontally opposed engine.

Yamaha

1955 - date

Race and then swept the top places in the ultra-light class of the first Asama Highlands Race of the All Japan Endurance Championships. It used an air-cooled, two-stroke, single cylinder, 123cc unit.

A deluxe YC-1 appeared at the Tokyo Motor Show held in Hibiya Park in April 1956. The YD-1 of 1957 took 'a 250cc for the Japanese,'

Two carburettors for the twin cylinder YL1.

YAMAHA Born in July 1955, Yamaha Motor Co., Ltd. was a relative latecomer in a market where as many as 150 motorcycle manufacturers competed for survival. New ones were starting up and others were folding at a tremendous rate, and few survived the challenge. At a time when motorcycle design was dominated by imposing, all-black styling, the YA-1 of 1955, Yamaha's first motorcycle, with its simple form and modern chestnut red coloring, quickly became known by the nickname 'Aka-tombo,' or the Red Dragonfly. It demonstrated its high performance by winning the third Mt. Fuji Ascent

A beautifully restored 1968 YL1, which used a 90cc, two-stroke, twin cylinder engine

as its key words and was given a compact and easy-to-ride body size that fitted the Japanese physique. It was Yamaha's first two cylinder engine, an air-cooled, two-stroke, 247cc unit. In 1959, there was further development on this machine to produce the sporty YDS-1 fitted with a 20hp engine on a steel pipe cradle frame. The third of the series, the YDS-3, arrived in 1966 and won great popularity in the United States. It was the first two-cylinder model to adopt the Autolube system along with other important upgrades.

The YG-1 appeared in 1963. This used an air-cooled, single cylinder, 75cc, rotary disk valve engine on a backbone-type, monocoque frame. It boasted a number of features such as waterproof brakes, a headlight nacelle and megaphone-type silencers.

The AT90 model appeared in 1965 as a dual-purpose bike that combined business utility with sportiness and had a small-displacement, high-rpm type, 90cc twin cylinder engine. The AT in its title came from its Autolube lubrication system. This forced lubrication mechanism achieved both high performance and low fuel consumption.

Winning an unprecedented following from the time of its release, the 1968 DT-1 started a worldwide boom in trail bikes. This model was the embodiment of a machine to take you 'beyond where the roads ends.' It was packed full of technology and features expressly designed to faciliate off-road riding. Ceriani type front forks, air-cooled, single cylinder, 5-port piston valve engine, wide-radius block-pattern tires and an engine guard. This model created the new genre known as 'trail bikes.' A pioneer of the 'mini-trail' category, the FT-1 appeared in 1970 and mounted a rotary disk valve, two-stroke, 50cc engine.

After making only two-stroke models for the first 15 years since its founding, Yamaha introduced its first four-stroke with the XS-1 of 1970. The goal was to build a lightweight, slim and compact, big-displacement sports model. A slim, air-cooled, ohc, two-cylinder engine of 653cc was mounted into a slim cradle frame, giving it an overall weight of 408 lbs.

In 1972, Yamaha introduced the TX 750, an air-cooled, four-stroke, single ohc, two cylinder, 743cc machine, their first production 750cc model to be sold on the market. It used dry sump

Generally known as a 'Fizzy' because of its designation of FS1-E, this is a 1973 50cc model.

Classic Yamaha colors and striping: a 1977 model FS1-E DX with two-stroke engine.

The tiny, 50cc engine of the 1977 FS1-E

lubrication, opposed-piston type double disc brakes and had the first aluminium frame ever employed on a street model.

Yamaha developed the 1973 TY250 as a competition model at a time when trial competition was booming. Mick 'the Magician' Andrews was one of the riders involved in the development. The TY250J was released as a model that could also be ridden on public roads. With its 250cc engine, it was known for its flat, torque characteristics and it was so strong that it could would move forward even when idling. Its many records in competition speak for themselves.

The TX500 of 1973 was the third model of Yamaha's four-stroke road sports category and, as the first road bike to have a DOHC, four-valve per cylinder, high output engine, was very different from its predecessors. Functions such as the world's first IC regulator, a CV carburettor, an aluminium frame and front disc brakes were also featured on this model.

The 1976 GX750 model adopted unique Yamaha technologies in features like its compact, laterally-aligned DOHC, three-cylinder engine and a maintenance-free shaft drive. The following year, the GX750II was introduced with a three-into-two exhaust and a big boost in power to 67 ps. Developed as a desert race

A break from the past, the XS750 was a four-stroke.

The shaft drive was tucked away behind the exhaust silencer.

A special edition 1.1 model in Martini livery.

enduro machine, the 1976 XT500 was released as a street-legal version of the TT500 enduro machine, launched the year before. For the first time ever, a forward inclining, upside-down rear suspension was used on a trail model. It was on an XT500 that the Sonauto Yamaha team's Cyril Neveu won the motorcycle division of the first Paris-Dakar Rally in 1979.

An export-only model, the 1977 XS1100 ushered in the over-one-quart era. The DOHC in-line, four-cylinder, 1102cc engine's awesome power created new excitement among European and American enthusiasts. The rear wheel was

Equipped with plenty of power and weight: the very sophisticated XS1100. The engine produces 95hp at 8000rpm.

shaft-driven. The European version had continental handlebars and an oil cooler. An American version with vertically handlebars was available.

The XS650 Special of 1978 was the model which started a boom in American-style bikes, based on the traditional, vertical twin engine of the TX650. With features like a teardrop tank and chopper style handlebars, along with a King & Queen seat and short, megaphone-type silencers, mounted on 16 in wheels, this model achieved a true, horseback-type riding feeling. In 1980, a supersport model was developed with the TZ250 as its base. The RZ250 was a huge sensation after its debut at the 1979 Tokyo

Wickedly fast: the 1978 RD400, two-stroke.

The RD400 engine, a twin-cylinder, 398cc unit with Reed-valve induction.

Motor Show. Its liquid-cooled, two-stroke, two cylinder engine pumped out high power equivalent to 140hp per liter of displacement.

It was mounted on a double cradle frame with a Monocross suspension and other features like lightweight cast wheels to produce unprecedented running performance. Even today, it remains a legendary model with a devoted following.

One of the models which embodied, perhaps better than many others, Yamaha's ideal of building 'slim, compact and fun to ride' motorcycles was the XJ750E, presented in 1981. The generator was located on the back end of the cylinders in an air-cooled, four-stroke, DOHC, in-line format, producing an exceptionally slim engine.

The XV750 Special of 1981 was an American-style model fitted with a newly developed, 75-degree, V-twin engine, and characterized by a powerful sense of torque that accentuated the solid, American-type ride. The model built an especially strong reputation in markets where longer riding distances are common.

With its 'world's first carburettor turbo system,' the XJ650 Turbo garnered much praise at the 1981 Tokyo Motor Show. This, added to the introduction of the electronic fuel injection turbo system on the XJ1100 Turbo, focused attention on Yamaha's turbo technology. The aerodynamically designed, full faring was the product of repeated wind-tunnel tests and employed much of the modelling technology and know-how from Yamaha's marine division.

Introduced in 1982, the XJ750D was the first model in Japan equipped with a full faring incorporating aerodynamic design. At the same time, it featured advanced Yamaha electronic technologies such as the YFIS (Yamaha Fuel Injection System) and the 'Yamaha Cycle Communication System,' which provided a man-machine interface to give the rider information concerning the condition of the machine.

The 1983 XVZ 1200D Venture Royale was the Yamaha motorcycle with the largest displacement and power output, developed as a long-distance tourer for the North American market. A liquid-cooled, DOHC, four-valve, 70 degree, V-4 engine with shaft drive and full comfort measures, including computer-controlled front and rear suspension system, this model was great for comfortable, long-distance cruising.

The 1984 Super Trail model DT 200R combined the mechanics, performance and even the image of Yamaha's YZ motocrossers with the design of a street-legal vehicle. Its two-stroke, liquid-cooled, single cylinder engine was the first to adopt both the YEIS and YPVS technologies on its engine, achieving a high power output of 30hp.

In 1984, came the RZV 500R, the world's first production model to mount a liquid-cooled, two-stroke, V-4 engine. As the flagship model embodying Yamaha's sporting spirit, it was also the fastest road-going model of its day. It was a direct descendent of the YZR500 works machine that Kenny Roberts rode to the championship title with six wins in the 12 rounds of the 1983 World GP. The engine boasted new advances in two-stroke technology, such as giving the for-

1978 500cc World Champion Kenny Roberts at full stretch on his Yamaha.

This is a 1985 AG 200. A real, reliable workhorse of a machine.

ward and rear banks of cylinders different induction systems, piston reed valve in front and crankcase reed valve in the rear. The FZ750 was presented at the Cologne Motor Show in Germany in the fall of 1984. Its five valve, DOHC, parallel four-cylinder, 45-degree, forward-inclined engine, a world's first, was the product of Yamaha's pursuit of increased power output and vehicle stability. This 'Genesis' concept has been passed on from the FZ to the FZR, and continues to evolve.

Inheriting the 'OW' in-house designation, the

The FZX from the mid-1980s had a 749cc, in-line, four-cylinder engine.

FZR750R of 1989 was a production model with many features which inspired by the Yamaha YZF750 works machine that competed in the TT-F1, four-stroke, road-racing class. It was a fully fledged works replica with a DOHC five valve, parallel, four-cylinder engine with titanium connecting rods.

The 1990s belonged to Yamaha. The firm won an unprecedented seven Paris-Dakar rallies, six by Stéphane Peterhansel on his XTE and XTZ. It was also a time when it further enhanced market winners such as the VMAX. The VMAX12 model debuted on the American market in 1985 and was very popular due to its unique styling and distinctive, powerful performance. The model, introduced in 1990, offered Japanese riders a fun cruising bike with the same kind of distinctive riding experience as the VMAX1200. It had a liquid-cooled, 1200cc engine.

The European Sports Tourer FJ, with its liquid-cooled, four-stroke, DOHC, four-valve, parallel, four-cylinder engine mounted on a high

The FZR 1000 was an awesome piece of machinery, with technology straight off the race circuit bikes.

Naked and powerful: the V-Max was very fast.

The engine of the V-Max was a powerful, 1200cc unit.

rigidity, lateral frame with Yamaha's unique vibration-reducing Orthogonal Mounting, made its debut as a 1100cc machine in 1984. Winning a big following among veteran European riders who really knew their motorcycles, the FJ was scaled up to 1200cc in 1989. Then in 1991, it was re-released in Europe and Japan as the FJ1200A, mounting a state-of-the-art ABS (Anti-lock Brake System). Packed full of the most advanced technology, the GTS1000 made its debut in 1992 as a new-generation sports tourer. The liquid-cooled, DOHC, five-valve, parallel, four-cylinder, 1000cc engine featured electronic fuel injection and a three-way catalyzer for cleaner emissions. Also, a newly developed, omega-shaped aluminium frame and a front wheel assembly separated steering function and suspension function for greatly improved handling stability.

1998 will long be remembered by motorcyclists as the year Yamaha launched the YZF-R1, widely acclaimed as the most remarkable supersport model of the decade. Equipped with race-bred engine and chassis technology, the R1 further underlines Yamaha's commitment to offering products that generate 'Kando' every time. In 2004, the R1 continues to amaze and astonish with its sheer power and cool handling.

In the same year, when many doubted he could do it, Valentino Rossi (Gauloises Fortuna Yamaha) secured the 2004 Riders MotoGP Championship at Phillip Island after winning an intense 27 lap battle with his main championship rival, Sete Gibernau (Honda). The win gave Yamaha its first title in the premier class since 1992 and Rossi has now won more victories in one season than any Yamaha rider in history.

As if this was not enough, the prestigious annual MCN Awards took place at the International Motorcycle and Scooter Show, where Yamaha came out trumps with Best Sportsbike, the YZF-R1 and Best All-Rounder, the FZS6 Fazer. These were just two of the awesome machines the company had lined up for 2005.

Yamaha's TDM engine is a liquid-cooled, four-stroke vertical twin.

The FZS6 with its 600cc engine is a load of riding fun.

Sit back and let the Majesty whisk you where you want to go.

This just has to be the ultimate experience, the awesome and latest R1 at full throttle.

Zenith

1905 - 1949

ZENITH Zenith trademark shows an early type of motorcycle imprisoned behind railings and featuring the words 'Barred.' This trademark is a reminder of 1910 when Zenith machines were so dominant in hill-climbs and similar competitions that organizers refused to allow Zenith riders to enter so that other machines could have a chance at the prize money.

Why were the machines so superior? The simple answer is the Gradua variable gear system, invented in 1908 by designer Fred Barnes, relied on the opening and closing of the engine shaft driving pulley, which altered the radius at which the vee-belt ran, in turn raising or lowering the overall ratio. The Zenith refinement was that the handwheel (or, on later versions, the crank handle,) which adjusted the pulley was arranged so that as the pulley diameter varied, the rear wheel was moved forward or rearwards in the fork-ends, and the belt tension was thus allowed to remain constant.

Zenith, however, goes back to 1905, when a machine, the Tooley's Patent Bicar, was exhibited at the Crystal Palace Show in London. Production of this machine started in 1905, but the name was changed to the Zenith Bicar. A man called Britton, once of Britton and Harley, became the works manager of the company formed to produce the machine, the Zenith Motor Engineering Company. This was based behind a row of cottages at 101a, Stroud Green Road, Finsbury Park, North London.

The Bicar was refined in the following years, and two tricars were added to the line-up. In 1907, Fred Barnes joined the company. His first machine was the 500cc, Fafnir-engined Zenette. When fitted with the Gradua system, it could climb hills which paralyzed other machines.

In 1909, the company moved to Weybridge, where it used the Brooklands test hill to test the machines. Hill-climbs and similar events were taken on and won. Barnes himself was a main contender and came away with a handful of medals.

By 1910, Barnes had a new model ready. It

This is a 1912 Zenith, fitted with the Gradua system which enabled it to climb hills other could not.

The 1912 machine used a single cylinder JAP engine.

The control pulley of the Gradua system.

was long and low and had a V-twin, JAP engine and the latest version of the Gradua system. It was formidable and earned the ban mentioned earlier. By 1914, the company moved to Hampton Court and a further model was introduced.

The First World War prompted the company to submit a sidecar model, with machine gun attachment, to the British Army. Unfortunately, it was declined.

In 1920, Zenith produced an oil-cooled, 500cc, flat twin, positioned fore and aft, designed by Granville Bradshaw. In 1922, an all-chain-drive Zenith appeared, a roadster with a 996cc, JAP engine. The following year, the Gradua system was dropped while a 350cc, single model was added.

By 1926, most of the machines were using JAP power units and Brooklands saw a lot of big, V-twin Zenith action with riders such as I.P. Riddoch, Oliver Laldwin, Paul Brewster, Joe Wright and Bert Le Vack. Le Vack, in the most

The 1914 Zenith Gradua used an 8hp, 976cc, JAP, V-twin engine and had a top speed of 68 mph.

Zündapp

1917 - 1984

appalling weather conditions, lapped Brooklands at over 100 mph on his Zenith. Joe Wright increased the lap record to 109.9 mph later that year. When Barnes produced two track specials, the pair Wright and Baldwin increased the lap record to 113.45 mph jointly during the same meeting. With Le Vack and Wright fighting it out for world records and Baldwin breaking records too, the Zenith Company was at its peak by the end of the 1920s.

Back at the works, however, the effects of the Depression were starting to be felt. A simple, 172cc, Villiers-engined, economy machine and a Super 8 were added to attract new customers. This did nothing to help, however, and by 1929, the work at Hampton Court was at a standstill.

This setback proved temporary, however, and by 1931, the company was back in business, now financed by a London dealer and working on a smaller scale. Machines were updated with saddle tanks and foot gear-change, but the Second World War bought another shut-down. Sadly, Fred Barnes was killed in an air raid during this period. After the war, Zenith was back with a JAP, 750cc, V-twin-powered machine. There was a 1000cc prototype on the drawing board when the company was forced to close its doors because of a lack of JAP and other suitable engines.

A slightly different version of the Gradua system can be seen here.

![ZÜNDAPP]

The factory was formed out of three companies as a munitions supplier, Zunder und Apparatebau Gmbh in Nuremberg in 1917. It changed its name after the First World War to Zundapp gesellschaft fur den bau von Specialmaschinen and manufactured tractors, turbines, cables and other products.

Although motorcycles were already part of the company make-up, most were imported.

The first machine produced in 1921 was described as the 'Volksmotorrader,' or Everyman's Motorcycle. It was designated Z22 and used a single cylinder, two-stroke, 211cc engine with belt drive. A sporty version was produced, the Z2G, and by 1923, the K249, which had a capacity of 249cc, three gears and slightly better frame, was also available.

The company participated in competition early on. In 1921, they entered the Wurgau hill-climb and took the first three places.

By 1924, more than 10,000 machines had been sold and the company was still producing at record levels. The Z249 was so popular that it remained in production until 1927, although it was updated in 1925 to the EM250 with a power increase to 4.5hp.

In 1928, the German government approved new legislation which exempted any motorcycle under 200cc from tax.

A 1927 Zundapp with 249cc, two-stroke, single cylinder model.

Suddenly the large-capacity Zundapp went out of favor and the decision was made to make smaller capacity machines. Thus the Z200 made its appearance. It used a single cylinder, two-stroke engine producing 4.5hp and had a three-speed gearbox with hand change.

The company moved to a new factory in Nuremberg-Schweinau, but during the next few years, the market went into turmoil and Neumeyer's son, Hans-Friedrich, became managing director.

The 1930 Zundapp S300 had a 298cc engine and top speed of 56 mph. It had three gears and chain drive.

During the early 1930s, production was low and the company faced hard times; machines were placed with dealers in the hope of generating sales. The 'S' range of machines consisted of the 200cc, 300cc and 350cc models, while the SS500 used a single cylinder Rudge Python engine.

Then motorcycle business started to pick up again, as did bike production.

Two utility machines were produced for 1932, the B170 and B200. At the Berlin Show of 1933, a new range was presented, designated DB175cc, K300, K400, K500, K600 and K800. The 'K' stood for Karden, confirming shaft-drive. The K400 and K500 had transverse, flat, twin engines while the K600 and K800 had transverse, flat, four-cylinder engines. All models were fitted with pressed steel frames and forks except the 175cc machine. The next few years saw the introduction of the K350cc two-stroke, along with the DS350 single cylinder, four-stroke machines.

In 1938, the company changed its name to Zundapp-GmbH Nurnberg. During the Second World War, production was military and the KS750 side-

The 791cc, flat, four-cylinder engine had four gears and shaft drive.

This is the huge Zundapp K800. The engine produced 22hp and the top speed was around 78 mph.

The sturdy K800 flat twin was an ideal military machine. It was robust and reliable.

car model was introduced. The DB200W single with twin exhausts and the civilian 500cc, 600cc and 800cc models were re-designated with a 'W,' indicating use by the Wehrmacht.

After the war, motorcycle production was not possible and the company helped with potato mashing and corn milling to help to feed the impoverished German population. This activity, along with the production of sewing machines, helped the company to re-establish itself in the motorcycle field and a number of DB200s were made in 1947. By now, Hans-Friedrich had been joined by his sister Elizabeth Mann and her husband, who were instrumental in developing future plans for the company. A new plant opened in Munich, leaving Neumeyer at the Nuremberg factory. The DB range had turned into the DB205 model by 1954, while the KS601 with transverse twin engine was introduced in 1950 and 1953 saw the introduction of the 'Bella' scooters. The Munich facility was selling the Falconette and Combinette 50cc mopeds and it became obvious that it was doing better than the one in Nuremberg, which was closed in 1958. Although the 'S' models continued until 1963 and the Bella scooters until 1964, the 50cc models kept the company alive.

During the 1970s, Zundapp produced a new 125cc machine which sold well in several different versions. It was used for sporting events and it won the 125cc World Motocross Championship in 1973 and 1974. It also went on to take the ISDT Trophy in 1975 and 1976. By 1978, the company was producing a new range of water-cooled, 50cc and 175cc models and the early 1980s saw the introduction of the sporty KS175 two-stroke. However, the company was again in dire financial straits. It was forced to close down in 1984.

The 1956 Bella model 151, 146cc, two-stroke Scooter.

Zundapp GS125, the German ISDT Wunderkind.

Index

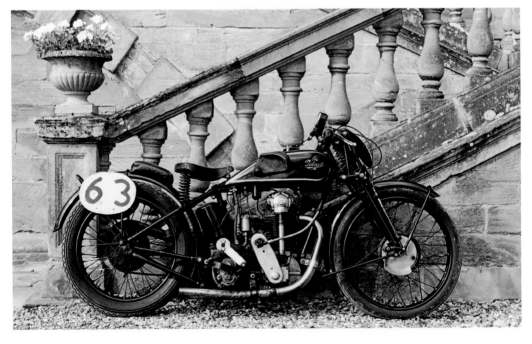

Acknowledgements

The author would like to thank the following people and organizations for their help and contributions:

Enrico Minazzi for his Aermacchi contribution.
Angelo and Pierluigi Cervini – for allowing me to photograph so many wonderful machines in their collection.
Andrew Morland Photo Agency, Butleigh, Somerset, England.
Don Morley International Sports Photo Agency, England.
Zweirad Museum, Neckarsulm, Germany – a special thanks to Peter and Hartmut.
The National Motorcycle Museum, Birmingham, England.
The National Motor Museum, Beaulieu, Hants, England.
Wheels Through Time Museum, Maggie Valley, North Carolina, USA.
Ray Jones of the Black Country Living Museum, Dudley, England.
North Leicester Motorcycles, Ellistown, Coalville, Leicester, England.
Arthur Farrow for his MM contribution.
DK Motorcycle, Newcastle under Lyme, Staffordshire, England.

The Curtiss Museum, Hammondsport, New York State, USA.
Myreton Motor Museum, Aberlady, East Lothian, Scotland.
Moray Motor Museum, Elgin, Grampian, Scotland.
Norton Motorcycles, Gladstone, Oregon. USA
MPC (Ural) motorcycles, Bitteswell, Leicester, England.
Barber Vintage Motorsport Museum, Birmingham, Alabama, USA.
American Classic Motorcycle Museum, Ashebro, North Carolina, USA.
Pininfarina design studio, Torino, Italy.
Aprilia; Benneli; Bimota; BMW; Cagiva: Ducati; Piaggio; Honda; Kawasaki; KTM; Morini; Moto Guzzi; MV; MuZ; Peugeot motocycles; Royal Enfield; Suzuki; Triumph; Yamaha.
Peter Gaffney Processing, Birmingham, England – thanks for processing all the film so beautifully.
Last, but not least, Sue, for all her encouragement, love and patience.
Many thanks to all.